Relating Hegel's *Sci*
Philosophy

Relating Hegel's *Science of Logic* to Contemporary Philosophy

Luis Guzmán
The New School, New York, USA

palgrave
macmillan

Softcover reprint of the hardcover 1st edition 2015 978-1-137-45449-2

First published 2015 by
PALGRAVE MACMILLAN

Palgrave Macmillan in the UK is an imprint of Macmillan Publishers Limited, registered in England, company number 785998, of Houndmills, Basingstoke, Hampshire RG21 6XS.

Palgrave Macmillan in the US is a division of St Martin's Press LLC, 175 Fifth Avenue, New York, NY 10010.

Palgrave Macmillan is the global academic imprint of the above companies and has companies and representatives throughout the world.

Palgrave® and Macmillan® are registered trademarks in the United States, the United Kingdom, Europe and other countries.

ISBN 978-1-349-49795-9 ISBN 978-1-137-45450-8 (eBook)

DOI 10.1057/9781137454508

A catalogue record for this book is available from the British Library.

A catalog record for this book is available from the Library of Congress.

To Luis and Irza, who once created me, and Caetano and Lautaro, who do not cease doing so

Contents

Acknowledgments

In my second year of undergraduate studies at Universidad Nacional de Colombia in Bogotá I was introduced to Hegel by Ramón Perez Mantilla, nicknamed "*el maestro absoluto.*" In a seminar dedicated to *Phenomenology* we barely made it to the inverted world. Twenty-five years later, I have barely made it through the Introduction. After a detour through Heidegger, I re-encountered Hegel at The New School for Social Research, at the hands of Agnes Heller and Richard Bernstein. It was Hegel's *Science of Logic* which now drew me in, with the argument that if one was to offer a non-metaphysical interpretation of Hegel, this was the work to test it against. A Dissertation Fellowship offered by The New School allowed me to spend 2000–2001 in Berlin, where I worked on what amounts to Chapter 4 of this book. I must thank Dmitri Nikulin, a member of my Dissertation Committee, who encouraged me to undertake this project. An abridged version of Chapter 3 was published in Spanish under the title "El Carácter Contingente de la Necesidad Absoluta en la *Ciencia de la Lógica* de Hegel" in *Ideas y Valores*, Universidad Nacional, Bogotá, Colombia, No. 131, August, 2006, under a Creative Commons Attribution 4.0 license.

Many fruitful discussions among a group of doctoral candidates at The New School helped shape various of the ideas offered here. I am grateful to Morgan Meis, Stephen Levine, Howard Ponzer, and John Blanchard, among others, for their dedicated probing. The connection between Hegel and certain neo-pragmatists was honed at various papers delivered and seminars held between 2011 and 2013 at Universidad Nacional de Colombia in Bogotá, Universidad Nacional Autónoma de México, and Universidad Autónoma de Mexico. I am grateful to William Duica and Efraín Lazos for extending invitations to offer month-long seminars on Hegelian philosophy and neo-pragmatist thought during Spring 2011 (Bogotá) and Spring 2012 (Mexico City).

On a more personal level, I cannot fail to mention Lucía Pulido, who insisted on sharing a life with someone who was busy sharing a life with Hegel. Lastly, this book is dedicated to my parents, whose perseverance, hard work, and selflessness were a simple matter of course.

Introduction

The year 1994 saw the publication of three major works highlighting various Hegelian themes. Robert Brandom's *Making It Explicit*, John McDowell's *Mind and World*, and Terry Pinkard's *Hegel's Phenomenology: The Sociality of Reason* helped bring Hegel back to a respectable seat at the table of contemporary philosophical debate in the Anglo-Saxon world. The themes that have found their way into these discussions are, among others, mediation, immediacy, the in-itself/for-consciousness distinction, and necessity; or in more contemporary terms: inferentialism, givenness, the conceptual scheme/content dualism, and analyticity.[1]

A frequent criticism of this Hegelian rehabilitation experienced in the last 20 years lies in the fact that it selects particular elements from the Hegelian system that, when plucked from their location and function within it, lose their Hegelian meaning.[2] These parts possess their meaning as elements of the whole. Separated from that whole they are no longer Hegelian. What we would have before us is not a rehabilitation of Hegel but rather a distortion of his philosophy and the masking of the metaphysical engine powering it. The task at hand is to offer a reading of Hegel from within his system, which would open spaces to be occupied by recent developments in analytic philosophy, instead of attempting to approach Hegel *from* these developments, setting aside what seems difficult to accommodate. This would require a defense of the whole structure of Hegel's philosophy, not merely of certain pillars and slabs belonging to the edifice. The question is whether this task is possible without ascribing to him a metaphysical position, which at the dawn of the twenty-first century would be difficult and probably unappealing to defend. If it is not possible, then Horstmann would be right: the Hegelian renaissance would not really be a renaissance but rather a plundering and decontextualizing of certain themes that are then recontextualized to make them sound appealing to our contemporary ears. To use Croce's vocabulary: what is living or dead in the philosophy of the thinker of totality and the absolute could only be that totality or absolute itself. One either takes the absolute or takes nothing at all.

However, what if the absolute itself ought to be understood non-metaphysically? What if its structure destabilizes all dogmatic claims made about what is really real insofar as its historical character constantly alters the content of these claims through time? We are then left with an absolute that resembles Heraclitus' rivers, where "different and different waters flow" every time we wade in. The existence of the absolute would consist in the existence of the question "What is?" and in the attempts to answer it (this is the starting point of the *Phenomenology*). The absolute exists so long as humans inquire about reality, However, it exists as a posit that always exceeds the inquiry. Now, what makes Hegel's philosophy unique and not merely an additional attempt at answering this question is that it itself constitutes the breaking point at which the structure of the absolute is revealed. Hegel's absolute is the self-consciousness of its structure, which consists in including all prior moments within it. It is the first conceptualization of the absolute as subject to time. Hegel's response to the question is to say that "what is" is the whole, and the whole is constantly changing, always constituted by the process that has led to it at each particular historical moment. If metaphysics is to be understood simply as the belief in a *necessary* and *definite* constitution of reality that is or can, under ideal conditions, be revealed to human beings,[3] then we might be willing to accept the Hegelian whole as non-metaphysical insofar as there are no ideal conditions under which it becomes a complete and necessary description of reality. The breaking point reached with Hegel lies, then, not in reaching the absolute and its necessary description of "what is," but rather in realizing that such a task is impossible and explaining why this is so.

The present work offers a non-metaphysical interpretation of Hegel's philosophy by focusing on five different topics that might serve as the ground on which to construct said interpretation. These topics have been selected because of their value in having bolstered an understanding of Hegel's philosophy as systematic, totalizing, and closed, thus paving the way for a rejection of Hegel's philosophical project as a whole as irrelevant to the various philosophical impulses informing the twentieth century. This positioning vis-à-vis Hegel unites thinkers as diverse as Russell, Popper, Gadamer, Adorno, Heidegger, Levinas, and Derrida, from schools of thought as varied as analytic philosophy, phenomenology, hermeneutics, critical theory, post-structuralism, and so on.

The five interpretive axes offered are Hegel's concepts of object, the infinite, necessity, rationality, and the absolute. The chapter on the object will be approached from the perspective of the "in-itself-for-consciousness" that appears in the second half of the Introduction to the *Phenomenology*. The chapter on the infinite will be culled from the section on Quality in Book One of the *Science of Logic*, where he deals with finitude, the ought, and the true infinite; the chapter on necessity will be based on the section on Actuality (*Wirklichkeit*) toward the end of Book Two; the chapter on rationality will be fleshed out by means of the syllogism, offered in the section on Subjectivity in Book Three; and the chapter on the absolute will focus on the last section of Book Three, that of the Idea. The goal is to be able to offer an interpretation of Hegel's philosophy that finds it very much alive and thus does more justice to any talk of a Hegelian renaissance than the isolated selection of certain Hegelian issues.

The present study does not offer a comparative analysis between Hegel, on the one hand, and contemporary thinkers such as Quine, Davidson, McDowell, Levinas, Derrida, and Brandom, on the other. It does not set itself the task of rescuing contemporary analytic topics from within the Hegelian texts.[4] Rather, it prepares the ground for such a goal by offering an interpretation of Hegelian philosophy that does not stand at odds with the philosophical impulse behind current analytic, neo-pragmatist thought, or behind philosophies of particularity.

The topics dealt with here have a direct link to contemporary issues. Reference to them is not designed to lend Hegelian philosophy a credibility sorely needed. Rather, the goal is to place Hegelian philosophy, not only certain rescued themes, at the center of current philosophical debates. With this in mind, each chapter shall begin by linking its interpretive axis to contemporary discussions as an example of its timeliness.

In the Introduction to the *Phenomenology* Hegel confronts certain epistemological issues that arise mainly due to the dualisms emerging in Kantian philosophy: spontaneity/receptivity, understanding/sensibility. He explains what the consequences are for a position that presupposes these dualisms, mainly skepticism and relativism, and attempts to reveal a prior unity behind them that would dissolve their aporetic structure. Some of the moves he makes parallel Davidson's claims against the conceptual scheme/content dualism, raised in his article "On the Very Idea of a Conceptual Scheme," where he shows the impossibility of having incommensurate conceptual schemes and, more importantly, the need for a shared background of true beliefs for there to be the possibility of error. The position Davidson takes against a relativism based on the dualism scheme/content mirrors Hegel's move in the Introduction against the skepticism entailed by Kant's transcendental philosophy.

In the section on finitude the issue whether there can be an irreducible other, a transcendence that escapes the pull of Spirit or thinking, comes up in the form of the distinction between the true and the bad infinite. According to a common interpretation the bad infinite seems to constantly place otherness in an unreachable beyond, whereas the true infinite would amount to its inclusion in the totality. The apparent impossibility of an absolute otherness in Hegel's philosophy has been a deep source of criticism raised against him early on, defining his thinking as the high point of logocentrism, a thinking that absorbs everything within it. This is the main critique lobbed at him by Levinas and Derrida. They attempt to rescue a remainder that escapes the all-penetrating force of reason and thinking. It is true that Hegel situates absolute otherness within reason. However, the interesting question is whether anything gets lost by doing so when this otherness located within thought itself can never be absolutely overcome. Is there a significant difference whether we confront otherness from the outside or from the inside? The elucidation of Hegel's concept of the true infinite will reveal that finitude is not overcome with the true infinite, but just more accurately grasped.

In the section on Modality Hegel reveals the structural connection between necessity and contingency as he moves from contingency to absolute necessity and proposes a complete identity between them. If there can be no absolute necessity that is not riven by contingency, then necessity is posited as presupposed, that is, it is made and not found. This would mean that the necessity of his system is posited as presupposed, placing his philosophical claims in a sort of anti-metaphysical parenthesis by revealing their own unstable ground. The first section of Quine's article "Two Dogmas of Empiricism" attempts to reveal the limitations of the concept of analyticity by showing the difficulty of reaching meaning invariance. He shows that meanings are processes that are not guided by any necessary force behind them but rather subject to change, disallowing any claim to absolute necessity. With the conceptual determination of "what is" as actuality Hegel reaches a stage in which the conceptual strategy for thinking "what is" determines it as a process instead of an object: it is its having become what it is. The necessity of this process can only be posited from its endpoint *as* having existed all along, powering and directing the process. Only in this way can actuality be made sense of or be assigned meaning. However, this process is always subject to further change given its historicity. Meaning is subject to a continuous transformation in the movement of recollection or remembrance (*Erinnerung*).

In the section on the syllogism Hegel makes the claim that "everything rational is a syllogism." What distinguishes us from non-rational animals is our inferential capacity: not only that we have beliefs about the world, but also and mainly that we give and ask for reasons for our beliefs. The truth of a claim lies in the inferential process that leads to it. Otherwise, as Hegel says: "One bare assurance is worth just as much as another." To be rational consists in giving and asking for reasons. The minimum unit of meaning lies for Hegel neither in the concept nor in the judgment, but in the syllogism. Using Wittgensteinian vocabulary, neither a concept nor a judgment makes a move in a language game; only an inference does. This is one of the main themes running through Robert Brandom's *Making It Explicit*. His starting point is to find out how to distinguish ourselves from non-rational beings: the difference between sentient and sapient beings. He takes over from Hegel mediation and determinate negation: relations of consequence and incompatibility, by means of which we commit ourselves, and our partners in conversation hold us accountable, to certain beliefs about the world. Rationality and inference are the birthplace of objectivity. The world comes forth in the constant "to and fro" of giving and asking for reasons.

In the section on the Idea one encounters the "most stubborn opposition." The ideas of the true and of the good constitute this most stubborn opposition since they are "eternally created and eternally overcome." The Absolute Idea in Hegel consists in grasping the oppositional structure contained in our theoretical and practical relation to the world. This most stubborn opposition takes the form of a gap between mind and world, to use vocabulary from McDowell's *Mind and World*. McDowell wants to steer a course between two different ways of running into an insurmountable gap between mind and world: the myth of the given, where there is a merely causal connection between both sides that cannot account for knowledge of any kind, on the one hand, and, on the other, a coherentism that leaves the external world in a hopeless beyond and the mind spinning frictionless in its beliefs about that beyond. His solution is not to attempt to bridge the gap but to start off with no gap in the first place, by means of the Aristotelian concept of second nature. We are always already in the (conceptually given) world. The role of the eternal creation of the stubborn opposition in Hegel is to guarantee the hardness of the world and avoid the frictionless spinning in the void. The role of the eternal overcoming of the stubborn opposition is to show that despite the fact that the opposition does not disappear, we are nonetheless on both sides of the gap and thus always already in objectivity.

Metaphysics and necessity go hand in hand. The conclusion of Chapter 3 consists in the belief that the necessity ascribed to Hegel's system is posited in recollection and thus riven by contingency. Therefore, the *Science of Logic* should not be read as exhibiting the necessary a priori sequence of concepts that determine our relation to the world. The concepts encountered in it are precisely those we have come up with when attempting to make sense of our world.[5] To assert that it is complete must not be understood as saying that the system offers a final and definite account of "what is", no longer subject to revision since subject and object, mind and world, work as like to like and completely interpenetrate each other.[6]

One of the impulses behind the present study is the attempt to make sense of the meaning and location of Hegel's statement regarding the most stubborn opposition, its eternal creation and eternal overcoming. To announce the completeness of a system while structuring it in such a way that it will eternally encounter opposition within it reveals that such completeness does not lie in its claims to particular truths (about nature or society) but rather in how truth claims work in general. They are historical, rooted in a linguistic community that has a certain relation to the world and gives itself the measure of their correctness. However, they are always subject to being falsifiable by human experience. The absoluteness of Hegel's system lies in his belief that he is the first to reveal this structure. He is the first to create a totality of meaning in order to explain the present as the result of all the preceding developments of thought and human experience. Aristotle set for himself a similar task in the first Book of his *Metaphysics*, though he did not think he was *constructing* this totality but rather uncovering different parts of it in his predecessors and offering it in full for the first time. He presupposed his system, whereas Hegel is positing his system *as* presupposed. He is the first to tell us that a system can only be posited, and that its universality, absoluteness, and objectivity are constructed and thus subject to change. There is no outside from or against which to measure our claims about the world and ourselves. The totality and completeness of Hegel's system does not consist in reaching final and definite claims about the world but in realizing that the only definite claim possible concerns the impossibility of definite claims.[7] Hegel's system is closed only insofar as we have its structure before us. However, its particular content will constantly be changing. This is distinguished from Pyrrhonian skepticism insofar as in the latter the opposing equipollent claims cancel each other since they are all equally justifiable, leading us to *epoche* in order to gain *ataraxia*. In Hegel's view opposing claims are an equally constitutive part of the truth since the truth is the whole. It is just that we never reach the "whole" whole.

Hegel's thinking constitutes the moment of self-realization of spirit: he is the first thinker to create a system that is absolute insofar as it does not purport to be absolute. The truth he reaches is the whole since it includes the totality of the process of thinking that leads to the present moment where what is true is understood as that conceptualizing process itself. The absolute character of the system lies in its permanence since what is held to be true will *always* be determined by the process of its search despite it being always different.[8]

1
The In-Itself-For-Consciousness: The Third Dogma

1.1 Introduction

In the Introduction to the section on the Idea Hegel asserts that it possesses the most stubborn opposition.[1] This stubbornness is grounded in the oppositions encountered in both the idea of the true and that of the good, that is, in theoretical and practical philosophy. These oppositions are being eternally created and eternally overcome. Human knowledge is eternally producing and overcoming an opposition between subject and object, concept and content, mind and world. The goal of philosophers from Descartes to McDowell has been to overcome this opposition once and for all. Different strategies have included God, forms of intuition and categories of the understanding, intellectual intuition, knowledge by acquaintance, second nature, coherentism, and so on. These strategies instead of overcoming the opposition have ended up producing either a loss of the world (frictionless spinning in a web of beliefs), a loss of our knowledge of the world (causal interaction without justification), or some type of dogmatism (appeal to God or to intellectual intuition). In the Introduction to the *Phenomenology* Hegel lays out the problematic of the idea of the true using as guiding thread the opposition between the object in itself and the object for consciousness. The "in-itself" is the content thought, what is real, undisturbed by its being thought, whereas the "for-consciousness" is what is thought about the content, the identification of it as something, determined by a particular scheme. Any identification of the content as object of thought would already imply a particular conceptual scheme without which that content could not be thought. The strategy he proposes in confronting the stubborn opposition is to transfer the two poles of content and scheme, in-itself and for-consciousness, into thought itself as the "object in itself for consciousness," though without collapsing them. This will not overcome the opposition, but rather reveal the structure due to which it is constantly created and overcome. That it is not completely overcome amounts to saying that it is intrinsic to human beings to always find themselves at theoretical odds with the world, to never be able to decipher it in a permanent manner, and thus to always be prone to having the world reveal itself as different than expected. This is what Hegel understands by *experience*. In this manner, he avoids losing the world without either falling into dogmatism or renouncing knowledge of it. We shall follow this strategy as it is laid out in the second half of the Introduction by means of the issue of the measure and its continuous alteration in experience. We give ourselves the measure against which we compare our beliefs about the world, while simultaneously altering this measure when we alter our beliefs in the face of our negative experience with the world. The Introduction emphasizes the dynamic at work between these two poles of consciousness and reveals the structural necessity of this opposition for the problem of knowledge and the constitution of human beings insofar as they are characterized by making truth claims. The source of objectivity, the hardness of the world, lies in our getting it wrong. The world only reveals itself in our false knowledge as being that *about which* our knowledge was wrong. Friction with the world is experienced only insofar as we err *about* it.

1.2 Detour via Davidson

In Donald Davidson's 1974 article "On the Very Idea of a Conceptual Scheme"[2] we find a variation of this stubborn opposition of the idea of the true. He calls it the third dogma of empiricism: the distinction between content and conceptual scheme. A conceptual scheme can be understood as a set of rules of construction by which content is unified or synthesized into the kinds of objects common sense takes as making up the world. If the content lies beyond the conceptual scheme representing it and is only accessible through this scheme, then it will forever lie beyond our reach in its independence since we will only relate to it as determined or formed (and therefore altered) by the scheme we approach it with. There will be no criterion or measure (*Maßstab*) from which to determine anything common to schemes since the content they are attempting to represent or depict lies outside their scope. If one grants the world independence yet does not believe in the myth of the given, in the possibility of an unmediated connection between the world and us that goes beyond the merely causal stimulation of nervous endings and impresses upon us facts that serve as justifications for beliefs about the world, then the independence of the world becomes an unbridgeable barrier and we are led to either skepticism or relativism. We are led to skepticism if we emphasize the fact that there is no measure or criterion accessible to us against which to compare our beliefs about the world. Thus we can never know if they are true, if they correspond to the way the world really is. We are led to relativism if we emphasize the fact that since there is no one measure or criterion accessible to us, we end up having an indefinite number of conceptual schemes, determined by the particular historical, cultural, or linguistic standpoint of the observer, making the truth of our beliefs relative to the particular scheme in which they are formed. Some of these beliefs may be incommensurable with others, that is, they might not share anything in common and thus be incomparable/untranslatable. This belief in the dualism of content/conceptual scheme is the third dogma of empiricism. Davidson's attack on it would, according to him, leave nothing distinctive to call empiricism.

By rejecting the third dogma, Davidson aims at regaining the world, at stemming the danger of relativism in which the world itself disappears into a multiplicity of perspectives. He concludes the article by saying: "In giving up the dualism of scheme and world, we do not give up the world, but re-establish unmediated touch with the familiar objects whose antics make our sentences and opinions true or false."[3] However, the truth of the sentences regarding this "unmediated touch" has been qualified in the previous sentence as remaining "relative to language, but that is as objective as can be." If Davidson clearly distinguishes between a causal interaction with the world and an epistemological one based on beliefs about the world, and the latter cannot be grounded on the former (*pace* the myth of the given), then "nothing can count as a reason for holding a belief except another belief."[4] The objectivity reached is not one understood as correspondence to an external, independent world, but rather as coherence among beliefs in a language. And as his article has attempted to show, truth relative to *a* language can be reduced to truth relative to language given the impossibility of having incommensurable languages. Any language as language must share enough common background with any other in order to be able to be identified as a language. This commonality of background among languages is what allows for divergences among them, that is, for error. Objectivity is to be found in the nature of beliefs themselves, not in their comparison to the external world. Davidson says: "The basic claim is that much community of belief is needed to provide a basis for communication or understanding; the extended claim should then be that objective error can occur only in a setting of largely true belief. Agreement does not make for truth, but much of what is agreed must be true if some of what is agreed is false."[5] Objectivity is given in belief due to the nature itself of beliefs.

However, as McDowell raises the issue,[6] if this is the case, what role does the causal transaction with the world play if it cannot justify our beliefs about the world? We are left spinning in a frictionless void of beliefs, without ever knowing with certainty whether they correspond to the world or not. What can the "antics" of the familiar objects consist of, which determine whether our statements and beliefs are true or false, if the causal space of perceptions and the logical space of reasons are kept separate? Davidson would need to either renounce any type of friction (as he seems to be doing when he says: "truth of sentences remains relative to language, but that is as objective as can be") or produce friction by coming up with some type of relation of justification between the simple causal transactions with the world, which determine (or co-determine) the antics of the familiar objects, and the beliefs formed about them. This second alternative would lead straight back to either the myth of the given or to skepticism/relativism.

Davidson seems to want to undo the dualism of scheme/content in order to save our immediate connection to the world, given that with it we fall into relativism. However, it would seem he just substitutes one dualism for another by substituting the term "belief" for "conceptual scheme." Instead of talking about the scheme/content dualism, we now have a logical space of reasons constituted by beliefs and a causal space of sensory information impinging on us ("experiential intake," in McDowell's vocabulary). The objectivity of our beliefs has not been sufficiently grounded insofar as we are left spinning in a frictionless void of beliefs cohering or not among each other, without any epistemological anchoring to the hardness of the world, except for the bombardment of nervous stimuli that cannot qualify as knowledge.

* * * *

Hegel's Introduction to the *Phenomenology of Spirit* can be divided into two sections. The first section would run from paragraphs 73 to 80, the second from paragraphs 81 to 89. Our main concern lies in the second section, which regards, in Hegel's own words, "the method of carrying out the inquiry."[7] In the next sentence he further clarifies what kind of inquiry this is: "an investigation and *examination of the reality of cognition.*"[8] I intend to focus on and analyze the structure appearing in the discussion of the "in-itself" and the "for-consciousness," understood respectively as content and scheme, and of the problem of the criterion. Before delving into the passages in question, an overview of the first section of the Introduction will help contextualize the discussion of the criterion. For this purpose I shall elucidate three main topics to be found in the first section: (1) certain epistemological paradoxes; (2) the starting point and drive of the *Phenomenology*; (3) the particularities of natural consciousness and its relation to the question of truth.

1.3 Introduction to the Introduction

1.3.1 Epistemological paradoxes

Hegel starts off by pointing to the paradoxes faced by an epistemological endeavor that separates cognition (*Erkennen*) from the true (*das Wahre*) and decides to focus on an analysis of the functioning of our conceptual schemes before dealing with content or "what truly is."[9] This does not mean that Hegel finds no value in epistemological endeavors that attempt to clarify the structure and limits of cognition, and that he merely wants to return to a pre-critical thinking that believes in an immediate access to "what truly is." As was mentioned above, the *Phenomenology* is itself an "*examination of the reality of cognition.*" Hegel is also a major foe of the immediate character of any type of knowledge. Science in its immediacy only "comes on the scene."[10] It is an appearance that has to exhibit itself as what it is. What Hegel criticizes from epistemological endeavors is the fact that they completely separate knowledge from truth, falling thus into the third dogma. This would lead to a renunciation of knowledge of "what truly is" and to its limitation to appearances, which would be a completely unacceptable compromise for Hegel regarding what knowledge should be about. This path describes in a general sense the move Kant makes in his *Critique of Pure Reason*: things in themselves are inaccessible to human cognition and to think about them leads to contradiction. Only appearances (phenomena) constituted by a manifold of sense data intuited through the pure forms of space and time and subsumed under categories of the understanding, united by a transcendental synthesis of apperception, make knowledge possible. There can only be cognition of things as they appear to us. It is by renouncing knowledge of the absolute that Kant is able to secure a universal knowledge against empiricism. Thus, he is able to overcome the limitations of both rationalism and empiricism. On the one hand, he renounces knowledge of the objects of reason, such as God, the soul and the world, due to the fact that there is no intuition of them (concepts without intuitions are empty). On the other hand, he nonetheless saves the possibility of universal knowledge due to the a priori character of both the pure forms of intuition and the categories of the understanding (by means of which not just the possibility of experience but also that of the objects of experience themselves is established). He merely limits the field of knowledge to phenomena, to things as they appear to us. Hegel has Kant in mind when he talks about "a type of cognition which, though it does not cognize the Absolute as Science aims to, is still true," and when he says that "cognition in general, though it be incapable of grasping the Absolute, is still capable of grasping other kinds of truth."[11] This is the "hazy distinction between an absolute truth and some other kind of truth,"[12] which Hegel cannot accept since it is already a compromise regarding his strongly asserted starting point "that the Absolute alone is true, or the truth alone is absolute."[13] A philosophy that settles for less than the absolute shall not bear such a name. The presupposition of the separation between scheme and content must be justified: why should one start from such a separation? This presupposition leads to the insoluble problem of separating scheme from content while simultaneously only having access to content through conceptual schemes: how does one have access to this content to verify if knowledge of it is correct, if the only access to it is precisely through our conceptual schemes? And if there were another type of access such as revelation or belief, why bother with epistemological matters at all?[14] Here one already sees emerging the problem of the "criterion." How does one know that the conceptual scheme being used to grasp reality does not distort it, if there is no direct access to this reality itself? This clearly brings out the problem faced by an opposition between two entities, one of which should account for the other: either there must appear a third element uniting them, or the two heterogeneous entities must be revealed not to be heterogeneous at all. The only way to approach the absolute is by means of reflection.[15] The only way to approach the true is by means of our knowledge *of* it. The content depicted by our conceptual scheme must already reside somehow in the scheme itself, in order to overcome an otherwise unbridgeable gap leading to skepticism or relativism.

The dead end that the separation of scheme from content leads to occurs when the scheme is taken as assuming an active role and as assuming a passive one. In the former it works as an instrument (*Werkzeug*), which leads to the problem of the effect it has on what it works on. It does not leave it unaffected, thus excluding all possibility of having access to "what truly is", independent of our attempt to grasp it via a particular scheme. In the latter it works as a medium

(*Mittel*) through which we are able to *see* "what truly is". This talk of knowledge assumed to work as a medium uses the metaphor of light and reflection, presupposing that light is what allows us to see objects as they truly are, without affecting them. Hegel wants to show, first of all, that it is a false metaphor insofar as we are equally blinded by pure light as by pure darkness. One must acknowledge the need for both light and darkness in their interplay in order to be able to distinguish objects. To grasp an object is to be able to distinguish it from what it is not. This requires negation, darkness.[16] Second, light is not just a neutral medium in which objects make their appearance for us, the subtraction of which would leave us with the pure thing "in-itself." Such a subtraction of the medium through which we cognize objects would leave us rather with "a pure direction or a blank space."[17] Hegel shares here with Kant his critique of the possibility of knowing things-in-themselves by means of a cognition separated from them by assuming either an active or a passive role. Either way, we would not have the thing-in-itself but only how it relates to us, organized and unified by our conceptual scheme. Whereas Kant gives up on knowledge of the in-itself, Hegel will challenge the absolute separation itself of scheme from content: why should one take for granted such a separation without analyzing it? It seems to be a presupposition unanalyzed and unaccounted for, that asserts "that the Absolute stands on one side and cognition on the other, independent and separated from it, and yet is something real."[18] The source of this unanalyzed presupposition seems to be a *fear of falling into error*: the more one fears error the farther and more isolated one sets up the absolute, as if trying to preserve it from being tainted by a false knowledge. The absolute stands beyond reach and only there can it maintain its fullness while all error and insufficiency fall upon the shoulders of cognition. Hegel suspects that the fear of error leads to an incapacity for taking up the absolute, and asks "whether the fear of error is not just the error itself?"[19] This does not amount to a move back to a pre-critical, immediate grasp of "what truly is". That the fear of error is considered to be the error itself does not mean that if we do not fear we shall not err, but rather that only by erring do we reach the absolute. If due to fear of erring we either become satisfied with a cognition of a lesser truth, or fall into the paradox of positing the absolute in a beyond while still using it as a criterion of the correctness of our knowledge about it, then we have renounced the absolute; we have committed the ultimate, absolute error insofar as it denies the possibility of any other error, and therefore, of reaching the true. The problem for Hegel is not that such an attitude errs, but that it errs in thinking that only by not erring can the absolute be reached. Hegel is not criticizing the fact that such an attitude is based on presuppositions, but rather that it is based on the presupposition of a "presuppositionless" true unaffected by our attempts at grasping it. He is criticizing a specific type of presupposition (that of a "presuppositionless" absolute). This can be seen through the fact that in the first sentence of the paragraph immediately following this talk of fear of error and of presuppositions, he lays down his own presupposition: "The Absolute alone is true, or the truth alone is absolute."[20] If Hegel is not criticizing an approach to truth from the standpoint of any presupposition, but rather an approach to it by means of the particular presupposition of a separation between the absolute and cognition, of a distinction between scheme and content, then he must show the advantage of his presupposition in order not to fall prey to his own criticism bluntly put in the Introduction: "*One* bare assurance is worth just as much as another."[21]

The difference lies in the fact that the presupposition of a separation between truth and cognition is self-defeating in either of the two paths it might lead to. The Kantian path is self-defeating insofar as knowledge of the absolute is renounced while simultaneously requiring a mysterious "thing-in-itself" to feed the understanding with content;[22] whereas the other path is also self-defeating insofar as it cannot offer a viable solution to the *paradox* expressed above, leading thus to skepticism. There is a further difference between the presupposition of a separation between cognition and truth, and that of an absolute that alone is true. While the former makes a specific claim to truth: "the Absolute stands on one side and cognition on the other,"[23] the latter is empty, a bracket to be filled with content in the form of any specific truth claim. In other words, while the former presupposition is a specific truth claim p, the latter consists in the need for there to be truth claims at all (p, q, r, etc.) if we are to know "what is." In asserting that "the Absolute alone is true" Hegel is just giving the *Phenomenology* its motor or drive, without asserting where it will lead, or filling it with a specific content. One could obviously say that if this is the case then it is perfectly legitimate to start with any type of truth claim insofar as it is a truth claim. Thus, it would be legitimate to start with the claim of a separation between cognition and truth. This is correct, and it is exactly what Hegel does: he follows up on this claim and reveals its self-defeating character and the need to go beyond it. In the last passages of the *Science of Logic* Hegel makes reference to this point, explaining why his first presupposition is superior to all others:

> The Method, which thus winds itself into a circle, cannot anticipate in a development in time that the beginning is, as such, already something derived; it is sufficient for the beginning in its immediacy that it is simple universality. In being that, it has its complete condition; and there is no need to deprecate the fact that it may only be accepted provisionally and hypothetically. Whatever objections to it might be raised – say, the limitations of human knowledge, the need to examine critically the instrument of cognition before starting to deal with the subject matter – are themselves presuppositions, which as concrete determinations involve the demand for their mediation and proof. Since therefore they possess no formal advantage over the beginning with the subject matter against which they protest, but on the contrary themselves require deduction on account of their *more concrete content*, their claim to prior consideration must be treated as an empty presumption.[24]

Hegel's presupposition is the truth of the Absolute.[25] He believes that the presupposition of transcendental philosophy (the prior investigation of the structure and limits of human cognition in order to clarify its possibility) is self-defeating (it renounces the absolute) and self-contradictory (the "thing-in-itself" is a contradictory concept). To presuppose the absolute would easily be taken as a dogmatic claim, in which case it could be challenged by any other dogmatic claim with the same pretension to truth. However, Hegel's presupposition is without content; it is a shell. To presuppose that the absolute alone is true is completely different from presupposing that the true is *this* here, or the *thing* with many qualities, or different *forces*; or that there is a separation between knowledge and reality. This separates Hegel from any dogmatic position.[26] One has to presuppose the absolute, be it what it may. To presuppose it is for it to already be present, in some form or another. Only by presupposing the absolute does one not close the door to its being reached. It should be made clear that to presuppose the absolute does not mean to presuppose having reached it. It only guarantees the *possibility*[27] of its being reached. In other words, what this presupposition excludes as self-contradictory is the dogmatic claim of academic skeptics, who assert that there is no truth.[28] A further consequence of this presupposition for Hegel is the denial of an absolute completely separated from knowledge, an "in-itself" *posited* as such, insofar as to posit something is to already establish a certain relation to it. From this perspective Kant would fall under the skeptical camp in his denial of the possibility of knowing things in themselves.[29]

1.3.2 Starting point and drive of the *Phenomenology*

Does natural consciousness belong to a specific historical period or is it rather a permanent feature, continuously encountered in the development of spirit? There are three references to it throughout the Introduction, by means of which a clearer idea can be reached of what such a consciousness consists in. In paragraph 77 Hegel says of it that it "presses forward to true knowledge,"[30] whereas in the following paragraph he says that "it takes itself to be real knowledge."[31] In the next paragraph Hegel talks of a "state of despair about all the so-called natural ideas, thoughts, and opinions...ideas with which the consciousness that sets about the examination [of truth] *straight away* is still filled and hampered, so that it is, in fact, incapable of carrying out what it wants to undertake."[32] I take the "*straight away*" (*geradezu*) to mean a lack of consciousness or analysis regarding the presuppositions from which a claim is asserted. As a perfect example of this one could cite the position that "presupposes that the Absolute stands on one side and cognition on the other, independent and separated from it."[33] Such a presupposition leads to contradictory consequences and must thus be overcome in order to reach the true. Natural consciousness seems to have then as its basic characteristic a claim to truth, whatever the content of that claim may be. The first consequence to be drawn from this is that it cannot have anything to do with a primitive being, immerse in nature, which has not yet torn itself from her, for which there is no consciousness of self, much less of truth.[34] In Part Three of the *Encyclopaedia*, in the chapter entitled "The Philosophy of Spirit," Hegel divides subjective spirit into soul, consciousness, and spirit, assigning them anthropology, phenomenology of spirit, and psychology, respectively. The natural consciousness the *Phenomenology* starts with is not the soul (which is itself divided into natural, feeling, and actual soul) but rather consciousness. The former "has not yet objectivized its notion, is still notionally undeveloped."[35] It is an immediate part of nature, still not grasping itself as different from or opposed to her. Such a soul would not be able to make any claim to truth, the major requirement of which is to establish a difference between itself and that which it takes to be true, between its knowledge and that which its knowledge is about.[36] Natural consciousness must be able to make a truth claim, to be aware of the possibility of being mistaken. It is not to be taken as a pure immediacy, at one with nature, but rather already split, capable of reflection.[37] However, if one reads the *Phenomenology* straightforwardly as leading to "the point where knowledge no longer needs to go beyond itself, where knowledge finds itself, where Notion corresponds to object and object to Notion,"[38] to "a point at which it gets rid of its semblance of being burdened with something alien, with what is only for it, and some sort of 'other,'"[39] then it would seem that the *Phenomenology* leads not only beyond natural consciousness, but also beyond reflection.[40] From one perspective this would seem to be true insofar as the *Science of Logic* consists of pure thought thinking itself, having overcome the separation between thought and object. Natural consciousness and, thus, reflection would seem to be overcome as philosophical starting points in the quest for "what is really real". However, there are two perspectives from which it is not overcome: natural consciousness is not a historical starting point. One should not tie it to a specific point in the development of humankind, the realization of which would bring it a step closer to "what is." Natural consciousness does not describe a specific historical moment, but rather a *position of thought* (*Stellung des Gedankens*). These positions are not historically but rather philosophically overcome. In other words, any quest for the true, at any given historical period, must make a gesture of reflecting on its own presuppositions and take them into account.[41]

However, natural consciousness is not overcome from a philosophical perspective, either. It would be wrong to assume that taken as a philosophical starting point it is completely overcome throughout the course of the *Phenomenology*, that there is no longer a reflection based on a subject/object separation, nor a consciousness "filled and hampered" by presuppositions, but rather a self-consciousness transparent to itself and at one with its objects. The movement itself of the *Science of Logic* belies this view and reveals that speculative thinking is not immune to the gap between subject and object (an object no longer posited as external to the subject, though). It is a reflection on this reflective activity.[42] We do not reach the world by overcoming the use of any conceptual scheme (myth of the given). We rather realize that it is precisely this dualism scheme/content that constitutes, and is the condition for reaching, it. Natural consciousness is to be overcome in the sense of realizing it *does* constitute what is true, though not in the way it thinks it does.[43]

What keeps the *Phenomenology* moving forward are not the actual claims to truth, but rather the contradictions they fall into and which they cannot remain in. Here we find another fundamental attribute of natural consciousness: its incapacity to withstand contradiction. It is impossible for it to remain in a contradictory position. When confronted by a contradiction, it cannot merely turn its back on it and continue unperturbed. There is something in its constitution that does not allow it to remain fixed to a certain claim when confronted by a claim that contradicts it.[44] When understanding posits a claim, it aims at the satisfaction of reaching a stable, unchangeable truth. However, it will find that what it had previously held as true reveals itself to be contradictory. This forces it to alter its claim. It is a constitutive part of understanding to follow the principle of non-contradiction.[45] The only alternative to being forced beyond by adherence to the principle of non-contradiction and the contradictory nature of things is for consciousness to turn its back altogether on any claim regarding what is and remain in the *barren ego*, a "paralysis, an incapacity for truth" that has nothing to do with philosophy and would contradict its first presupposition: the absolute itself.

1.3.3 Natural consciousness and the question of truth

In paragraph 80 Hegel defines consciousness as being

> explicitly the *Notion* of itself. Hence, it is something that goes beyond limits, and since these limits are its own, it is something that goes beyond itself. With the positing of a single particular the beyond is also established for consciousness, even if it is only *alongside* the limited object, as in the case of spatial intuition. Thus, consciousness suffers this violence at its own hands: it spoils its own limited satisfaction.[46]

The German makes use of the term "for-itself": "*Das Bewußtsein aber ist für sich selbst sein Begriff*" (Consciousness is "for-itself" its own concept). This sole characteristic must explain the uniqueness of consciousness and thus its relation to making truth-claims. Consciousness is opposed here to what is limited to a natural life, which in turn is characterized as not being able to "by its own efforts go beyond its immediate existence."[47]

What characterizes consciousness is that it has a concept of itself. It is split between what it is and the concept it has of what it is. However, for our purposes and those of the second half of the Introduction, the focus will be the more general fact that any object of consciousness, be it itself or an object, is split between *it* and whatever is said (or meant: *gemeint*) about it, between content and conceptual scheme. The important issue for Hegel here is not only that consciousness has a concept of itself but mainly that whatever it may be conscious of (there can never be a pure consciousness without content), there will always be a gap between what it is conscious of and the belief it has about it. In other words, Hegel is interested in a consciousness always already conscious *of* something *as* something, split into the content of its consciousness and its concept or belief regarding that content. It is not the case that an *I* stands all alone, without a world, and discovers itself, forming a concept of itself. Consciousness already means consciousness of something, with a specific content. It does not merely have a content, but always has a belief about the particular content it has or is conscious of. Consciousness is always split between the content it *means* at a specific moment and the concept it has of such a content. The sentence immediately following the definition of consciousness talks about limits and a beyond. The word *limit* should be understood to refer to the belief consciousness has, the conceptual scheme it uses to relate to the content. It is limited insofar as it is merely *for consciousness*. What will take it beyond (*jenseits*) itself to the content is its referent. The belief immediately refers back to something it is a belief *of*, an "in-itself."[48]

Thus, the reading given to the definition of consciousness as what is for itself its own concept brings out the connection to the second half of the Introduction regarding the measure insofar as consciousness is shown to always have a belief regarding what it is conscious of. It is structurally split between an "in-itself" and a "for-consciousness," between the content it has at a specific moment, and the manner in which that content appears to it, the *Sinn* in the famous Fregean distinction between *Sinn* and *Bedeutung* (meaning and reference). The problem of truth takes place in the field opened by this gap, in the non-correspondence between these two poles, and in the movement generated by this non-correspondence. This is why truth is a problem specific to natural consciousness and its peculiar structure, and why natural consciousness *can find no peace* as long as it thinks, since to think is to think *that*, to take something *as* something.

1.4 The problem of the criterion or measure

The second half of the Introduction is described by Hegel as dealing with: "a way of *relating Science* to *phenomenal* knowledge, and ... an investigation and *examination of the reality of cognition*."[49] The first part of this description reveals the problem of justification. The term *Science* can be substituted here for the absolute, "what truly is", the true, and so on. How can it reveal and justify itself as true? How does phenomenal knowledge show itself to be what it claims to be? Any claim to truth can only be verified by a comparison to that which it is a claim about. Verification requires a standard or criterion against which to verify whatever is being asserted as true. Hegel calls this criterion a presupposition: "it would seem that it [the exposition] cannot take place without some presupposition which can serve as its underlying *criterion.*"[50] The use of the word *seem* might easily point toward a Hegelian critique of the assumption of a criterion for confronting the problem of truth. However, as will be shown below, the critique is directed rather against the external nature assigned to this presupposed underlying criterion. It attempts to show that such a presupposition is in truth a *positing* by consciousness itself, though this by no means would deny its necessary character for the search for truth. The problematic of the criterion is what the *examination of the reality of cognition* consists in. One should be aware that what is being dealt with in the Introduction and the first three sections of the *Phenomenology* is precisely this cognition. The examination occurs despite the fact that for Hegel the prior analysis of the cognitive power leads to contradiction and insoluble paradoxes, and that Science, "in the absence of such scruples gets on with the work itself, and actually cognizes something."[51] The examination does not occur in the Kantian sense developed in the first *Critique*, but rather in a phenomenological sense of merely observing natural consciousness at work in its claims to truth. Hegel's starting point is similar to Kant's: to realize how the faculty of understanding works. However, he does not limit its application by renouncing the Absolute. Rather, he reveals how the Absolute shows itself *as* understanding. Hegel does not fall into a contradiction by, on the one hand, asserting that the starting point of epistemology leads to contradiction and paradoxes, and, on the other, starting with "an investigation and *examination of the reality of cognition.*" He does not share the deficiency of the epistemological endeavor he is observing (its unchecked presupposition of an Absolute on one side and cognition on the other). He is merely following its development. Kant's problem was not his focus on epistemological concerns, but rather his overlooking the fact that such a starting point was not without presuppositions. Hegel, on the other hand, neither follows Kant's path, presupposing that the Absolute is opposed to cognition, nor starts straight off with the Absolute. He realizes there has to be an examination of cognition, precisely because it is where the Absolute reveals itself (as what cognition is *about*).

The obvious paradox emerging from the problem of the criterion consists in the following: How does one have access to this criterion in order to examine the claim to truth? A content cannot justify or validate itself. A direct relation to the world or reality occurs at a purely causal level that would preclude any possible justification insofar as a truth claim takes us from the causal space of perceptions to the logical space of reasons. Any claim to knowledge requires a conceptual ability that would take us beyond the purely given. As Hegel will show in the chapter on sense-certainty, one can neither say nor think the given *as* given. The attempt itself already takes us beyond it. There is no non-inferential perception of particulars that can qualify as knowledge since at the very least the particular must be able to be re-identified, which cannot occur without a conceptual apparatus.[52] How can the content function as the criterion by which we determine whether our beliefs about it are accurate? What assigns our conceptual schemes the objectivity they aspire to if what they are about lies beyond their reach? How do we avoid relativism/skepticism? The solution to this paradox lies in the definition of consciousness: it is for itself its own concept, although in paragraph 82 Hegel uses other words to describe it:

> Consciousness simultaneously *distinguishes* itself from something, and at the same time *relates* itself to it, or, as it is said, this something exists *for* consciousness; and the determinate aspect of this *relating*, or of the *being* of something for a consciousness, is *knowing*. But we distinguish this being-for-another from *being-in-itself*, whatever is related to knowledge or knowing is also distinguished from it, and posited as existing outside of this relationship; this *being-in-itself* is called *truth*.[53]

A natural consciousness with a claim to truth distinguishes the content of its claim (what its belief is about) from the belief it has about such content (what it knows about that content). In this context Hegel ascribes the terms "in-itself" to the former and "for-consciousness" to the latter. Thus we have knowledge and "being-for-consciousness" as referring to the way the object is taken by consciousness based on a conceptual scheme, and truth and "being-in-itself" as referring to the object independent of consciousness. Taking into consideration the fact that this is a split internal to consciousness, we then have natural consciousness being conscious, on the one hand, of itself as knowing—having a determinate belief with a claim to truth—and, on the other, of the object its determinate belief is about; of a conceptual scheme that allows the object to appear to it in a certain way, and of the object it has conceptualized.

1.4.1 Criticisms raised against Hegel

What does natural consciousness understand by truth and knowledge at the beginning of the *Phenomenology*? Its aim is to lead phenomenal knowledge on the path to Science or absolute knowledge. This already requires as starting point a consciousness whose desire is to reach "what is." Therefore, its main characteristic is that it makes claims to truth. Hegel is interested in a consciousness that claims *that* such and such is the case, a consciousness constituted by a "holding-as-true" or believing (in the sense of *meinen*).[54]

The "abstract determinations of truth and knowledge as they occur in consciousness"[55] are not what Hegel himself understands by them, but rather what natural consciousness takes them to be in an immediate manner. After giving a description of them as they occur in consciousness, Hegel says: "Just what might be involved in these determinations is of no further concern to us here. Since our object is phenomenal knowledge, its determinations too will at first be taken directly as they present themselves."[56] What is involved in these determinations is the concern of the *Phenomenology* as a whole, and only at its end will it become clear what truth and knowledge are. There is also a distinction between what natural consciousness understands by truth and knowledge, and these determinations *as they occur in it*.[57] The determinations given of these two concepts in paragraph 82 are not the response natural consciousness would give when asked what truth and knowledge are. They are, rather, the presuppositions underlying a consciousness with a claim to truth, in which it takes something as something. In other words, underlying any immediate cognitive claim regarding reality lies a distinction between what is being talked about and what is being said about it. This necessarily occurs in consciousness when it makes a claim to truth. Whatever natural consciousness might believe truth and knowledge to be, whatever definition it might give of them, its truth claims will presuppose this distinction. This distinction takes the structure of the conceptual scheme/content dualism, in which the content is what is being talked about, whereas the conceptual scheme consists in how that content appears unified for consciousness in the form of a belief about it, the *as* as which it appears to consciousness. This reading of the phrase: "abstract determinations of truth and knowledge as they occur in consciousness" corresponds well with the phenomenological character of Hegel's analysis. What is being observed is natural consciousness asserting a claim to truth. A claim to truth is not a claim about *truth* but rather about *what is true*.[58] Evidence of this is sense certainty's deictic attempt at grasping what is true in the form of *this* here and now. If this is the case, then Hegel, in order to reach an understanding of what truth and knowledge are for natural consciousness, has to observe it in its attempt to figure out what is true, and extract from this the presuppositions underlying its answers, instead of questioning it directly. Natural consciousness has the reflexive nature of attempting to reach "what truly is", but not yet the self-reflective nature of realizing how it itself is constitutive of "what truly is"; it is not yet capable of transforming the question into: "How is truth structured?"

Any criticism regarding natural consciousness's understanding of what truth and knowledge are[59] would then be unfounded insofar as the natural consciousness with which the *Phenomenology* begins is not being asked directly what it understands by these concepts, but merely being observed in its claims to truth, which point toward a certain structure underlying them.

Knowledge *as it occurs in consciousness* is the *determinate aspect* of the relating of consciousness to an object that it simultaneously distinguishes from itself. Given that natural consciousness is to be understood in the sense of "holding-as-true," "*determinate aspect*" here should mean the *as* as which the object I am conscious of appears. It is determinate precisely because it is a specific belief. There can be no knowledge of objects insofar as an object can be neither true nor false.[60] It is important to keep in mind that what Hegel offers as "knowledge" at the beginning of the *Phenomenology* is a claim that still needs to be verified or falsified; it is neither true nor false. It is merely a determinate belief of consciousness, which, when asserted in its constituting a claim to truth, is worth just as much as any other. Thus, the determinate aspect of the relating of consciousness to an object includes within it all types of opinions, errors, and illusions since they will be revealed to be such only in retrospect. These are all different types of knowledge, still to be confirmed or falsified, homogeneous in their claims to be true.[61]

This explains Tugendhat's misreading of Hegel's understanding of "knowledge."[62] Tugendhat understands belief (*meinung*) as a "holding-as-true" that has not yet been grounded, has not yet given reasons for its being taken as true. It is a wider category than knowledge. This description of belief matches precisely what Hegel understands as knowledge: it is a claim to truth that has not yet shown itself to be what it claims to be. This is the case with each of the stages of consciousness in its search for truth. The emphasis underlying both Tugendhat's *Meinen* and Hegel's *knowledge* is the need for it to be justified, to show itself to be true. This need keeps the *Phenomenology* in motion. Thus, contrary to what Tugendhat asserts, giving reasons for a claim (showing itself to be what it claims) is the fundamental character of what knowledge is for Hegel insofar as he criticizes all attempts at immediate knowledge and intellectual intuition, which would obviate the need for such a grounding.

What, then, does Hegel understand as *Meinen* if his concept of knowledge can be equated to what Tugendhat understands as *Meinen*? The first chapter has as its title "Sense-Certainty: or the 'this' and "Meaning" (*Meinen*)." What characterizes this shape of consciousness is its lack of consciousness of the role of language or universals in its claim to truth. It believes it can express precisely what it has in its mind, what it *means*, in all its particularity, not realizing that the moment it is expressed in words it becomes a universal. What Hegel understands by *Meinen* here is total particularity, what *one means* to express before expressing it, before it becomes something shared and thus universal. The critique lies in the fact that one cannot mean the most particular without already expressing its opposite: a universal. The act itself of "*meinen*" is a contradictory one. In the *Science of Logic*, in which the object of thought is itself internal to thinking, there are also various contradictory acts of thought itself. When "being" is thought, what is meant is the most determinate, but what ends up being expressed is the most abstract and empty: nothing. Thus, *Meinen* is what is meant, intended in language or thought, which, when expressed, ends up being the opposite of what was meant.[63] Taking into consideration the differences between what Hegel understands by *Meinen* at the beginning of the *Phenomenology* (where consciousness attempts to grasp "what is" non-linguistically) and in the *Science of Logic* (where thinking is expressed in language), what seems to distinguish *Meinen* from knowledge is the unreflective or immediate character of its assertion, due to which it does not realize that it is saying exactly the opposite of what it meant. The difference between knowledge and meaning, then, would be one of degree: whereas all knowledge is a holding-to-be-true that will be revealed to be false when asked for the reasons grounding it, meaning is an extreme version of this holding-to-be-true insofar as it is not even "aware of what [it] is saying,"[64] or, put more precisely, insofar as it says the opposite of what it means to say. Hegel seems to reserve the use of this concept of *Meinen* for those extreme situations in which the assertion itself of consciousness or of thinking already *explicitly* includes within it its own opposite.

With regard to Tugendhat's concept of *Wissen*, the two characteristics that constitute it are: (1) it is true; (2) it can be justified as true by giving reasons.[65] The *Phenomenology* as a whole is a continuous endeavor to accomplish the latter. The movement from shape to shape is nothing but the realization that the reasons given for their truth have led to contradiction and thus have falsified their claims. The former is merely the consequence reached through the fulfillment of the latter, which is its necessary and sufficient condition. What can it mean for something to be true if not that good reasons (no better reasons appearing yet on the horizon) can be given in its favor? The only path for reaching the conclusion that something is true is by accepting the reasons given for such a claim. According to Hegel, when this point is reached we will have arrived at truth (absolute knowledge), having sublated (*aufgehoben*) knowledge. The *Phenomenology* should be read as a continuous attempt at progressing from knowledge to truth.[66]

The main criticism against Hegel's concept of truth as it appears in the Introduction is that it is not propositional.[67] As was mentioned above, the definition of truth given in the Introduction is not Hegel's own, but has to do with natural consciousness. Furthermore, it is not even natural consciousness's explicit understanding of truth but, rather, what is implicit in its claims to truth, the presuppositions underlying such claims. Is Hegel blind to the propositional character of truth? Considering the fact that consciousness, as understood by Hegel, is not merely consciousness of something, but rather of something *as* something, thus distinguishing the object it is conscious of from that *as* which the object appears to it, and thus from itself, it never relates directly to objects as true or false, but rather to propositions: that such and such is the case regarding an object. For truth to be at stake something must be said or predicated about something. At a cognitive level there can be no relation to a pure "in-itself"; it is only through the object's being for-consciousness that consciousness can relate to it, only by taking it *as* something, by asserting something about it. The space for truth lies in the correspondence or non-correspondence between these two poles of consciousness: between what we assert about an object, which requires a conceptual scheme applied to it, and the object itself or content.[68]

1.4.2 The nature of consciousness

Hegel's solution to the problem of the measure will lie in the nature of the object of investigation. The *Phenomenology* is an "investigation and *examination of the reality of cognition*." What is being investigated is knowledge itself, or rather consciousness in its claims to truth. The nature of consciousness is to be for itself its own concept. Thus, the object of investigation is this "being for itself its own concept." This means that the object of investigation is an activity: consciousness is an activity. As such there is no separation between what it is "in-itself" and the concept it has of itself insofar as its "in-itself" is precisely the activity of being "for-itself," of having a concept of itself. Consciousness "in-itself" is the concept it has of itself. It is whatever it thinks it is insofar as it is constituted only in this thinking. This solves the paradox of the measure since consciousness reveals itself to have both moments within it: what it is and the belief it has of what it is. One should be careful not to ascribe to Hegel a collapse of these two poles into one, which would justify a claim of complete self-transparency for consciousness. First of all, consciousness is not an object but an activity; it is in constant movement and change. Second, as Hegel mentions in paragraph 80, insofar as consciousness is for itself its own concept, what it is is always more than its beliefs about itself. The content of consciousness is never exhausted in the peculiar properties it ascribes to itself. It always goes *beyond* what it thinks it is, and cannot be tied down to any particular properties. It is constituted precisely by what it ascribes to itself and nothing more, while simultaneously always being more than what it thinks it is.

In paragraph 84 a second sentence is offered regarding consciousness: "Consciousness provides its own criterion from within itself."[69] The German reads: "*Das Bewußtsein gibt seinem Maßstab an ihm selbst*" (consciousness gives its criterion to itself). Miller's translation emphasizes the fact that the origin of the measure lies within consciousness itself. However, the German *an ihm selbst* seems to lay the emphasis elsewhere, as Heidegger correctly notes,[70] insofar as it does not use the reflexive conjugation (*an sich selbst*), but rather the dative. This would place the emphasis on the *separation* between consciousness and the measure despite consciousness's own active role in giving itself the measure. There is an objective element in the measure that is not totally absorbed by the fact that it is consciousness that gives itself the measure.[71]

In this same paragraph Hegel seems to want to show how the examination of our knowledge in its comparison to what is true works either way, be it that we take the concept or belief as knowledge and the object or content as what is true, or that we take rather the concept or belief as what is true and the object or content as given to us in its appearing. In the former, the examination consists in comparing our scheme to the content, whereas in the latter it consists in comparing the content in its appearing to our concept or scheme. What is important for Hegel here is that either way both poles fall within consciousness. In this context of showing how consciousness is internally split between its content and the concept it has of it, Hegel is right in his assertion "that the two procedures are the same."[72] It is worth dwelling on this assertion that they are the same, since it seems to go against Hegel's own distinction between mere correctness and truth.[73] Correctness occurs when our subjective knowledge corresponds to objective reality, and its proof or verification is just an empirical matter. What is called external reality is the criterion used, and the relation of consciousness to it is by means of perception and the senses. There is a different type of object concerning which what is at stake is no longer correctness but truth. In this case, the object must correspond to the concept being ascribed to it. It is an objective concept insofar as it is not constituted by a particular individual and her perception, but rather by a society or culture throughout its development, and thus it determines reality in its correspondence or non-correspondence to such a concept. Examples of these objects are beauty, justice, goodness, friendship, and so on. A specific object is true or not depending on its correspondence or non-correspondence to its concept. Given this reading, the two procedures cannot be taken up as the same since in them both the concept of concept and that of object vary. In the first, we have a subjective concept: what I as individual believe or mean to be true; whereas in the second we have an objective concept: a universal concept determined throughout time by cultures, societies, or institutions. Regarding the object, in the first procedure it is the object posited as beyond our particular perception of it, the pure "in-itself" untouched by us, whereas in the second it is the particular in its particularity, perceived by us. Using Hegelian terminology, there is both an object "in-itself" and one "for-itself," and a concept "in-itself" and one "for-itself." The object is split between the appearance and that which it is an appearance of,[74] whereas the concept is split between the subjective concept determined by the object it is a concept of and the objective concept, which determines the object as adequate to it or not. This distinction would seem to create a sort of gradation of types of being, some located closer to the absolute than others. To assert that the two procedures are the same, on the other hand, would allow us to avoid this gradation of being. They are the same insofar as either way, be it that we are dealing with certain types of objects such as states, works of art, human actions, and so on or with grains of salt, the objects *always already* require concepts for them to appear *as* such objects. For an object to be given to us in consciousness, for us to know a particular, it must appear *as* something, which itself requires a conceptual ability. In hermeneutical jargon, for any object to be thematized, it must appear from within a horizon that gives it the meaning it possesses in its being thematized. In Sellars's terms, there can be no non-inferential knowledge without there already being a conceptual world within which those non-inferential experiences are given.[75] There is no knowledge at the purely causal space of perceptions. Content without concepts would not be able to be recognized as content. This is the lesson learned by sense-certainty.

Before continuing on with paragraph 85, let us clarify an important grammatical distinction appearing in the original German, which gets lost in its translation into English. It has been said above that consciousness is split between its belief about an object (that such and such is the case), and the object it has knowledge of. Insofar as both form part of consciousness itself, they are both for consciousness, obviously in different ways. This distinction is made explicit by Hegel all along paragraphs 84–87 through a corresponding grammatical distinction. What we have called the belief of consciousness or the "for-itself" (knowledge) is referred to by Hegel by means of the preposition *von*: *Wissen von einem Gegenstand* (knowledge *of* an object). This illustrates what was said above concerning the fact that we cannot know an object but rather *of* an object that it is so and so. There is only one reference to this belief that, instead of using the preposition *von*, uses the direct object in the accusative form: "The object it is true, seems only to be for consciousness in the way that consciousness knows it."[76] Obviously, this "in the way" means *as it appears to consciousness*; it does not presuppose that consciousness knows an object but that it knows it *as* something: in the way it appears to it. Some of Miller's renditions of the "*wissen von*" discard the use of the preposition and therefore collapse the distinction between knowing an object and knowing something of an object, the latter being Hegel's position concerning knowledge, the former being impossible for him. For example, Miller translates: "But the distinction between the in-itself and knowledge is already present in the very fact that consciousness knows an object at all."[77] The distinction is present since consciousness knows *of* an object *that* it is such and such. Between paragraphs 83 and 87 there are a total of eight uses of *von* plus the dative case and one use of "*the way consciousness knows it*," to refer to consciousness's knowledge. On the other hand, the object of that belief, the "in-itself," is referred to by Hegel with the dative case: *ihm*. Within these four paragraphs such a use of the dative occurs eight times. The problem concerning Miller's translation is that this use of the German dative (*ihm*) can only be translated into the preposition *for*, which would extinguish any distinction between these two poles of consciousness. Only once does Miller attempt to save the distinction by forcing the English and translating: "At the same time this other is *to* consciousness not merely *for it*, but is also outside of this relationship, or exists *in itself*."[78] This strangely sounding *to* is a direct translation of the German dative *ihm*, which Hegel uses to refer to the content about which consciousness has a belief, that of which it knows something. Another way to grasp the difference between the *for it* and the *to it* (*ihm*) is to equate the latter to the subject of a sentence, the content being referred to, and the former to the *that* clause asserted of it, which requires a conceptual scheme by means of which we can have an object at all. The subject is *presupposed* as independent of all predicates, but is in truth *posited* as independent only through its predicates.[79]

1.4.3 The instability of the object: paragraph 85

Returning to the problem of the alteration of the object by means of the alteration of our knowledge of it, this is a perfectly sound conclusion derived from the split existing in consciousness insofar as the only reference to the object "in-itself" is by means of our knowledge of it, of its being "for-itself." This is the case due to the following: the object "in-itself" is posited by consciousness as being "in-itself." It is a sort of shadow[80] projected by our knowledge. All knowledge is knowledge of something *as* something. The object "in-itself" is the *of* projected by means of its appearing to us *as* something. Being the only connection to it, the moment this knowledge we have of it is falsified, the object too will be altered, just as a change in an object under the sun determines a change in the shadow it produces. As Hegel says, the object "essentially belonged to this knowledge."[81] It is fundamental for Hegel to assert that the object is also altered with the alteration of the knowledge about it. This is a critique of the idea of a "thing-in-itself," a *beyond* completely unrelated to our knowledge of it, a content lying beyond all conceptual schemes. This critique does not mean that Hegel opens the door to the "thing-in-itself"; it is not a relapse into a certain metaphysics in which access to "things-in-themselves" is granted. Rather, with the assertion that the object is altered with the alteration of our knowledge of it Hegel is showing that we simultaneously have and do not have access to the "thing-in-itself," that insofar as we *posit* it as a shadow, we are related to it, but insofar as we posit it as a *shadow*, it will never be transparent to us. It is not the case that it is unknowable because we can never reach it due to our being affected only by how it appears to us. Rather, it is unknowable because it is nothing but appearance, constituted in its appearing as *what* appears as such and such. It does not give rise to its appearances *as* something, but is originated in these appearings. The world is not made of sense-data, things with qualities, or forces. Rather, our different conceptual strategies project back onto the world entities as shadows of our knowledge.

Hegel says: "Hence it comes to pass for consciousness that what it previously took to be the *in-itself* is not an *in-itself*, or that it was only an in-itself *for consciousness*."[82] The in-itself does not remain untouched by our knowledge of it. If this were the case, there could be no knowledge of it since there would be no possible access to it. It would be a content lying beyond any conceptual scheme attempting to grasp it. In my truth-claim the object "in-itself" is constituted by what I claim is the case regarding it. The moment this claim is falsified, that object "in-itself" reveals itself to have only been for me, posited by a false knowledge. There is no such thing as a *hypokeimenon* to which I ascribe accidents, that remains what it is through the process of revealing these accidents to be false. This supposed *hypokeimenon* is always already in alteration, being determined by the accidents predicated and denied of it.[83] The object "in-itself" is altered with the alteration of knowledge since it is pure alteration. It is not the case that I assert that the table is red, after which, through empirical corroboration, I assert that the table is not red, but purple, while the table remains as a substratum all along. Rather, I assert that the red table is red (since the only relation I have to the table is its being red[84]), then I find my claim falsified and conclude that it is false that the red table is red, but rather the purple table is purple. There is a double movement occurring in knowledge: (1) the table "in-itself" posited in my claim concerning its redness becomes a mere table-for-me when this claim is revealed to be false (according to this, knowledge seems to always be equivalent to, or be revealed as, false knowledge); (2) a new object "in-itself" is posited the moment I alter my claim to truth regarding that previous "in-itself," constituted by the new belief of consciousness.[85]

Let us attempt to clarify what Hegel means with this alteration of the object by making use of the hermeneutical vocabulary of horizon and theme proposed by Theunissen.[86] "Being-for-consciousness" is a thematizing of something, that is, an appearing of something *as* something. All thematizing is possible only through a horizon it comes out of, which is itself in constant alteration. This horizon works as the condition of possibility for something to appear *as* something. The thematizing of an object (its appearing *as* something to consciousness), and more importantly, its being revealed not to be the case, will alter the horizon from which the object came in its appearing. This horizon is never totally revealed.

1.4.4 The negativity of experience: paragraph 86

Paragraph 86 deals with what Hegel calls *experience* and with the two objects it is constituted by: the disappearing into nothingness of the first, and the appearing of the second as a new object. The movement from the one to the other is what Hegel calls *experience*: not only the alteration of consciousness's belief but also that of the object itself, the continuous emergence of a new object in the quest for truth. The first object is the "in-itself," posited by means of my knowledge that an object appears to me as such and such. In being posited the "in-itself" is the shadow of my knowledge. To continue with the example of the red table, when I perceive a red table I immediately posit the table as the "in-itself" to which I ascribe the attribute of redness, notwithstanding the fact that the table could only have emerged through the appearance for me of one or many of its attributes. When I realize that my knowledge of the table (as red) is false, the table posited as "in-itself," the shadow of my knowledge, becomes "for-consciousness," that is, it becomes the table of a false knowledge, falling into nothingness as false knowledge. This means that both the redness ascribed to the table and the table itself are falsified. The only content the table had, its only relation to consciousness, was its being red. Nothing subsists beyond my knowledge of it, unperturbed by the falsifiable character of knowledge, because then knowledge itself would be impossible (this is part of the meaning of Hegel's assertion that the Absolute is "with us, in and for itself, all along"[87]). If we maintain the dualism scheme/content, knowledge would be impossible. If the first object, posited "in-itself," disappears into nothingness when it becomes part of a false knowledge, when it becomes a "being-for-consciousness" of an "in-itself," what is the second object and where does it come from? Hegel's reply would seem to point merely toward the becoming for knowledge of the first object, of the "in-itself," as the second object. He says:

> But, as was shown previously, the first object, in being known, is altered for consciousness; it ceases to be the in-itself, and becomes something that is the *in-itself* only *for consciousness*. And this then is the True: the being-for-consciousness of this in-itself. Or, in other words, this is the *essence*, or the *object* of consciousness. This new object contains the nothingness of the first, it is what experience has made of it.[88]

One has to be careful here not to ascribe the character of being the true to something that is only for consciousness. Let us remember that the alteration of knowledge (the disintegration of the first object into nothingness and the emergence of the second object) occurs only insofar as it is falsified, revealed as contradictory. This is what experience means for Hegel: something is revealed as not being what it was thought to be.[89] What Hegel wants to show with this talk of the second object issuing from the dialectical movement, of this new object being the true, is that experience does not occur in a vacuum, it does not appear *ex nihilo*. The falsifying of knowledge does not empty the claim to truth it produced. Rather, it immediately exchanges it for another. When we discover that the red table is not red, we are not left with a color-less table; the discovery of non-redness is simultaneously the revealing of another color. Knowledge consists in a constant process of change and alteration in its claims to truth.[90] This means that the becoming "for-consciousness" of the "in-itself" (the revealing of the red table as not being red) is simultaneously the emergence, not of a new truth claim about *it* (that it is *x*-colored), but of a new object "in-itself" (that the x-colored table is x-colored). False knowledge is only revealed as such by a new truth claim. Both the first and second are objects in-themselves, the first being revealed in the process of experience as merely "for-consciousness," as our (false) knowledge *of* it; the second being the "in-itself" *posited* by consciousness as "in-itself" through its experience of its new knowledge: as soon as the new object appears to us *as* something it also appears retrospectively as independent of our knowledge of it. There are four objects in the process of experience: two objects in-themselves and two objects for-consciousness. The second object is not the "being-for-consciousness" of the first "in-itself" but rather the "in-itself" of the second "being-for-consciousness," of our new knowledge. The *thing* with multiple properties is not the "being-for-consciousness" of the *this* here but rather the "in-itself" of the new object appearing *as* a grain of salt after the *this* vanished in the midst of its contradictory nature, becoming "for-consciousness".

Obviously, the newness of the new object should not be taken so literally. Just as it is new in the sense that it appears as something different, thus *being* something different (since it *is* its appearing), it is also not new in the sense that nothing completely new can appear from nowhere. There can be no thematization of something without a horizon from which it is thematized. Hegel himself, by saying that the "new object contains the nothingness of the first,"[91] shows that they share a horizon from which they are thematized, the second as a negation of the first. The specific pre-understanding shared by human beings of a particular society or culture holds experience together and gives it a sense of continuity, despite its negative element.

Given this reading of what Hegel means by first and second objects in the process of experience, the nothingness mentioned is not opposed to the content, but belongs to it.[92] It is *determinate* nothingness, the negation of a specific content. An appropriate way of grasping what this positive value of nothingness consists in, is by means of the concept of becoming: to negate an object is to reveal the dynamic nature of being, to reveal how it is intimately tied to its opposite: nothing.[93] Nothingness does not negate existence; it negates static being, a dead thing. That the *new object contains the nothingness of the first* reveals how what Hegel is dealing with here is becoming. The content becomes other than itself while our knowledge of it is revealed to be false. What experience has learned of the new object is what it is not. "Nothingness" is what the "in-itself" ceases to be in its becoming something other through human experience; it is determinate insofar as experience is made *of* it. The emphasis on becoming determines not only a change in our truth claims or conceptual schemes, but also in the content, which is constantly altering in the alteration of our knowledge of it. Hegel says: "In other words, the criterion for testing is altered when that for which it was to have been the criterion fails to pass the test; and the testing is not only a testing of what we know, but also a testing of the criterion of what knowing is."[94] The conceptual scheme/content distinction is overcome, though not insofar as the concept embraces the content with no remainder. It is rather overcome insofar as the content is constantly being posited or projected from the conceptual scheme as the shadow cast by it. We are one with our shadow since we cannot shake it off. However, every attempt to embrace it keeps us at a certain remove from it. In this manner, the third dogma of empiricism amounts to the most stubborn opposition encountered in the idea of the true and as such co-constitutes the absoluteness of the absolute idea.

* * * *

The problem of the examination of knowledge with respect to "what truly is", and of the criterion by which such an examination is to take place, has brought up an *internal* dualism between knowledge of what is, the conceptual scheme, and the reality it is a knowledge *of*, the content. It has revealed the impossibility of having pure and unmediated access to a content untouched by its being known by consciousness. However, this move by itself would lead to a frictionless spinning in a void, as McDowell calls Davidson's coherentist position, in which all objectivity and hardness of the world are lost. Hegel's move to avoid the loss of the world is to make sure that the internalization of this dualism does not amount to the collapse of its two sides: scheme and content. Consciousness is structurally constituted by this gap. The fact that the objective pole of consciousness (the "in-itself" which is to it [*ihm*]) lies within consciousness itself, does not lead to its complete revelation, to a total transparency by means of which "what truly is" appears in all its plenitude; nor does it lead to a frictionless spinning in a void having severed any anchoring to the world. On the contrary, the human experience *par excellence* is that of negativity: realizing that what was thought to be the case is not so.[95] To posit that "what truly is" is not a reality external to and independent of consciousness but rather given to us *in* the conceptual schemes we (as Spirit) posit of such a reality does not lead to the fulfillment of correspondence between thinking and what is thought. Nor does it lead to a coherentist fitting among beliefs, without any bite on the world. The structural gap constituting the thinking *of* reality also constitutes the thinking *of* conceptualized content, as the whole development of the *Science of Logic* attests to. Following McDowell's terminology, the objective logic follows the conceptual strategies used to think what is when it is thought as *outside thinking*, whereas the subjective logic follows the conceptual strategies used to think what is when thought as internal to thinking. In neither case can the content thought lie *outside what is thinkable*.

The structure revealed in the second half of the Introduction by means of the problem of the criterion is not overcome with the *Phenomenology* since it is constitutive of thinking as such. All thinking is thinking of something (be it external object or concept) that such and such is the case. The fact that there is no pure transparency in the thinking of conceptual schemes, that there is a gap structurally inherent to thinking that simultaneously makes it possible to talk of truth (of an "other" to knowledge posited by knowledge) and bars access to such truth, determines the idea of the true as a *most stubborn opposition* not to be overcome. Proof of this is that it is determined as such in the last sections of the *Science of Logic*. The opposition between conceptual scheme and content cannot be dissolved. Knowledge is always *of* something. "What is" always lies just beyond knowledge *of* it.

Hegel by internalizing, without collapsing, the dualism scheme/content, confronts the specters of relativism and skepticism, which state that given the gap between scheme and content, either we will never know if our knowledge matches the world it is about, or truth is relative to us, to a particular conceptual scheme.[96] The first move, that of internalization, is realized by the fact that the in-itself is, as in-itself, already in-itself-for-consciousness. It is posited by consciousness as in-itself. We are on both sides of the gap since the other side, the content, is the shadow projected by our conceptual scheme. This would seem to lead to a pure frictionless position, where the world disappears within our beliefs about it. Hegel counters this result with the second move. He avoids the collapse of the two poles through his essentially negative concept of human experience: we are constantly hitting ourselves against the hardness of the world. This experience consists in our beliefs about the world turning out to be wrong. In this sense, we *are* connected to the absolute, though via falsehood. Only insofar as we are wrong in our beliefs about "what is" do we relate to it. The absolute is revealed through what it is not. We cannot relate to it positively since it is constantly changing. By positing a becoming, historicized absolute, Hegel avoids the epistemological dead-ends of rationalism, empiricism, and transcendental philosophy. And the friction required in order to avoid coherentism or relativism is offered by experience itself insofar as it is negative. Negativity is the source of objectivity. Without hardness we would not experience error. However, only the experience of error reveals such hardness to us. This hardness is a staple of human experience. It consists in the opposition between what we believe and what turns out to be the case. Being human consists in not being able to overcome this opposition, or, in Hegel's words, in eternally creating and eternally overcoming it. The absolute idea will amount to the consciousness of this structure and of its necessary character, along with its parallel in the idea of the good.

2

The True Infinite and the Idea of the Good: Internal Excess

2.1 Introduction

If, as Hegel states in the *Encyclopaedia*, the true infinite is "the basic concept of philosophy,"[1] then much turns on how this concept is to be understood. Its interpretation might strengthen the view of Hegelian philosophy as undermining and subsuming difference within an all-encompassing totality that reduces all things to a mere moment of the whole that grants them their identity. Hegelian philosophy in this view would represent the pinnacle of the absoluteness of reason, where being is being thought (logocentrism). It is a philosophy of identity (between being and thinking), sameness, and presence. What gets lost in this picture would be particularity, difference, otherness, alterity. There would be no place for an other to thinking that is not already absorbed by thought. A reaction to this logocentrism is the impulse behind the philosophy of many post-Hegelian thinkers, among them Kierkegaard, Nietzsche, Adorno, Levinas, Deleuze, and Derrida.

The sections on the infinite in the *Science of Logic* and the *Encyclopaedia* are followed by a remark on idealism. In the *Encyclopaedia* Hegel says: "But the truth of the finite is rather its *ideality*... This ideality of the finite is the most important proposition of philosophy, and for that reason every genuine philosophy is *Idealism*."[2] Philosophy, insofar as it is the activity of thinking "what is," is already idealism. From Thales's water as the basic element to Levinas's face of the other, every philosophy is always already, and cannot but be, ideal. So the issue for Hegel is not whether there is something irreducible to thought, since the activity itself of coming to terms with that irreducibility already undermines its absolute otherness to thought. The pivotal issue is rather whether by revealing this posited character of the absolutely other we deny human experience something fundamental to it, be it in thought or in action. The above-mentioned thinkers base their critiques on this denial. If it turns out that the *experience* of absolute alterity is not denied in Hegel, then the distinction between him and these critics might be reduced to making the same claim from supposedly opposite sides of a supposedly solid barrier.

The dynamic at work within the Idea of the good toward the end of the *Science of Logic*, what determines it to be a *most stubborn opposition*, strictly parallels that encountered in the duality finitude/infinity. By means of the analysis and interpretation of what is at stake in this duality, we will be in a better position to do justice to the stubbornly oppositional character of the Idea of the good. Therefore, this chapter shall deal with the aforementioned section and, by means of this, prepare the ground for an understanding and interpretation of Hegel's absolute Idea, to be offered in Chapter 5. If the idea is possessed by the *most stubborn opposition*, then Hegel's resolution of the opposition between the finite and the infinite cannot consist in doing away with this opposition, but rather in offering a description of its structure and the reasons for its stubbornness. In order for it to maintain this stubbornness, it must consist in an opposition that does not contradict itself since this would lead to its overcoming. Or, it must consist in a contradiction that can sustain itself, as opposed to all other contradictions encountered both in the *Phenomenology* and the *Science of Logic*. The task of the present chapter will be to shed light on this opposition in order to acquire a better grasp of the stubbornness constitutive of the idea of the good.

2.2 Detour via Levinas/Derrida

In "Violence and Metaphysics"[3] Derrida follows Levinas in critiquing Hegel's concept of the true infinite as doing injustice to particularity and the otherness of the other insofar as the attempt to make the other one's own through comprehension leads to a distortion or alteration of its otherness. As Derrida says: "There is no concept of the Other."[4] The problem with Hegel's true infinite is that it disallows transcendence, which is the only possible realm for absolute particularity and alterity to exist. Anything short of transcendence is an imposition on the other insofar as it is no longer what it is in itself but has become merely for us, giving up all resistance to the power of sameness emanating from thought.[5] As Derrida and Levinas read Hegel, immanence, sameness, identity, totality, and infinity all mutually implicate one another. Immanence imposes identity on what lies within it insofar as it reveals beings to be part of a totality that determines their being. Infinity consists in the identification of all beings as parts of this totality, whereas finitude would consist in the illusory belief in independence from it, in a false sense of otherness or alterity. Derrida imagines Hegel asking himself, puzzled: "How can alterity be separated from the 'false infinity'? Or inversely, how could absolute sameness not be infinity?"[6] For Hegel, according to Levinas and Derrida, absolute alterity would be an illusion impossible to sustain without sameness and identity. Only by belonging to the totality can one particular being be different from another. This makes difference parasitic on identity, though without disappearing in it.[7] The idea thus understood is a "return to self-presence," the realization that the other to thought is conceptualized as other to thought, and thus always already with us. Derrida continues: "Under these conditions, the only effective position to take in order not to be enveloped by Hegel would seem to be, for an instant, the following: to consider the false-infinity (that is, in a profound way, original finitude) irreducible."[8] Nothing escapes Hegel's true infinite. The limitation of the finite would lie in its transitory character, in its constantly becoming something other, without being able to maintain itself in its irreducibility to thought. This irreducibility is what Derrida attempts to rescue. Toward the end of the text Derrida says:

> In having proffered the *epekeina tes ousias*, in having recognized from its second word (for example, in the *Sophist*) that alterity had to circulate at the origin of meaning, in welcoming alterity in general into the heart of the logos, the Greek thought of Being forever has protected itself against every absolutely *surprising* convocation.[9]

The limitation of logocentrism, of the metaphysics of presence, is its domestication of the utterly surprising. For Derrida, the human experience of coming up against a hardness that cannot be domesticated or accommodated within one's thinking or one's acting is what constitutes human finitude. We will never exhaust that experience. There will always be a beyond not quite within reach, which keeps us on our toes, so to speak. In Derrida's reading of Hegel's true infinite, this experience disappears insofar as everything humans confront has always already been made our own, tailored to us; more boldly put, only by being made our own, by being tailored to us, can there be anything at all to confront us.

* * * *

The concept of the infinite in Hegel's philosophy stands out due to the lavish vocabulary with which it is described. One might think that in the *Science of Logic* the absolute makes a rather early appearance disguised in the garb of the true infinite.[10] However, it is still far from appearing in- and for-itself. The following are excerpts of the descriptions of the infinite found in both the *Phenomenology* and the *Science of Logic*:

> This simple infinity, or the absolute Notion, may be called the simple essence of life, the soul of the world, the universal blood... Infinity, or this absolute unrest of pure self-movement, in which whatever is determined in one way or another, e.g. as being, is rather the opposite of this determinateness, this no doubt has been from the start the soul of all that has gone before, but it is in the inner world that it has first freely and clearly shown itself.[11]
>
> it [the infinite] is the true being, the elevation above limitation. At the name of the infinite, the heart and the mind light up, for in the infinite the spirit is not merely abstractly present to itself, but rises to its own self, to the light of its thinking, of its universality, of its freedom.[12]

If the Hegelian commonplace according to which the absolute appears in each and every stage of the journey of its search is true, then the concept of the infinite must be one of its paradigmatic exemplifications. To encounter this talk of soul, essence, blood, and freedom at such an early stage must be a sign that the absolute is especially sensitive to the infinite, that in some way or another this concept reflects its structure or constitution, allowing us to catch an early, albeit furtive, glimpse of it.

In the *Science of Logic* one is no longer dealing with a natural consciousness in its quest to grasp "what truly is". This natural consciousness first believed it could encounter "what truly is" in the outer world, merely taking it in as it is (Consciousness). It then thought it could take its own self as measure of "what truly is" (Self-consciousness). It finally came to realize that the conditions of possibility, not only for the determination of "what is", but also for there to be such a quest for truth, lay beyond any particular consciousness, being actually embedded in the whole development of Spirit. Only a particular consciousness that belongs to Spirit is able to raise the question of "what is true" or "really real". The starting point of the *Science of Logic*, then, is precisely the endpoint of the *Phenomenology*. However, one should not imagine the *Science of Logic* as a different, more advanced segment of a continuous line, going beyond the segment the *Phenomenology* went through. It is rather a turning back into itself of Spirit, observing the same development mapped in the *Phenomenology*, though from a different vantage point.[13] It presupposes not only that what is really real is conceptually constituted, but also that the conceptual constitutor is Spirit, not a particular human being. It is a description of and reflection on the concepts used in the quest for truth, thinking through those presupposed by natural consciousness and its quest for truth in the *Phenomenology*. Therefore, the *Science of Logic* is a mapping of the different conceptual strategies and their failures, insufficiencies, and contradictions, traversed in the history of Western thought while attempting to grasp "what is." Since the starting point of the *Logic* presupposes the conclusions reached in the *Phenomenology*, it will reveal the historical character of such concepts, becoming thus a sort of lexicon of Western philosophy.[14] This explains why, when dealing with specific concepts, reference is constantly made to philosophers such as Parmenides, Heraclitus, Spinoza, Leibniz, and Kant, all of whom conceptually constituted "what truly is", though in a partial manner.

The development of the *Science of Logic* runs parallel to that of the *Phenomenology*, albeit no longer blind to the historical nature of its quest.[15] However, the parallel nature of these two works should not be taken to mean that the same stages of development are reflected in the same order. One should not hold the *Science of Logic* to the test of faithfully reflecting the development of natural consciousness. Just as different vantage points reveal different relations among objects while losing others from sight, so pure thinking reflecting on concepts will reveal certain aspects hidden to natural consciousness while losing from sight other aspects of the experience of natural consciousness.

The *Science of Logic* is the process in which pure thinking reflects on the conceptual strategies it has used throughout its becoming conscious of itself in its quest of thinking "what truly is".[16] It will run parallel to the *Phenomenology* insofar as it starts with objective concepts of being (concepts used to think "what is" as immediately given through perception, i.e., sense-data or perceptions of things), and then goes on to objective concepts of essence (concepts used to think "what is" as existing behind the immediately given). The parallel would run as follows: doctrine of being > sense-certainty and perception, doctrine of essence > force and understanding. However, this parallel breaks down once we get to the section on spirit in the *Phenomenology* and to that of subjective logic in the *Science of Logic*.[17]

2.3 Introduction to the issue of the infinite

2.3.1 Being

The following is a very schematic and introductory sketch of the path of pure thinking to the point where it thinks the concept of the finite. The starting point of the *Science of Logic* runs parallel not only to that of the *Phenomenology* in its degree of abstraction and presupposed immediacy, but also to that of the history of Western thinking itself. Spirit reflecting on itself and its development realizes that with Parmenides there is a qualitative leap in terms of thinking "what truly is". He stands in opposition to his predecessors the physicists. A similar leap is described by Kant in the Preface to the second edition of the *Critique of Pure Reason,* when he asserts that mathematics enters "the sure path of science" by means of the demonstration of the properties of the isosceles triangle.[18] Parmenides is the first to think a concept of the absolute separate from any tie to the sensuous. This allows Hegel to say of being that it "could be regarded as the first, purest, that is, most abstract definition of the absolute."[19] It is not a concept *of* or *about* something but rather a "self-determination of thought,"[20] that is, dependent only on itself for its content, which is what the *Science of Logic* will deal with:

> What we are dealing with in logic is not a thinking *about* something which exists independently as a base for our thinking and apart from it, nor forms which are supposed to provide mere signs or distinguished marks of truth; on the contrary, the necessary forms and self-determinations of thought are the content and the ultimate truth itself.[21]

This concept of being, however, is so abstract that it means *nothing; nothing* is thought when being is thought without any determination. Thus, we reach a second concept: that of nothing, which, as empty as being is, *is* a concept nonetheless, thus remitting us back to the concept of being. We find a double contradiction here: a being that is empty, *nothing,* and a nothing that in its emptiness is determined *as* empty, thus no longer being empty.[22] Any attempt to think through either of these concepts will lead to its opposite, providing thus a third concept: becoming, a constant "turning into an other." Becoming is the truth of being and nothing. It has a pre-eminence over these insofar as it explicitly exhibits an element of negation constitutive of all concepts, making them dependent on others for the realization of what is *meant* by thinking them. This dependence sets up the movement from concept to concept in the *Science of Logic*. Whereas the element of negation is implicit in being and nothing insofar as they lead to what they are not when they are thought (both fail to bring to light what was meant by them), in the concept of becoming this negative element is explicit insofar as becoming is either from nothing (coming-to-be) or to nothing (ceasing-to-be). Nonetheless, the explicit character of negation in becoming is not sufficient for allowing it to grasp what is meant with it, either. Replicating what occurred with being and nothing, becoming *objectifies*[23] its meaning and makes it inadequate for its expression. It requires a further concept to complete it. The concept of becoming falls short of adequately expressing what is meant by it insofar as it is dependent on the concept of determinate being (*Dasein*); otherwise it would remain in a ceaseless flux of being turning into nothing and vice-versa. Becoming is dependent on *something* that becomes; otherwise it would undermine itself. Pure becoming seems to be as empty and impossible as pure being and pure nothing. It requires some minimum identity that becomes: a being-*there*. Constitutive for the concept of *Dasein* is the element of becoming it contains: to be *there* is to be in the process of becoming.

2.3.2 *Dasein*

The *thereness* of determinate being is revealed by its qualitative nature. To be *somewhere* is to have qualities, to be determined. To think of quality brings in the concepts of reality and negation. To determine a being-*there* is to underscore its qualities; this in turn requires a negating, a limiting off from other qualities. The chapter on Perception in the *Phenomenology* comes to mind. In order to determine a being-there positively, one must both limit its qualities from all others and also determine each quality, the amount that pertains to it. Let us take the example of the grain of salt. The reality of that grain of salt *there* is constituted both by the list of qualities it possesses—white, cubical, tart, and so on—and also by limiting itself to a specific proportion of these qualities, by cutting itself off from all others. Thus, negation in the form of this *cutting itself off from* is constitutive of *Daseine*. A purely positive being not limited by anything else, not cutting itself off from any other being, would be pure abstraction since it would not have any determination by means of which to grasp it. Any concept that collapses all determination and that has nothing limiting it becomes an abstract nothing:

2.3.3 Something

When reality is given its limits, when it accepts that it needs negation to be what it is, we reach the concept of "something." "Something" is a positive or reality that includes the negation of quality within it. With it one reaches a certain degree of identity insofar as what is identical to self can only be so opposed to what is different from it. "Something" is *Dasein* that has come back to itself through mediation, through its qualities. Hegel calls it *In-sich-sein*: "being-within-self." It negates its first negation by taking it up, and achieves its identity by putting limits to its qualities. There is now a "something" that becomes, either coming-or ceasing-to-be.

With the concept of "something" a stability is reached that does not allow its dissolution into pure change, though *it* still disappears in its ceasing-to-be. "Something" is insofar as it negates what it is not. It needs, however, *not* to be what it is not. There is no identity in pure immediacy; it is acquired through mediation. The concept of "something" can only have come about by negating what it is not, by setting limits.

Insofar as "something" is "being-within-self," insofar as it has reached a certain degree of identity amid difference, it takes itself to be self-sufficient, independent of any *other* to it. However, nothing can be said about a "something" *as* "something" to distinguish it from other "somethings." Since it cannot rest on qualities due to their permanent alteration its identity must rely on its opposition to what it is not: to its "other." It does not realize, though, that in its opposition to an "other" it itself is an "other" since its other is also a "something." Thus, it becomes other to itself. This means that in order to be what it is it is dependent on what it is not. What was thought (*gemeint*) to be "in-itself" became "being-for-other." One cannot think of a "something" in itself without thinking of what that "something" is not. Coming back to the chapter on Perception in the *Phenomenology*: a thing cannot merely be the exclusive one, completely unrelated to the "also," the community of qualities; nor can it be merely the "also" of its qualities, completely unrelated to the exclusive character of the one.

> Something *preserves* itself in the negative of its determinate being [*Nichtdasein*]; it is essentially *one* with it and essentially *not one* with it. It stands, therefore, in a *relation* to its otherness and is not simply its otherness. The otherness is at once contained in it and also still *separate* from it; it is a *being-for-other*.[24]

"Something" is revealed to be constituted by its "being-for-other": it is what it is in its relations to others. At this point Hegel introduces three interrelated concepts constitutive of what "something" is. They are: determinateness (*Bestimmtheit*), determination (*Bestimmung*), and constitution (*Beschaffenheit*). We shall focus on the concept of determination since by means of it we may reach a better understanding of the move Hegel makes with the concepts of the finite and the infinite. It may also help us understand why the discussion on the finite and the infinite seems to exceed the particular setting in which these concepts appear (qualitative being) and touch on moral issues. There are three closely connected aspects tied to this concept of determination, which will bolster the particular reading of the finite and the infinite proposed in this chapter. These are: (1) the apparent *qualitative leap* realized in these passages when, all of a sudden, humankind and the moral realm appear; (2) the appearance of the German dative term *an ihm*—already encountered in the Introduction to the *Phenomenology*—in the definition of what determination is; (3) the fact that *Bestimmung* also has the meaning of *vocation*.

2.3.4 Determination, determinateness, and constitution

"Something" was both an exclusive one, limiting itself off from others, and the "also" of a community of others. It was "being-within-self" and "being-for-other'. A middle term is required to bring these two sides together. In this case the middle term is determinateness since, on the one hand, the fact that "something" is determined by *x*, *y*, and *z* links it to what it is not insofar as *x*, *y*, and *z* are universals that are not exhausted by their determining that "something." They determine what "something" is in its relation to what it is not. Hegel calls this constitution: "But it is the quality of something to be open to external influences and to have a *constitution*."[25] On the other hand, looked at from the inside, so to speak, it determines "something" as being different from the "others." Being *x*, *y*, and *z* determines it as what it exclusively is, limited off from the "others." Here, however, in contrast to what occurs in the chapter on Perception in the *Phenomenology*, it is not merely a matter of determining "something" as different from every "other" by means of the qualities that make it up and the particular configuration they assume. There is an extra element Hegel adds, which will explain why by means of an apparent qualitative leap he introduces talk of humans and of a moral realm (ought) after having been referring only to determinate beings, qualities, and "somethings." This step is fundamental for understanding what is at stake in the concepts of finitude and the infinite. It will also allow us to conceptualize "what is" beyond a mechanicist view of "somethings" that are subject to external forces and cannot maintain themselves in their being, thus constantly altering into other "somethings." This will be the first step in conceptualizing the organic world.

The extra element has to do with the German dative pronoun *ihm*, encountered in the Introduction to the *Phenomenology* when talking about the problem of the measure and of the "in-itself" posited as such. In that discussion the conclusion was reached that the *an ihm* emphasized the objective pole of consciousness; it stressed the separation, although internal to consciousness, between its knowledge and what it knows, which appears *to it* as "such and such" in its knowing it. Hegel says:

> Determination is affirmative determinateness as the in-itself with which something in its determinate being remains congruous in face of its entanglement with the other by which it might be determined, maintaining itself in its self-equality, and making its determination hold good in its being-for-other. Something *fulfils* its determination in so far as the further determinateness which at once develops in various directions through something's relation to other, is congruous with the in-itself of the something, becomes its filling. Determination implies that what something is *in itself*, is also *present in* it.[26]

In the German text there are three uses of the dative in this passage. The first two pertain to the fact that "something" is or remains congruous with the "in-itself" despite its being determined by an "other." The German original uses *gemäß sein* or *gemäß bleiben*, which takes its object in the dative. An "other" determines "something" to be what it is (insofar as "something" is a determinate being it must be determined by its "other," it must have relation to an "other"). Nevertheless, this "something" is not totally determined by the "other," but simultaneously remains congruous with its "in-itself." Being determined by an "other" becomes the filling of its being congruous with its "in-itself." There is a strong similarity between this passage on determination and those on the measure and the "in-itself" in the Introduction to the *Phenomenology*. What does it mean for "something" to be congruous with its "in-itself'? Although "something" is determined as what it is by its entanglement with and relation to others, it also achieves a self-identity not totally collapsed into the determinateness it is due to its relations to others. This self-identity lies beyond its being determined by its others, though only comes to be through its being determined by them. In the Introduction to the *Phenomenology* we had consciousness determining the "in-itself" as more than the knowledge consciousness had of it ("for-itself"), albeit only as a shadow projected by this knowledge; both poles never collapse into one. In the same manner we have here what "something" is-as its "in-itself," its having returned to itself after having been determined by what it was not. It has returned to itself through the relations to the others it is not. Being determined by what it is not is its *filling*. Nonetheless, it is the filling *of* "something"; that is, however much it is determined by what it is not, it still projects a certain independence from what it is not, though not enough to survive beyond the alteration of its qualities.

The last sentence of the passage quoted contains the third use of the dative: "*Die Bestimmung enthält dies, daß, was etwas an sich ist, auch an ihm sei*": "Determination contains this, that what something is *in itself* is also *to it*" (my translation). When Hegel talks about the problem of the measure in the Introduction to the *Phenomenology* he says: "*Das Bewußtsein gibt seinem Maßstab an ihm selbst,*" which I translate as "Consciousness gives its criterion to itself." There is a separation between an objective and a subjective consciousness. This gap allows objectivity and the problem of truth to appear. Concerning determination, it is the return to what "something" is "in-itself" after having been determined by what it is not. However, this "in-itself" can no longer be pure immediacy, but rather a positing of immediacy through mediation, a return to what "something" is beyond its being determined by "others" (qualities), only through its being determined by them, nonetheless. The determination of "something" brings us back to its identity as itself, sustained only through its entanglement with "others," without collapsing and being only this entanglement. In the Introduction to the *Phenomenology* the "in-itself," understood as reality, could only be determined through its "being-for-us" (our knowledge of it), though as being different from that knowledge. A similar move occurs here: "something" can only be determined "in-itself" by means of its being determined through its relation to "others," though its character of being "in-itself" is not limited to this being determined. The gap described in the *Phenomenology* as existing within consciousness is shown here to exist within the concept of "something": every "something" is split between its being determined by "others" and its self-identity, achieved only by means of such being determined by "others" but not identical to it.

What Hegel seems to be saying is that in thinking "what is" as a "something" there is a disparity between what it shows itself as (its being related to "others") and a self-identity it must have in order to be thought. This self-identity cannot consist in the mere totality of its relations to "others." Qualitative thinking of beings can only hold on to the relations they have with "others" due to the universal nature of the qualities constituting them. However, to hold on to this being thought thinking must project an identity onto it, given through its relations to "others," but going beyond them. This identity amid difference is what Hegel's use of the dative reflects. If thought only grasped beings in their qualitative nature, in their relations to "others," there would be a constant turning into an "other" insofar as qualities spill out beyond their qualifying "something" and lead to many other "somethings." The conceptual tool to think an identity beyond a mere sum of qualities is *determination*. It will allow us to think life and beyond that, the infinite.

We have a syllogism in which the two extremes, "being-within-itself" and "being-for-other," or determination and constitution, respectively, are brought together by a middle term: determinateness.[27] This parallels the syllogism found in the Introduction to the *Phenomenology*, consisting of the two extremes of knowledge ("for-itself") and reality ("in-itself"), mediated by consciousness insofar as it was shown to posit both as extremes: to posit its knowledge of something and to posit that of which it has knowledge. Determinateness can be taken as part of the constitution of "something," in which case it determines that "something" in relation to "others"; and it can be taken as part of the determination of "something," in which case it separates it from all other "somethings." However, this separation effected by the middle term does not yield an "in-itself" completely untouched by its qualities and relations to "others" but rather a posited or mediated "in-itself," an *an sich an ihm ihm* or *"in-itself" to it*, as was translated above. It is constituted *by* its relations to "others," *as* being different from them.

2.3.5 Determination as vocation

The term *Bestimmung* means not only determination, but also vocation.[28] This shall allow us to understand why Hegel introduces the term "ought" at this point.[29] To exemplify what he understands by determination, Hegel leaves behind all talk of qualitative "somethings" and "others," and brings in humankind (*der Mensch*). Thought qualitatively, a human being is determined by natural existence (*Natürlichkeit*), sense-nature (*Sinnlichkeit*) and thinking reason (*denkende Vernunft*). It shares the former two determinatenesses with animals; the latter distinguishes it from them. However, thinking reason as a determinateness of a human being "in-itself" (what separates it from "others") still does not do justice to what it is to be human. For this, a human being must be taken as a determination, as a tendency toward, in order to be fully grasped in her humanity. Hegel says:

> But thought is also present *in* him [an ihm]; man himself is thought, he actually exists as thinking, it is his concrete existence and actuality; and, further, since thought is in his determinate being and his determinate being is in thought, it is to be taken as *concrete*, as having

> content and filling; it is thinking reason and as such the *determination* of man. But even this determination again is only *in itself* as something which *ought* to be, that is it, together with the filling which is incorporated in its in-itself, is in the form of the in-itself in general, *in contrast to* the determinate being not incorporated in it, which at the same time still confronts it externally as immediate sense-nature and nature.[30]

Since determination is the ought, it is in itself insofar as it is posited as not accomplished. In this paragraph the filling is working as the middle term since it can be taken both in its external character (the determinate being determined by its relation to "others"—immediate sense-nature and nature) and as incorporated in the "in-itself." This occurs since from it, unbeknownst to itself, finite being posits the determination, the unfulfilled ought. This ought, the determination posited by finite being as beyond its reach, is determined by finite being's determinateness, without being collapsed with it, however.

To think being as a "something" constituted in its relations to "others" does not capture the richness and tension that being entails. The sudden emergence of this talk of human beings and the ought in the midst of a discussion of the concepts of "something" and "other" points toward the limitations thinking suffers when thinking "what is" by means of them. The concept of determination reveals this lack on behalf of thinking by means of its dual meaning as determination and vocation. Beings cannot limit themselves to being determined by qualities they share with "others"; nor can they limit themselves to what they are "in themselves" (thinking reason). Neither of these accurately reflects the *actual* nature of certain types of being (organic beings, the exemplar of which is humankind). In other words, certain qualitative beings are always more than their qualities, since if they were only their qualities, they would constantly change into their "other."[31] This concept of changing into their "other" means that they would disappear and become "other" since they are completely dependent on "others" for their being and non-being. They would not have a stability to give them unity and thus would dissolve into their components. To determine humans as thinking beings (understanding what thinking is strictly in opposition to non-thinking, as that which non-thinking beings lack) does not capture what it is to be a human being. Beyond being a determinateness "in-itself" of what it is to be human, thinking must also be *to it* (*an ihm*). To be human means to tend toward thinking, to constantly realize it while simultaneously falling short of it. It is not a finished state, but rather a constant summons, a permanent taking up the task. It is the vocation of human beings to think reasonably. This makes them what they are. Just as the measure is *to* consciousness, that is, just as consciousness posits the measure as something to attain through its knowledge, in the same manner the determination/vocation of humans is *to them*; it is posited by them as something to be attained. We posit ourselves as reasonable thinking beings and permanently strive to fulfill such a task.

The only way to grant permanence to a qualitative being is in its character of striving toward what it is. In this way the qualities constituting it converge and do not disappear in "others." To think of "what is" merely in terms of piles of qualities, so to speak, of objects understood as sums of qualities, contradicts the more complex phenomenon of life. Therein lies the importance of the term *Bestimmung*: determination/vocation. It not only gives unity to a cluster of qualities and constitutes objects but also brings movement to "what is" in the form of a *tending toward*, an *inclination to*. This will open the space for Hegel to begin to talk about the moral realm and the ought given the paradigmatic role of humankind among living beings. There is an inclination by means of which qualitative beings tend toward "something." This does not allow them to disappear in the universality of their qualities. A being is inclined to be. In order to account for a world full of movement and life, a living (*lebendige*) world, the concept of being must be one constituted by an inclination to be, a striving toward.

2.4 Finitude

At this point Hegel will show that the attempt of "something" to realize itself in its determination, its claim to self-dependence, will reveal it to be dependent upon what it is not, what it limited itself off from through its determination. Thus, we had a "something" constituted by its qualities: its constitution (*Beschaffenheit*). There it was shown that for it not to dissolve into the qualities making it up, it had to posit certain stability amid change. It had to be inclined to be "something," to strive toward "something" since at the qualitative level a being has no essence or substance underlying and sustaining its constant change. This "striving toward" was called its determination. Now, due to it "something" believes it has achieved independence by thinking it can cut itself off from its "others." By showing how the concept of limit is determined by and determines both what is limited and what it is limited against, Hegel reveals the co-dependent and co-constitutive character of the two sides of a limit. He reveals how these two sides are determined not only as what they are, but also as their opposite. This leads to the conclusion with which the concept of the finite is reached: "Something with its immanent limit, posited as the contradiction of itself, through which it is directed and forced out of and beyond itself, is the finite."[32] Let us analyze this sentence in light of the previous discussion on determination, determinateness, constitution, and limit. The concept of limit contains within it the tension revealed in the "something" between its determination and its constitution. "Something" that in order to be what it is limits itself off from what it is not (the other side of the limit), makes itself dependent on that other side since only through it is the "something" what it is. The limit as constitutive of it makes it come into contact with what it is not. Therein lies the contradiction: "something" has within it itself as *Dasein* and what it is not. Both elements co-constitute it. "Something" needs its "other" in order to be. The fact that it makes the attempt of limiting itself off from what it is not, shows not only that it is in contact with it but also that it is so through its own activity; it has posited what it is not.[33] The concept itself of independence is negative since it negates dependence. Therefore, it depends on the very same thing it negates. The finite is the first concept to posit its own contradiction. All previous concepts merely stumbled upon it in their *meinen*. The concept of the finite is constituted by lack. It determines itself as incomplete, as dependent on something: "finitude is the negation as *fixed in itself*, and it therefore stands in abrupt contrast to its affirmative."[34]

This contradiction of being constituted both by what it is and by what it is not reveals that it will never be able to be what it is insofar as in its being there will always be an element it is not. Its being is a striving toward, an inclination to be, which is never quite fulfilled since it is constitutive of it to be what it is not. Paradoxically, precisely for the same reason, as will be shown further below, it actually is what it is by being what it is not: its nature is to be so constituted. "But the development of this negation, so that the opposition between its determinate being and the negation as its immanent limit, is itself the being-within-self of the something, which is thus in its own self only a becoming, constitutes the finitude of something."[35] This being constituted by itself and by its "other" reveals being once again as a becoming. However, now the becoming is not "in-itself" or pure but has been posited by that which itself becomes: *werden an ihm selbst*. Following the translation of *an ihm* offered throughout, we would have *a becoming to itself*, instead of Miller's "in its own self [only] a becoming." This will allow us to better understand the moral implications of the finite/infinite discussion.

> When we say of things that *they are finite*, we understand thereby that they not only have a determinateness, that their quality is not only a reality and an intrinsic determination, that finite things are not merely limited—as such they still have determinate being outside their limit—but that, on the contrary, non-being constitutes their nature and being. Finite things *are*, but their relation to themselves is that they are *negatively* self-related and in this very self-relation send themselves away beyond themselves, beyond their being. They *are*, but the truth of this being is their *end*. The finite not only alters, like something in general, but it *ceases to be*; and its ceasing-to-be is not merely a possibility, so that it could be without ceasing-to-be, but the being as such of finite things is to have the germ of decease as their being-within-self; the hour of their birth is the hour of their death.[36]

This passage illuminates the crucial step beyond thinking "what is" as "something." The reality of a "something" is determined by its qualities and thus by the external character of its being. This could only lead to an alteration from one batch of qualities to another. A world consisting of "somethings" that alter in their relations to "others" is a mechanical world in which they change place, break up into smaller "somethings," and so on. Alteration is determined by other things external to what suffers that alteration. By means of the concept of determination and the element of vocation that it includes within it we have reached a qualitative being constituted as such by its *not* being what it is, by its striving toward or being summoned to what it is not. The negative element constituting any qualitative being has now been internalized, it lies within the being itself: "non-being constitutes their nature and being." To be is not to be "something" but to strive to be. Being is constituted by what it *lacks*. A human being is not merely a list of qualities by which it both relates to and distinguishes itself from what it is not, that is, sense-nature, natural existence, and thinking reason. In addition, it is a striving to be what it is, a becoming what it is. As a striving or becoming it never quite fully actualizes what it is. This striving reveals what Marcuse called the *motility of beings*, and points already toward the conceptualization of the phenomenon of life.[37] Only by means of this striving can such phenomenon be thought. Only in a being whose nature is constituted by non-being can one account for the motility of living beings.

The concept that allows for the thinking of life and its motility is shot through by lack or insufficiency. This lack constitutes living beings and gives them their motility. A movement internal to beings themselves, as opposed to a mechanical one, requires that these beings be constituted by a lack or limit posited by themselves *as* limit (this positing of a limit as limit is called a limitation—*Schranke*). Only in this way can movement be explained internally, beyond a mere alteration of "somethings" and "others."[38]

Hegel first points toward the contradictory nature of the concept of the finite, encountered in its immediacy.[39] It is an immediately contradictory concept. To say that all beings are finite is to oppose the finite character of things, their perishing nature, to the universality of the claim that all beings are finite, through which the finite itself cannot perish, but rather must remain.[40] Hegel says:

> But the point is, whether in thinking of the finite one holds fast to the *being* of finitude and lets the *transitoriness* continue to be, or whether the *transitoriness* and the *ceasing-to-be cease to be*. But it is precisely in that view of the finite which makes *ceasing-to-be* the *final* determination of the finite, that this does not happen.[41]

The two options laid out are: either ceasing-to-be is absolute since all things as finite cease to be; or ceasing-to-be itself ceases to be. Hegel's choice is the former since it is the nature of finite things to cease to be. Thus, if ceasing-to-be itself ceased to be, beings would no longer be finite. Ceasing-to-be has to remain as "the final determination [*das Letzte*] of the finite." In order to hold on to the concept of the finite by limiting it off from its opposite the infinite so as not to let it escape through one's grasp, one would posit a contradiction, an absolute, nonperishing finite: "incapable of union with the infinite, it remains absolute on its own side; from the affirmative, from the infinite, it would receive affirmation, and would thus cease to be; but a union with the infinite is just what is declared to be impossible."[42] This contradiction would bring about the destruction of the concept of the finite. The only path remaining in order to avoid the second option, that of a ceasing-to-be that ceases to be (which would lead the finite directly into its opposite), is to allow the finite to perish. This, however, would only lead it to abstract nothing:

> If it is not to remain fixed in its opposition to the infinite but is to cease to be, then, as we have already said, just this ceasing-to-be is its final determination, not the affirmative which would be only the ceasing-to-be of the ceasing-to-be. If, however, the finite is not to pass way in the affirmative, but its end is to be grasped as the *nothing*, then

> we should be back again at that first, abstract nothing which itself has long since passed away.[43]

Thus, the price the concept of the finite will have to pay for its contradictory nature in order not to be related to its opposite the infinite is either to fall into contradiction or to fall back into nothing. This leads Hegel to conclude:

> and the development of the finite shows that, having this contradiction present within it, it collapses within itself, yet in doing so actually resolves the contradiction, that not only is the finite transitory and ceases to be, but that the ceasing-to-be, the nothing, is not the final determination, but itself ceases to be.[44]

What perishes is not the finite but rather perishing itself. The finite does not disappear when the infinite is thought, but is rather taken up by it, included in it. To better understand what Hegel might mean when talking of the ceasing to be of ceasing-to-be, one could refer to Aristotle. In Aristotle an organic *tode ti*, thought of in itself, has as its *telos* its perishing, its death. One would not be able to conceptualize it beyond a mere pointing: *tode ti*. However, from the perspective of the species this *tode ti* has eternal being as its *telos*. Even though it will perish as an individual, perishing itself perishes as a species. The finite character of the *tode ti* does not disappear. It is taken up by the infinite character of the species. Its *final determination* is to not cease to be. Although it does cease to be at one point, it does not do so totally.

2.4.1 Limitation and the ought

The relation between determination and constitution that takes place at the level of "something" and "other" will now be replayed here by substituting these concepts for those of the ought and of limitation, respectively, where what is dealt with is no longer the concept of "something" and "other," but that of finite, living beings. Hegel also calls this concept "an explicit, self-determined totality,"[45] giving as examples of it instinct, life, and ideation. By bringing in this talk of the ought Hegel will not only be able to display a particular example of the concept of the finite, whose habitat is the moral realm—which he seems to hold as paradigmatic for the problematic character of such a concept—but also overcome its contradictory character. "In the ought the transcendence [*hinausgehen über*] of finitude, that is, infinity, begins. The ought is that which, in the further development, exhibits itself in accordance with the said impossibility as the progress to infinity."[46] What is limited is, in a sense, indifferent to what limits it. It shares the limit with what it is not. Thus, the limit is an external relation of things that, although constitutive of what a thing is, as was shown above, nonetheless constitutes it externally. With "limitation" we are dealing with finite beings that as finite are constituted internally by a lack or a striving. The concept of a finite being is characterized as having a negative content: it *is* its lack, its desire and striving. And although it is determined by the ought in the same manner in which "something" was determined by its determination, it is determined by it negatively, as striving toward it. The concept of limitation reveals this aspect insofar as it pulls being out beyond itself: "and since the limit is in the *determination* itself as a limitation, something transcends *its own self*."[47] To have limits means to be affected from outside. To have limitations means to act out beyond oneself.

The other side of the coin, so to speak, of the concept of limitation is that of the ought. Whatever has a limitation must also have (or more precisely, lack) that toward which it strives due to such a limitation. This is the ought. Thus, the limitation is posited as the finite, whereas the ought is posited as the "being-in-itself."[48] Both are inseparable and presuppose each other. The ought is posited as ought by the finite being; it is immanent to the finite being to strive toward an ought. However, that this is so does not do away with the ought as a constitutive element of what it is to be a finite being. Just as Hegel did with the concept of the finite, and then of limitation, the first step he takes with respect to that of the ought is to show its unstable nature. This instability brings the concept to life. Its instability lies in the fact that it simultaneously is and ought to be. It exists but as not being, as a lack. Hegel says:

> What ought to be *is*, and at the same time *is not*. If it *were*, we could not say that it *ought* merely *to be*. The ought has, therefore, essentially a limitation. This limitation is not alien to it; that which *only* ought to be is the *determination*, which is now posited as it is in fact, namely, as at the same time only a determinateness.[49]

2.5 The spurious and the true infinite

Seen from one side, the ought reveals itself as lack, as unfulfilled striving or determination: it is what beings tend toward, never quite fulfilling it since, if it were fulfilled, it would cease to be an ought. Seen from the other side, as this lack it *does* determine beings positively as what they are; it is a determinateness. In other words, without this striving or lack, beings would not be what they are: *an explicit, self-determined totality*. The paradoxical nature of the ought lies in the fact that its existence depends precisely on its non-existence: it is insofar as it is not. Thus, its realization or fulfillment cannot consist in the fact that what ought to be comes to be, since this would destroy the ought, but rather in the fact that it *is* in its ought to be. This movement replicates that encountered in the concept of the finite: if it realizes itself it disappears, while if it remains separate from the *is*, it will never be.

Thus, already in the passages dedicated to the ought one finds hints of both what the spurious and the true infinite will consist of. The spurious infinite relates to the unreachable aspect of the ought, its separation from what is finite. It emphasizes the character of the finite of not being able to reach its "other." The ought is taken as perennial, due to which the finite is made absolute. The ought cannot be realized since then it would itself disappear. Thus, in order to maintain itself as ought, the transcendence of the finite by means of the ought must be extended to infinity. The progress to infinity does not allow the collapse of the two: finitude and the ought. The ought is a transcending of the finite, but limited insofar as it is never fully achieved: "the ought is the transcending, but still only *finite transcending*, of the limitation."[50] Hegel gives as example of the process one taken from the moral realm:

> and those too who, reasoning from the level of the understanding, derive a perpetual satisfaction from being able to confront everything there is with an ought, that is, with a "knowing better"—and for that reason are just as loth to be robbed of the ought—do not see that as regards the finitude of their sphere the ought receives full recognition.[51]

No human act, insofar as it is human, can be determined as strictly fulfilling the ought since the moment it were determined as such the ought itself would disappear, collapsing the distinction. Hegel's point goes further, applying not only to those who believe a *knowing better* can always be brought up in opposition to an act, but also to those who merely confess it is impossible to be certain that a specific act strictly fulfilled the ought. Put in Kantian terms, it is impossible to know whether an act was done for the sake of duty or whether it was heteronomous. Finite beings are such, not insofar as they cannot act for the sake of duty, but rather insofar as they can never be certain they have done so. To be certain of acting for the sake of duty is to do away with such a concept. It is a self-destructive concept, so to speak: its realization brings about its own destruction. The alternative to its self-destruction is a spreading out in a progress to infinity.

The reflection of the true infinite in the concept of the ought surfaces in the fact that, when positing a limitation, one also posits what lies beyond it:

> it is asserted that the limitation cannot be *transcended*. To make such an assertion is to be unaware that the very fact that something is determined as a limitation implies that the limitation is already transcended. For a determinateness, a limit, is determined as a limitation only in opposition to its other in general, that is, in opposition to that which is *free from the limitation*; the other of a limitation is precisely the *being beyond* it.[52]

Seen from this perspective, the ought is realized precisely in its not being realized; it is its nature not to be reached. If finite beings, determined by their limitations, were to realize the ought, they would cease being finite. Thus, they realize their nature as finite beings by not realizing the ought. It is a realization through non-realization.

> The finite as the ought *transcends* its limitation; the same determinateness which is its negation is also sublated, and is thus its in-itself; its limit is also not its limit.[53]
>
> the finite in its ceasing-to-be, in this negation of itself, has attained its being-in-itself, is *united with itself*.[54]

The concept of the finite carries within it the true infinite. The true infinite is the "in-itself" of the finite; it merely has to realize that this is the case.[55] This does not mean that the limits are broken. They remain and do not remain. The finite is the true infinite. It just needs to be taken in, so to speak, as a whole rather than extended to infinity.[56] This idea of taking in the whole is described in terms of the self and its feeling pain. He says:

> The sentient creature, in the limitation of hunger, thirst, etc., is the urge to overcome this limitation and it does overcome it. It feels *pain* and it is the privilege of the sentient nature to feel pain; it is a negation in its *self*, and the negation is determined as a *limitation* in its feeling, just because the sentient creature has the feeling of its *self*, which is the totality that transcends this determinateness. If it were

> not above and beyond the determinateness, it would not feel it as its negation and would feel no pain.[57]

Through the feeling of limitation or pain the self determines itself as totality, though negatively: it is the totality that the limitation prevents. Nonetheless, only through this limitation does the *totality that transcends this determinateness* reveal itself as totality. In its appearing negatively as feeling pain, or as not realizing the ought, the totality reveals itself, not as different from the limitation (limitation + what is lacking), but rather as being a totality *of* limitation, a totality structurally built to have a limitation.[58] The self-determined totalities are structurally built on limitation or lack. Within them there is a gap not to be filled or realized. The fact that the self is a *totality that transcends determinateness* does not mean that the feeling of its self is one in which all lack is overcome and all ought realized. To have a feeling of self is to have a feeling of limitation *as* limitation, that is, not of a particular limitation it is striving to overcome, but rather of the structural character of limitation within itself. The true infinite is the consciousness of this structure.

Those for whom a lack or an ought is something without the realization of which finite beings remain unfulfilled are to be set next to those Hegel describes in the Introduction to the *Phenomenology*: they attempt to grasp the true by subtracting from the whole experience of knowledge that brought in by the instrument of knowledge.[59] The only difference is that, for the former it is a matter of addition (adding that which is lacking to the finite being to make it complete), whereas for the latter it is a matter of subtraction (subtracting "from the representation of the Absolute which we have gained through it whatever is due to the instrument, and thus getting the truth in its purity"[60]). Hegel agrees with Kant and Fichte, then, in the impossibility of reaching completion by merely adding the fulfilled ought to the finite being, since this would bring about the destruction of the ought itself and of finite beings understood as such. He agrees that the ought should be maintained *as* an ought. However, he disagrees with them insofar as they do not realize that the totality has already been reached in its character of being structurally lacking. Thus, they remain caught in a progress to infinity, at each step of which the finite being remains unfulfilled and incomplete: "The philosophy of Kant and Fichte sets up the ought as the highest point of the resolution of the contradictions of Reason; but the truth is that the ought is only the standpoint which clings to finitude and thus to contradiction."[61]

The overcoming of the finite has to do with knowledge of the structure of the ought. Fichte thought he had solved the opposition between self and not-self by transposing it from the theoretical to the practical realm and extending it in a progress to infinity. Every time one attempts to reach the not-self by theoretical means one realizes one has *posited* it *as* determining the self. To avoid this constant positing masked as presupposing, one arrives at the practical in which one posits oneself as positing the not-self. One becomes conscious of one's own activity of positing. However, one can never reach an absolute positing since as an activity of positing it will always limit itself in this positing. Hegel's solution to this progress to infinity lies, not in reaching the absolute positing beyond Fichte's reach, but in returning to the theoretical and realizing *that* this is the case. In the Addition to § 234 in the section on Willing in the *Encyclopaedia*, after criticizing Kant and Fichte's philosophy, Hegel says with respect to finitude:

> Therefore the will itself also requires that its purpose shall not be realized. This correctly expresses the finitude of willing. But we must not stop at this finitude, of course, and it is through the process of willing itself that this finitude is sublated, together with the contradiction that it contains. The reconciliation consists in the will's returning-in its result-to the presupposition of *cognition*; hence, the reconciliation consists in the unity of the theoretical and practical Idea. The will *knows* the purpose as what is its own, and intelligence interprets the world as the Concept in its actuality. This is the genuine position of rational cognition.
>
> What is null and vanishing constitutes only the surface of the world, not its genuine essence. This essence is the Concept that is in and for itself, and so the world is itself the Idea. Unsatisfied striving vanishes when we *[re]cognize* that the final purpose of the world is just as much accomplished as it is eternally accomplishing itself.[62]

The solution to the contradictory nature of the ought does not lie in the practical (one continues acting, conscious of the ought one must follow, though never having the certainty that one follows it for its sake), but in the theoretical, in coming to grips with the structure of the ought. The knowledge achieved regarding the practical realm does not dissolve it. The world *eternally accomplishes itself*. The concordance of *is* and *ought*, by which Kant and Fichte are overcome, is a concordance in non-concordance. This determines it as process: "it constantly brings itself about."[63]

The immediate characterization of the concept of the infinite will reveal it as self-contradictory insofar as it stands opposed to the finite, thus itself being finite. This is not the infinite but the non-finite.[64] As long as "it is the nature of the finite to transcend itself, to negate its negation and to become infinite,"[65] as long as the infinite is "the nothing of the finite...all determinateness, alteration, all limitation and with it the ought itself, [are] posited as vanished, as sublated."[66] Either concept will lead to the destruction of both. Here Hegel applies the process already experienced in the passages of "something," "other," and the limit, to the finite/infinite opposition in order to reveal its contradictions. They are co-dependent, presupposing and positing each other, contradicting themselves in their claim to independence. The process constituting this spurious infinite is parallel to that constituting the relation between being and nothing: the moment one is thought it gives rise to its opposite, and so on to infinity. There is, however, a difference: the process between being and nothing is more immediate. Being thinks itself to be self-subsistent, the richest concept. It then disappears into its opposite, whereas it is the nature of the finite, as determinate being, to disappear into its "other." The finite is characterized by its lack, by the infinite it is not. Thus, it is its nature to disappear insofar as it is finite. To think the finite separate from the infinite is to make it infinite; whereas to think the infinite separate from the finite is to make it finite. Each becomes its "other," becoming then the "other" of its "other," and so on, in a progress to infinity.

The spurious infinite can be characterized as being the transformation of the finite into the infinite, or of the infinite into the finite (due to their contradictory nature). However, in this transformation both are still maintained as opposites to each other. The finite taken as opposed to the infinite, becomes itself infinite insofar as it absolutizes itself by not relating to an "other" to it. On the other hand, the infinite, since it does not include its opposite the finite, becomes finite itself. As long as the unity of these two concepts is not realized, they will remain in a spurious infinite.

There are two important characteristics that determine the difference between the spurious and the true infinite. The first is the fact that there is no new element added to the spurious infinite to transform it into the true infinite. It is merely a matter of *reflection*.[67] The second, directly related, is that reflection on the spurious infinite reveals that what was taken one-sidedly as consisting of isolated acts, is rather a totality or process. Thus, the spurious infinite is merely the non-realization of the totality. It is the incapacity to look beyond the immediate opposition of the finite and the infinite and their transformation into their "other" and to see that they are realized in the act of transforming themselves into their "other." To remain in the spurious infinite is to take the lack that drives finite beings to be external, beyond reach (finite beings are thus incomplete), while it is actually internal, constitutive of what it is to be a finite being. This lack is part of the structure of a self-determining totality. Hegel says:

> In the first place, the negation of the finite and infinite which is posited in the infinite progress can be taken as simple, hence as separate and merely successive. Starting from the finite, the limit is transcended, the finite negated. We now have its beyond, the infinite, but in this the limit *arises* again; and so we have the transcending of the infinite. This double sublation, however, is partly only an external affair, an alternation of the moments, and partly it is not yet posited as a *single unity*; the transcending of each moment starts independently, is a fresh act, so that the two processes fall apart.[68]

When the finite, taken as opposed to the infinite, transforms itself into its opposite the infinite, this new infinite is still taken as opposed to the finite. Taken as such, it becomes its opposite: the finite. This process continues, though its character of being a process is only seen from an external viewpoint. As long as the finite and the infinite are taken as opposites, we have before us not a process of transformation, but one *fresh act* after another, a *monotonous alternation*.[69] Returning to the moral realm, not to realize that the ought as ought cancels the possibility of its own realization (more specifically, of our being certain of its realization) is to bring about an unhappy consciousness since one is not a totality, one lacks something without which realization as a human being would not be possible. Every human act would then be the confirmation of the impossibility of being human, and as such, a source of constant unhappiness and frustration. Put in a moral context, the true infinite does not consist in realizing the ought, in being certain that one acts for the sake of duty, but rather in realizing that in not knowing if one reaches the ought one fulfills it insofar as the attempt at achieving the ought is what constitutes the nature of moral beings. When one realizes that it is our nature never to be able to know if we act for the sake of duty, the unhappy consciousness and the frustration of not being a totality disappear. One accepts one's finitude, realizing that it is precisely not a finitude. One neither becomes God, reaching the certainty of having acted for the sake of duty, thus dissolving the concept of duty itself, nor does one become amoral, turning one's back on the ought due to the consciousness of its unreachable character.[70] The concept of the ought must be preserved for us to fulfill ourselves as moral beings in our striving toward it. Both to stop acting morally and to have the certainty of having acted morally lead to the same result: ceasing to fulfill our being. Thus, Hegel's view on the ought does not lead to our turning our back on acting morally. Neither does it lead to a relativistic position in which "anything goes." Hegel's main foe seems to be any type of moral a priori. However, to be wary of the certainty of a moral a priori is not equivalent to rejecting normativity altogether. Normativity, nonetheless, cannot lie beyond history since there is no such beyond. It is rather constituted by history itself.

There is a passage in Hegel's *Relationship of Skepticism to Philosophy* that clearly reveals how the true infinite adds nothing new or different to the spurious infinite.

> The science of philosophy, too, only repeats for ever one and the same rational identity, but new cultural formations spring forth from the former ones in this repetition, out of which it builds itself up into a complete organic world, which is [re]cognized both as a whole and in its parts as this same identity. Whereas the eternal repetition of that antithesis which leads to organic breakdown and the *nihil negativum*, is on its negative side a perpetual pouring of water into a sieve, and from its positive side, it is the continual and mechanical application of one and the same rule of understanding, wherein no new form comes forth from the old, but always the same mechanical work is done; this application of the rule is like the labor of a woodcutter who ever strikes the same blow, or of a tailor who sews uniforms for an army.[71]

There are two types of *repetition*. One could also say there are two types of progress to infinity.[72] Their difference lies in the reflective character of the one constituting the true infinite. This reflective character takes in the whole totality at once and views the progress to infinity as a process, whereas the spurious infinite parallels a mechanical view that does not see beyond each separate act; it is led back step by step in its search for a first cause.

Throughout the passages on the spurious and the true infinite one finds references to a *reflection* on the spurious infinite, on the opposition between the finite and the infinite, through which the true infinite is achieved. What will take us from a mere *eternal repetition* to the *repetition* of *rational identity* is simply a matter of reflecting on this progress to infinity.

> The infinity of the infinite progress remains burdened with the finite as such, is thereby limited and is itself *finite*. But this being so, the infinite progress would in fact be posited as the unity of the finite and the infinite; but this unity is not **reflected on**... This transition from one to the other and back again constitutes the external realization of the Notion. In this realization is *posited* the content of the Notion, but it is posited as *external*, as falling *asunder*; all that is required is to **compare** these different moments which yield the *unity* which gives the Notion itself; the *unity* of the infinite and the finite is-as has often been remarked already but here especially is to be borne in mind-the one-sided expression for the unity as it is in truth... In *saying* what the infinite is, namely the negation of the *finite*, the latter is itself included in what is *said*; it cannot be dispensed with for the definition or determination of the infinite. One only needs to ***be aware*** *of* [*zu wissen*] *what one is saying* in order to find the determination of the infinite in the finite.[73]

The spurious infinite can also be characterized as an external activity that brings to mind the association of this *eternal repetition* to a mechanistic view of things, brought up in the passage quoted above. That the finite becomes infinite and vice-versa is posited as an external activity that does not occur due to the finite or the infinite themselves, but rather to their being posited as opposite each other. What moves the infinite to become finite is its having as opposite the finite insofar as the infinite becomes finite when it is posited as opposed to it. Thus finite and infinite would seem to be brought together externally: "This double sublation, however, is partly only an external affair, an alternation of the moments, and partly it is not yet posited as a *single unity*."[74] Right before this passage Hegel asserts that for the understanding, which keeps the finite and the infinite separate, their unity in each *fresh act* of the spurious infinite is an "external bringing together of them... an incongruous combination alien to their own nature."[75] Hegel himself contributes to the view that what is at stake in these passages seems to be the distinction between mechanical and teleological beings, by using the concepts of cause and effect understood form a mechanical point of view as an exemplification of what the spurious infinite is. However, the point being made here is not the association of the spurious infinite with a mechanical view of beings, always regressing in search of a cause external to them, and of the true infinite with a teleological view of beings, in which they are self-caused, self-determined totalities. The passage quoted above from *Relationship of Skepticism to Philosophy* was intended merely to bring to light the fact that there is a way of understanding the idea of repetition or of progress to infinity that does not consist merely in an endless "one after another."

The whole section on determinate being should be taken as the conceptual movement that occurs in thinking objective being qualitatively, from "something" and "other" (in which being is completely dependent on its "other," on its relations to its "others" for its being), to "being-for-self" (in which being is completely self-subsistent, a self-determined totality). However, one should not apply the development from a mechanical view of being to a self-subsistent teleological one encountered here to the discussion of the step from the finite to the infinite since finite beings are already self-subsistent beings, they have their telos within them. They are not driven by their relations with "others" in an external manner but rather internally, in a self-subsistent manner. Their truth is their *end*: "They [finite things] are, but the truth of this being is their *end*."[76] The step from the finite to the infinite is rather a reflection on what this *having their end as their truth* means. As much as what is being dealt with here is the concept of a self-determined totality leading toward the concept of "being-for-self," the emphasis placed in the specific discussion of the spurious and the true infinite is on the character of this totality being constituted by a lack. It does not cease being self-determined since it is only a totality when it includes this lack *as* a lack. In other words, the stress Hegel lays on the concept of the true infinite is that as a totality it is constituted by a sort of blind spot, the structure and necessity of which can be reflected on, but which can never be erased. Thus, what is at stake in the step from the spurious to the true infinite is not mechanism vs. teleology, or material vs. final causes, but rather non-fulfillment due to lack vs. fulfillment through lack. The overcoming of the finite nature of beings does not consist in their fulfillment by means of reaching what was lacking (ought). It consists in their fulfillment by means of revealing the constitutive character of the unrealizable nature of the ought, of what they lack.

The concept of the true infinite can be characterized as a coming to terms with finitude, whereas the concept of the finite can be understood as the belief that completion or fulfillment lies external to it and is therefore unreachable. To come to terms with finitude means to realize that by positing their fulfillment as being unreachable finite beings have already achieved it, they have determined themselves as being what they are, becoming thus a "being-for-self." The unfulfilled character of finite beings, insofar as it is posited by them as being unfulfilled, is fulfilled. In the section on the Idea of the good in the *Science of Logic* Hegel says:

> Now, if it is supposed that the end of the good is after all not realized through this mediation, this signifies a relapse of the Notion to the standpoint occupied by it before its activity-the standpoint of an actuality determined as worthless and yet presupposed as real. This relapse, which becomes the progress to the spurious infinity, has its sole ground in the fact that in the sublating of that abstract reality, this sublating is no less immediately forgotten, or it is forgotten that this reality is in fact already presupposed as an actuality that is intrinsically worthless and not objective. This repetition of the presupposition of the unrealized end after the actual realization of the end consequently assumes this character, that the *subjective bearing* of the objective Notion is reproduced and made perpetual, with the result that the *finitude* of the good in respect of its content as well as its form appears as the abiding truth, and its actualization appears always as a merely *individual* act, and not as a universal one. As a matter of fact, this determinateness has sublated itself in the actualization of the good; what still *limits* the objective Notion is its own *view* of itself, which vanishes by **reflection** on what its actualization is *in itself*. Through this view it is only standing in its own way, and thus what it has to do is to turn, not against an outer actuality, but against itself.[77]

Here we find both characteristics mentioned above as determining the difference between the spurious and the true infinite. Nothing new is brought to the true infinite that is not already there in the spurious infinite. It is merely a matter of reflection. The true infinite or self-determined totality has been reached. However, it does not *view itself* as such since it *forgets* to keep itself in view as a whole, so to speak. To do this it requires *reflection on what its actualization is in itself*. This leads us to the second characteristic. What the finite being forgets is that the end of the good cannot be realized, that *this reality is in fact already presupposed as an actuality that is intrinsically worthless and not objective*. In other words, it forgets that it cannot fulfill the ought since if it did it would cease to exist. Each time it attempts to realize it, finite being considers it a *fresh act*, a merely *individual act*. It does not realize that it is the nature of the ought itself not to be achieved, that all human acts insofar as they fall short of achieving the ought are to be taken as a *universal act*, being constituted by their falling short. The moment finite being remembers the universal nature of all its acts, it no longer has before it an endless succession of individual acts, but rather the process that constitutes it as being finite and thus the actualization (in non-actualization) of the good. The good is actualized in striving to actualize it: "the final purpose of the world is just as much accomplished as it is eternally accomplishing itself."[78] Only insofar as there is a continuous striving toward accomplishing an ought is it already accomplished. There is an agreement (*Übereinstimmung*) between *the is* and *the ought to be*; however, it is not *rigid and unmoving*. The agreement lies in a constant striving to achieve their agreement.[79] In the previous chapter it was seen that there is an *Übereinstimmung* between knowledge and truth, not insofar as they coincide, collapsing into each other, but rather insofar as only from knowledge is truth posited *as* truth, *as* being the *of* that knowledge is *of*. In the same manner the *ought* is in *Übereinstimmung* with the *is* insofar as it is posited as ought: "the final purpose of the world, the good, only *is*, because it constantly brings itself about."[80] In the section on the finite Hegel hints at this taking up of actuality as the outcome of the constant and permanent production of the good and accomplishing of the final purpose of the world, the permanent *Übereinstimmung* between being and the ought:

> But in the world of actuality itself, Reason and Law are not in such a bad way that they only *ought* to be-it is only the abstraction of the in-itself that stops at this-any more than the ought is in its own self perennial and, what is the same thing, that finitude is absolute.[81]

The reading of the true infinite proposed here, in which a progress to infinity is not cut short but rather viewed structurally as a whole and as constitutive of what a finite being is, is confirmed by the emphasis Hegel lays on not dissolving the difference between the finite and the infinite completely in their being sublated. The true infinite does not amount to unity reached after overcoming difference. It is unity of unity and difference. The difference between the finite and the infinite is maintained. This maintains the process: the continuous accomplishing of the purpose of the world. However, insofar as it is reflected on it is also overcome; it realizes that the finite turns into the infinite and vice-versa. Their unity is given by reflection on their difference. If the difference were to cease to be, the motility of being would also cease to be. The unity of the finite and the infinite merely reflects that the nature of a finite being is to be constituted by a lack, to be a totality in lack since this lack determines it *as* totality. Thus the true infinite should be understood as the unity of the unity between the finite and the infinite, and their difference.

In a highly confusing passage, even for Hegelian standards, he attempts to clarify how this unity reached with the true infinite should and should not be understood.[82] The difficulty of grasping it is that it consists in the attempt at conceptualizing life itself, a task difficult for the understanding since it always works one-sidedly, avoiding contradiction. The motility of life cannot be conceptualized by a spatial alteration occurring at different points of time. This merely reveals change of place, which could occur to a "something" or an "other" by external forces. To grasp life one must be able to grasp the spatial alteration as originated internally by being, one must see a process and not isolated results. This is what Hegel has in mind when he discusses two types of unity of the finite and the infinite: a simple and a double unity, neither of which is capable of reflecting the motility of beings. The simple unity is one in which the finite, insofar as it is opposed to the infinite, becomes infinite, and the infinite, insofar as it is opposed to the finite, becomes itself finite: F/I. In this unity all difference disappears, resulting in pure unity. This result is similar to what one would have in pure becoming without a determinate being (*Dasein*) to become. The double unity results from uniting a finite that became infinite and an infinite that became finite: F/I I/F. This is still unsatisfactory since understanding jumps from one to the other without grasping the movement, due to the same reason: on one of the poles the finite is taken as opposed to the infinite and thus turns into the infinite; on the other the infinite is taken as opposed to the finite and thus turns into the finite. The result of this double unity is the same simple unity: F/I.

> Just as before, the simple unity of the infinite and finite was falsified by the understanding, so too is the double unity. Here too this results from taking the infinite in one of the two unities not as negated, but rather as the in-itself, in which, therefore, determinateness and limitation are not to be explicitly present, for these would debase and ruin it. Conversely, the finite is likewise held fast as not negated, although in itself it is null; so that in its union with the infinite it is exalted to what it is not and is thereby infinitized in opposition to its determination as finite, which instead of vanishing is perpetuated.[83]

The true infinite must reveal this becoming of each into its other while simultaneously holding them separate.[84] Only by also holding them separate does it capture the totality instead of seeing a ceaseless change of the finite into the infinite and vice-versa. By holding them separate it realizes that in the constant movement of their turning into each other they come back to themselves. They maintain themselves in this constant becoming. Their becoming is what gives them their identity.

We have then a finite that is both itself, taken as opposed to the infinite, and itself and the infinite since it becomes the infinite, and an infinite that is both itself, taken as opposed to the finite, and itself and the finite since it becomes the finite: F/F-I I/I-F. We may now go beyond saying that at a specific moment the finite is the finite and at another the infinite (in this case we would only see unrelated *fresh acts*).[85] Now the finite is itself and its *becoming* the infinite:

> The finite has the double meaning of being first, only the finite *over against* the infinite which stands opposed to it, and secondly, of being the finite and *at the same time* the infinite opposed to it. The infinite, too, has the double meaning of being *one* of these two moments-as such it is the spurious infinite- and also the infinite in which both, the infinite and its other, are only moments. The infinite, therefore, as now before us is, in fact, the process in which it is deposed to being only *one* of its determinations, the opposite of the finite, and so to being itself only one of the finites, and then raising this its difference from itself into the affirmation of itself and through this mediation becoming the *true* infinite.[86]

Transposed to the moral realm, finite beings are simultaneously finite in the sense of lacking something, of having the ought as external to them, and infinite in the sense of fulfilling this ought by striving toward it, becoming infinite by being finite: F F/I. The fact that there are two poles maintains the progress to infinity. However, each time the finite posits the infinite by determining itself through it as opposed to it, this infinite is realized in its non-realizable nature.

The images Hegel chooses for representing the spurious and the true infinite are the straight line and the circle, respectively. The circle would seem to confirm the present reading of the true infinite insofar as it has no end, though its structure is revealed as a totality in itself. One can take it in as a whole, whereas the line always leads beyond the point where one sets one's eyes.

To be wholly present without end is what was called above realization through non-realization, totality of limitation. The progress to infinity is not cut short or dissolved. It is just reflected on, by means of which its constitutive nature comes to light. It ceases to be what denies finite beings their fulfillment, leaving them with an unhappy consciousness, and becomes their fulfillment precisely insofar as they are fulfilling what it is to be a finite being.

Although the true infinite has been reached wherein the opposition between the finite and the infinite is sublated (*aufgehoben*), and "being-for-self," a self-subsistent independent being, has appeared, we are still within the Doctrine of Being, that is, we are still dealing with concepts of Objective Being. This has as a consequence that, from the point of view of Hegel's first definition of finite things given in the first Remark to Becoming: "It is the definition of finite things that in them the Concept is different from being, that Concept and reality, soul and body, are separable and hence that they are perishable and mortal,"[87] we are still dealing with the concepts of finite things separate from their concept, although the concept is their truth. There are two levels in which Hegel uses the concept of the finite. We have been dealing with the internal one, so to speak, which occurs within the chapter on Determinate Being. However, the other level in which the finite has a place in the *Logic* occurs on a larger scale. All concepts of Objective Being, appearing in the doctrines of Being and of Essence, can be taken as finite insofar as in them "Notion and reality, soul and body, are separable."[88] Hegel's excursus into the concept of the ought in the passages just analyzed already points toward the overcoming of the finitude of Objective Being. This overcoming will be encountered in the Doctrine of the Notion and will be treated in Chapter 5 when dealing with Hegel's Idea.

Looking back at the structure brought to light in the previous chapter concerning the problem of the measure, one finds that the concept of the infinite shares many of its characteristics. Truth understood as reality is posited by knowledge of it *as* being beyond such knowledge insofar as knowledge is always of something that something is the case. What knowledge is of is posited through this knowledge but as distinct from it. It is its shadow, only revealing itself as not being such and such when its knowledge is falsified. In other words, only in revealing knowledge as false does what is true appear, *as* not being that. As Michael Theunissen says: "The real content of the truth of that which is held as true comes to light-in an apparent paradox-precisely with the unmasking of its untruth."[89] Concerning the ought all human acts posit it as their shadow, as beyond them, insofar as it is constitutive of a human act never to have the certainty of having occurred for the sake of duty. Thus, the ought is also confirmed negatively, as that for the sake of which no act can be known to be realized. The ought is the shadow projected by each human act. Truth always appears *as* that which knowledge is of, although it lies beyond knowledge (insofar as knowledge is *of*...). It is realized by fulfilling its function of determining knowledge as being knowledge *of* … . Truth and knowledge could never collapse into one since then both would disappear. Truth is only reached through knowledge; thus it has always been reached and is always being reached in a constant unmasking of knowledge as false (of truth as being other than what we *meant*: experience). In the same manner, the fulfillment of the ought would spell its own dissolution. It cannot be realized. For the same reason it is constantly being realized in its non-realization, in the attempts of moral beings to act morally. The purpose of the world is constantly accomplishing itself. Without the structural gap between the "in-itself" and the "for-itself" there would be no human cognitive experience. Without the structural gap between the *is* and the *ought* there would be no moral action. The true infinite is the realization that our finitude is already what makes us infinite beings. The fact that we do not leave behind our finitude, that we always come up short against the ought while nonetheless realizing it, is what determines the stubborn nature of the idea of the good, which accounts for the insurmountable opposition that characterizes the Hegelian Idea as it appears in Section III of the Doctrine of the Notion.

* * * *

The excess found lacking in Hegelian philosophy seems to exist right at its center. The fundamental question is whether its immanence necessarily undoes the depth of its otherness. If the only characteristic one can come up with regarding what lies beyond conceptuality in order to recognize it as lying beyond consists in the experience of always falling short of it, both theoretically and practically, then there seems to be no difference between Hegel's position and that of his critics, except for his renouncing as quixotic the attempt to non-conceptually gesture toward the non-conceptual. The assertion that "there is no concept of the other" is not surprising. It is also self-undermining in Hegel's view. What would be absolutely surprising, completely non-Greek, would be the *concept* of an immanent or internal excess, a concept of the other that does not deny this other its absolute otherness. This is what the stubbornness of the opposition of the idea of the good encountered toward the end of the *Science of Logic* consists in. On this reading, Hegel's idea of the good would amount to the only possible relation to a pure being (the other) that simultaneously respects its otherness to me by my always coming up short against it.[90] Whereas Levinas and Derrida would seem to emphasize treating the other as an absolutely other, Hegel emphasizes the impossibility of treating the other as an extension of myself.

She is always more than I can identify and reduce her to, although the only way I have of relating to her is through myself, through who I am and take myself to be. I can only encounter the other as the other by projecting myself onto her. Nonetheless, I always come up short in my projections. The other stubbornly surprises me time and again.[91]

3
Necessity Is Contingency: The Analytic/Synthetic Distinction

3.1 Introduction

A characteristic of metaphysical systems is that they purport to give a true account of "what is". In doing so, they ascribe it necessity: "what is" is necessarily so and cannot be otherwise. In this manner, the Leibnizian account of the world describes it as necessary due to a combination of God's goodness and omnipotence, despite the fact that from our human, finite perspective, truths of fact are racked with contingency. The Spinozist substance "exists from the necessity of its nature alone."[1] Regarding the absolute idea Hegel says of it that "its essential nature is to return to itself through its self-determination or particularization," and in the *Lectures on the History of Philosophy* he asserts that to know it in its necessity is the present standpoint of philosophy. It would not seem uncharitable to establish a running metaphysical thread between Spinoza's substance, Leibniz's monad of monads, and Hegel's absolute idea as attempts to reveal the necessity of "what is" or of reality. However, in Hegel's case, the underpinning concept of necessity requires a closer look. Since it is in the *Science of Logic* where we find the exhibition and explanation of the concepts by means of which philosophical thinking has thought "what is," this text will reveal what Hegel understands by necessity and what role it plays—what contradictions it resolves—in the attempt to think "what is." Any attempt to offer an interpretation of Hegel's philosophy, be it metaphysical or non-metaphysical, must come face to face with his concept of necessity and decipher what it amounts to for Hegel to ascribe necessity to his system. When one realizes how structurally connected necessity and contingency are, then Hegel's whole system would seem to be standing on unstable ground. If this is the case, the development of Spirit to the point of becoming conscious of its own becoming in Hegel's Idealism could just as well not have taken place.

3.2 Detour via Quine

Quine in his article "Two Dogmas of Empiricism" attempts to undermine the validity of two main tenets of empiricism advocated by logical positivism: the analytic/synthetic distinction and reductionism. The latter consists in the idea that "every meaningful statement is held to be translatable into a statement (true or false) about immediate experience."[2] For Quine's purposes it does not matter whether immediate experience be understood as sense data, objects, or even facts. According to this position, for a statement to have meaning it must be able to be traced back to the point of contact between mind and world, conceptual scheme and content, in such a way that this would provide its objectivity. Quine rejects the idea that meaning can be given in any other way than through science as a whole. In other words, the meaning provided for sense data, an object or a fact of experience can only exist through a prior theory about the world, a *Weltanschauung*, which, according to him, would be science: "The unit of empirical significance is the whole of science."[3] No word or statement can be confirmed or disconfirmed separately, by relying on our perception of simple ideas (Locke) or on our acquaintance with sense data (Russell). Confirmation or disconfirmation takes place from a pre-established horizon of meaning in which nothing lies beyond the possibility of being falsified.[4] There is no one-to-one point of contact between mind and world. This leads us to the first dogma: the analytic/synthetic distinction. If nothing lies beyond possible falsification then there is no such thing as an analytic statement. A statement cannot be true (or false) on the basis of meaning alone. Quine's attack on analyticity is mainly an attack on the concept of the necessity of meaning divorced from any empirical basis. An attempt to ground meaning through definition leads to use, which in turn, is empirical and thus subject to change. An attempt to ground it through synonymy presupposes analyticity instead of explaining it. The concept of analyticity only applies to logical tautologies and as such is meaningless.

For Quine "no statement is immune to revision,"[5] "there are no free-floating, linguistically neutral meanings."[6] To assert that two sentences have the same meaning is to assert that they are inter-translatable. However, given his theory of the indeterminacy of translation, which means that sentences have more than one acceptable translation due to various under-determinations, there is no possibility for identity or sameness of meaning. A correct translation does not preserve meaning. What it does is allow prediction of behavior or of events in nature. But this only happens from within a conceptual scheme already, which could be different and which, from an epistemological standpoint, makes "the physical objects and the gods differ only in degree and not in kind."[7] In the concluding section of the article Quine describes science, or the totality of our knowledge or beliefs, as a field of force that on its edges borders with sensory experience. The closer we get to the center of the field, the farther removed we are from our sensory experience. Therefore, the more abstract and conceptual our theories are the closer to the center of the field they lie. The outer edges are the point of contact between mind and world but they do not determine the field. All statements within the field, regardless of how close to the periphery they lie, are underdetermined by the periphery. Therefore, no statement is analytically true, that is, immune to revision, not even the principles of logic. There is no absolutely necessary statement, nothing that works as a fixed point from which to determine other statements occurring in the field. There is no free-standing necessity independent of a system or conceptual framework from which it is determined to be necessary relative to that system. An extreme example Quine offers is the law of excluded middle and quantum mechanics, within whose system such law need not apply. Necessity is thus determined as such by pragmatic considerations: "our vaguely pragmatic inclination to adjust one strand of the fabric of science rather than another in accommodating some particular recalcitrant experience."[8]

This metaphor of the "man-made fabric" or the "field of force" perfectly illustrates the third dogma of empiricism that Davidson finds still presupposed by Quine. He still works within the dualism of conceptual scheme/content, or interior/edges. The content impinges on experience along the edges, and science (the totality of our knowledge or beliefs) unifies, organizes or synthesizes the information received through our sensory apparatus (stimulation of nerve-endings). This leads Quine to posit truth as "relative to a conceptual scheme" since he maintains the causal space of perceptions separate from the logical space of reasons.[9] The end result of this separation is either relativism or skepticism.

* * * *

What follows is an analysis of the chapter on Actuality (*Wirklichkeit*) in the *Science of Logic*, which shows how the concept of absolute necessity not only includes within it but also contains as its structural element the concept of contingency.[10] In this manner a deflationary interpretation will be generated in which any ascription of necessity in Hegel's philosophy should not be immediately taken as pointing toward a pre-established end or telos inexorably guiding a process (be it of spirit becoming conscious of itself, or of actuality being determined as rational[11]) but rather toward an interpretive movement, in recollection, of the whole process. Let us begin by focusing on the directionality of the chapter, which always starts off with actuality itself and then goes back to possibility, and its importance in understanding the interpretive movement occurring in any constitution of actuality.

3.3 Location of the chapter on actuality within the *Science of Logic*

The first issue that arises regarding this section is its placement. *Pace* Kant, it is not located in the Subjective Logic, but rather finds its place in the Objective Logic. For Kant, such categories of modality "only express the relation of the concept to the faculty of knowledge." They do not express a "what" but rather a "how": "how the object, together with all its determinations, is related to understanding and its empirical employment, to empirical judgment, and to reason in its application to experience."[12] Modal categories are the only group within the table of categories that does not deal with content, but merely with its relation to the understanding (B100, B110). They do not add any information about the object thought. However, no object can be object of a judgment without being subsumed under one of the modal categories.

Why Hegel places modality within the Objective Logic can be explained by focusing on the difference between the Kantian project in the *Critique of Pure Reason* and that of Hegel in the *Science of Logic*. In the *Critique* Kant wanted to describe the structure and functioning of human understanding that would account for objective knowledge. His was a synchronous project.[13] Under this characterization, all reality, in order to be objectively known by the understanding, must be constituted by a quality, must have a certain quantity, must be in certain relations to other reality, and must be related to the understanding in a certain manner. After having revealed in the *Phenomenology of Spirit* that "what is," is not other to thinking, but "on the contrary, the necessary forms and self-determinations of thought are the content and the ultimate truth itself,"[14] Hegel attempts to grasp what is true as concept. This makes it a processual task insofar as the concepts used to think what is true always fall short: they either lead to contradiction or reveal themselves as other than what was originally meant by them. Thus, the appearance of each concept brings with it the tools for its own overcoming, by which the contradiction it led to is sublated. We might then conclude that in Kant the categories of modality (like all other categories) are conditions without which no object can be objectively thought; whereas, if one keeps in mind that the starting point of the *Logic* is the conclusion (derived from the *Phenomenology*) that the object of philosophy, the Platonic *ontos on*, is constituted by the concepts by which this *ontos on* or the true is thought, then the concepts of contingency, possibility, actuality, and necessity appear at a particular moment of the process of thinking this *ontos on*: when it is thought as actuality. Thus, when "what is" is thought in terms of being or essence, modal concepts do not yet constitute it. The difference, then, with Kant is twofold: on the one hand, these modal concepts do determine what is true (as do all concepts encountered in the *Logic*), although they will all be revealed to be insufficient to think what is true due to internal contradictions; on the other, what is true will not appear completely in these concepts since they still belong to objective logic (concepts used to think "what is" as external to thought). One should not lose sight of the location of these modal categories at the threshold of the subjective logic, the last section of which will reveal the true *ontos on*: the absolute idea, one of whose determinations is its absolute necessity.

For Hegel these four concepts are interrelated: to think one of them through entails being led to think the others. This requires being able to deal with them only when they can all be ascribed, including necessity. Such an event occurs with the concept of actuality.[15] The concepts of contingency, possibility, and necessity are posited from the appearance of actuality. There is no gradual build-up from mere possibility to absolute necessity. Rather, the moment the concept of actuality is thought when thinking what is true, it unfolds from within it those of contingency, possibility, and necessity. Thus, to think "what is" in a qualitative or quantitative manner implies not to be able to think it yet as contingent, possible, actual or necessary, but only as Being. There is neither necessity nor contingency in Being. Modal concepts appear at a specific moment in the process of thinking what is true. They are posited only when "what is" is thought as being actual. Actuality is not a mode of being thought (taking thought as opposed to Being), next to possibility and necessity. It is a mode of Being (taking Being as being thought), richer and less abstract than thinking "what is" in terms of qualitative or quantitative Being, or in terms of Essence.

These modal concepts constitute the chapter on Actuality, the second chapter of the section under the same name, which in turn constitutes the third section of the Doctrine of Essence. The other two sections are: "Essence as Reflection Within Itself" and "Appearance." Starting off with the three sections comprising the Doctrine of Essence, Actuality, as the third, is the unity of Essence and Appearance, of that which appears and that as which it appears. Actuality sublates all two-tiered concepts as which "what is" was thought in the Doctrine of Essence: essence/illusion, inner/outer, ground/grounded, condition/conditioned, world-in-itself/appearing world, thing-in-itself/existence. Actuality no longer manifests its essence but itself: "the absolute is manifestation not of an inner, nor over against an other, but it is only as the absolute manifestation of itself for itself. As such it is *actuality*."[16] This passage already hints at the main characteristic of actuality, which appears in the following section on "The Absolute Relation": it is cause of itself, not dependent on something other to it. The moments constituting actuality are in themselves "the *totality*... the complete *content* of the whole...,"[17] whereas the moment of the conditioned required that of the unconditioned, the moment of the outer that of the inner, and so on. This unity of essence and appearance is "the ground in which they [reflected determinations] have been engulfed [*untergegangen*]."[18]

Seen from a different angle, Actuality, as the third and last section of the Doctrine of Essence before continuing on to the Doctrine of the Concept, is the unity of Being and Essence. It is already the concept, though still in-itself, in need of displaying itself and becoming for-itself. Being was immediate, just taken up as a given. Essence mediated Being by devaluing it, making it dependent on an other to it, making it a mere manifestation of an other through it. Being was thus revealed as mere illusion (*Schein*), a placeholder for some other that gave it its content or meaning. With actuality, Being and essence are thought together. The immediacy of Being is posited, not presupposed. However, it retains all its wealth insofar as it contains its essence within it; what manifests itself is essence, or rather, its essence is its existence. Actuality is the manifestation of itself for itself. There is nothing hidden behind Being supplying meaning to it; nor is "what is" purely given, merely presupposed. It is now revealed to be posited as "what is."

The three chapters comprising the section on Actuality are (1) The Absolute; (2) Actuality; (3) The Absolute Relation. The modal concepts appear in the second chapter. Actuality is first revealed as the absolute: "The Absolute is the unity of inner and outer as initial, implicit unity."[19] One already sees in this definition its limitation: its immediate nature.

To illustrate this immediate unity of inner and outer, Hegel mentions Spinoza, from whom he takes the idea of "cause of itself," a substance whose essence includes existence or appearance.[20] The first and third definitions given by Spinoza in his *Ethics* are, respectively:

> I. By cause of itself I understand that whose essence involves existence, or that whose nature cannot be conceived except as existing... III. By substance I understand what is in itself and is conceived through itself, i.e., that whose concept does not require the concept of another thing, from which it must be formed.[21]

Here we find those characteristics ascribed above to actuality: unity of essence and appearance, and independence from something other to it. However, the immediate nature of the absolute will not allow it to account for what is true since this must be shown to be the case. Hegel rejects an immediate absolute presupposed as purely given. The absolute must manifest itself as what it claims to be in order not to be dismissed as a bare assurance. Hegel's critique of Spinoza's substance is that it does not become what it is. It is unmoved identity, the equivalent of pure abstraction and emptiness.[22]

3.4 The concept of actuality

Actuality is the manifesting itself of the absolute, the movement of the exposition by which the absolute reveals itself to become (or to have become) what it is. What is to be kept in view is not what it is, but that it manifests itself to be what it is, that it has *become* what it is. Actuality shows how it has done so.

> Or the content of the absolute is just this, to manifest itself. The absolute is the absolute form which, as the diremption of itself is utterly identical with itself, the negative as negative, or that unites with itself, and only thus is it the absolute identity-with-self which equally is indifferent to its differences, or is absolute content. The content, therefore, is only this exposition itself.[23]

We are no longer dealing with content separated from form. The emphasis has shifted from that which "what is" is, what it appears as, to the process of becoming and manifesting itself as what it is. We are going beyond the doctrines of Being and of Essence, beyond taking "what is" as content, in order to take it as an activity or movement.[24] What is actual does not have a particular, immediate content. Nor is it a thing-in-itself determining its appearance in the mediated sense of essence/appearance. The content of an appearance is determined by its essence.

One could understand the Objective Logic as an objectifying thinking, incapable of thinking what is true as actual, as a process in which "what is" becomes what it is, since this objectifying thinking congeals its movement and masks its dynamic character.[25]

However, to be a process is not a sufficient condition for it to be actual. With the definition of the absolute just quoted above it seems that all natural processes are also excluded from being actual insofar as they manifest a particular pre-existent essence. An acorn cannot but produce (or actualize in the Aristotelian sense) an oak, a dog cannot but beget a dog; and what constitutes an oak or a dog consists of particular biological characteristics that do not alter. Natural processes can only reproduce themselves, guaranteeing the permanence of their essence. Here Hegel would diverge from Aristotle insofar as he is not interested in establishing as actual this *energeia* of natural beings but rather processes in which the content is the manifestation or exposition itself. They are processes in which what is manifested is the process itself. These processes are spiritual as opposed to natural. In the Addition to §161 in the *Encyclopaedia* Hegel says: "What corresponds to the stage of the Concept in nature is organic life."[26] The limitation of the world of nature as opposed to that of spirit lies in its lack of freedom. There are no actualities in nature. Let us take a human life as example. The manifestation of a human life is not the manifestation of certain particular biological attributes that constitute what being human is. Rather, it is a manifestation of itself insofar as it determines itself to be what it is. In other words, the essence of a human being is to be free. It is not pre-determined to become what it becomes. Its identity-with-self is indifferent to its differences: there are no particular differences that necessarily constitute a human being (taken as a whole, that is, as an actuality determining itself in its becoming, as a self-developing process, not as member of a biological species). Each individual human being has particularities that separate it from other human beings. However, these are in constant alteration. Identity-with-self is absolute content: it can take up any content, regardless of its particularities.

This limiting of what is actual to spiritual, as opposed to natural, processes sheds some light on a topic that does not concern us directly here: Hegel's concept of concept. This occurs insofar as it was said above that actuality is the concept, though still in-itself, in need of development. We find confirmation of this limitation of the actual to spiritual processes in the fact that when dealing with the concept all the examples Hegel gives deal with spiritual processes: freedom, right, duty, God (*Science of Logic*); friendship, work of art, state, act (*Encyclopaedia*).[27] In the *Encyclopaedia* the concept is defined in the following manner:

> As the *substantial might which is for itself* the Concept is what is *free*; and since *each* of its moments is *the whole* that *it* is, and is posited as inseparable unity with it, the Concept is *totality*; thus, in its identity with itself it is what is *in and for itself determinate*.[28]

Keeping in mind the above given definition of the absolute as having the manifestation of itself as its content and as being indifferent to its differences, none of these concepts seems to have a particular content determining it. Rather, their content only arises from their manifestation; and this manifestation is always different insofar as what is determined as beautiful, rightful, and so forth, is constantly being reconfigured. There is no fixed essence of beauty, for example, more or less accurately manifested throughout different historical periods. Rather, it is determined from the manifestation itself of what is considered to be beautiful in each period. This lack of essence accounts for the freedom of the concept, its self-realization: it is constantly realizing itself by reconfiguring its content. It is the negative as negative, not negation of something, but pure negation: always the same concept yet always different.[29]

With the concepts of the absolute and of actuality something new seems to enter the constitution of "what is," something that evades the grasp both of a mechanical and of a teleological (as applied to organic beings) explanation. Hegel's talk of freedom, absolute negativity, negation as negation, and absolute content, does not point toward the model of organic being, but rather toward that of the Hegelian concept. We are now dealing with objects that in their constitution follow the model of Hegel's concept of concept.

3.5 Movement of the concept

Let us begin, then, with the analysis of the modal concepts. The first point to be noted is that the starting point is not possibility but actuality. Thus, the order is actuality, possibility, and necessity. They are not built up from possibility all the way to necessity, but rather are posited with actuality, and then branch out toward possibility and necessity. Only thinking "what is" (as actual) can one think of it as possible and as necessary.[30] In terms of the modal concepts, what is immediate is "what is" (as actuality); possibility is reflection-into-self, mediating it; and necessity is their relation to each other.[31]

Before dealing with each of the three subsections, I shall mention three simultaneously developing processes at work throughout the section, apparent in the titles themselves of the subsections. These processes lead: (1) from a formal through a real to an absolute level; (2) from actuality through possibility to necessity; (3) from contingency through relative necessity to absolute necessity. The latter two are further connected: the unity of actuality and possibility taking place in (2) leads to contingency, which in (3) is united with relative necessity, leading thus to absolute necessity (or absolute actuality).[32] These various processes at work reveal the interconnected nature of the modal concepts, none of which can exist independently of the others.

3.5.1 Contingency, or formal actuality, possibility, and necessity

We start off with the concept of "what is" as actual. This beginning, as all others, is pure immediacy, highly abstract. It is what is actual in general. Therefore, we begin with a formal level before going on to a real and then to an absolute one (process 1). Insofar as it is a beginning it has no content. As pure immediacy it is formal. The only assertion that can be made is an empty tautology: everything that is (actual) is (actual). For this reason we begin with contingency (process 3). Immediate actuality is contingent since it has not yet shown itself to be necessary. A bare assurance is, as such, contingent until it shows itself to be (to have become) what it claims to be. Another characteristic of formal actuality is that it is non-reflected, it takes up substance (unity of inner and outer) in an immediate manner as a given, not constituting it in reflection. However, actuality is not a pure immediacy; it is rather arrived at, mediated immediacy. This introduces the reflection-into-self of actuality: it unfolds into possibility. As an immediacy that is arrived at actuality reflects on itself as having arisen out of possibility: "*What is actual is possible.*"[33] The only immediate cause for an actual to be an actual, which means that it cannot have an external cause, something other to it, is its having been possible. The only self-cause at this level of immediacy and formality is possibility. Formal actuality leads back to formal possibility. The only assertion to be made of what is actual in its immediacy, of what is cause of itself, is to say that it is actual because it was possible, that its possibility determined it to actuality.

Reflection on the formal concept of possibility leads beyond the actual and pierces its limits. What is actual is a subset of what is possible. This leads directly to the first, positive concept of formal possibility, based on the principle of non-contradiction: everything that does not contradict itself is possible. To think of the possible in itself means to say that everything is possible. "But to say this is equally to say *nothing*, just as in the formal law of identity."[34] When thinking of the possible, not in itself but in relation to others, one reaches a second, negative concept of formal possibility: what is possible is not actual, it is "*only* a possible and the *ought-to-be* of the totality of form."[35] Whenever one thinks of a possible one can also think of its opposite as possible. This seems to be enough for Hegel to cancel the possible as impossible: "Possibility is therefore in its own self contradiction, or it is *impossibility*."[36] The concept of formal possibility includes within it its opposite. This reveals its contradictory nature since it simultaneously needs its other to be what it is and in positing its other it destroys itself.[37] This leads back to the actual we started off with, though now not immediately but in a reflected manner by having been mediated by possibility. It has become the unity of actuality and possibility: "This actuality is not the primary but the reflected actuality, *posited as unity* of itself and possibility."[38] Formal actuality taken up immediately leads to possibility, which in turn, leads to a reflected actuality, which includes possibility as a moment in it.

Hegel calls the unity of actuality and possibility contingency.[39] This is because the only characteristic ascribed to the actual is its having been possible. Consequently, its opposite could also have been possible. An actual that exists only insofar as it was possible for it to exist is contingent since it could have been otherwise, its opposite could also have existed. Using the actual and not the possible as starting point Hegel avoids the dilemma of the actualization of a possible: why does a particular possible become actual? The possible for Hegel is posited from the actual as its only source when the actual is taken in its immediacy. There is a difference between saying "X is actual because it was possible" and saying "X is possible and therefore it will become actual." That about which it can only be said that it is actual since it was possible reveals itself to be groundless. The possibility out of which it arose could have also been otherwise. This is the first side of contingency, in which possibility is taken immediately. However, if what is actual is such only insofar as it was possible then it must have been possible for it to become actual. Possibility here is no longer taken up immediately but rather reflected on from the perspective of actuality. In other words, the actualization of something out of its possibility shows that it fulfilled the only condition it needed to become actual. It could not have been otherwise since, had it been so, it would not have been actualized.[40]

To take possibility in an immediate manner means to take up its unity with actuality immediately: they are one. This reveals its contingent nature: insofar as it has only its possibility as a condition for actualization its opposite could also have been actualized. To take possibility as reflectedness-into-self emphasizes the fact that the possibility of each actual, from which it originated, is *its* possibility, being thus necessary for such an actual to be actual. Possibility and actuality still form a unity, though it is no longer immediate. Reflected possibility contains within it its actuality. This clears the space for necessity to appear since there is no necessity in immediacy: "This *absolute unrest* of the *becoming* of these two determinations is *contingency*. But just because each immediately turns into its opposite, equally in this other it simply *unites with itself*, and this identity of both, of one in the other, is *necessity*."[41] Contingency and necessity are not two mutually exclusive modal concepts that cannot be ascribed to the same process. Rather, all actuality is both contingent and necessary: "The contingent, therefore, is necessary because the actual is determined as a possible."[42] All actuality, in order to be what it is (self-caused), has to be possible. This positing of the actual as possible leads to it being both contingent (it could be otherwise) and necessary (it is not otherwise, and becomes precisely what it is). This unity of contingency and necessity is not to be understood in the sense of Leibniz's truths of fact, which are both contingent and necessary depending on whether they are taken up by God or by humans. Contingency in Leibniz merely reveals a limitation on the part of humans due to their finite nature. It is an apparent contingency viewed from the absolute standpoint of God. Hegel does away with this apparent character of the contingent and reveals how absolute contingency is the precondition for necessity since there is no absolute standpoint. A consequence of this will be that all standpoints become absolute. Thus, for Hegel something must be absolutely contingent in order to become necessary. If it were not absolutely contingent, its necessity would depend on something external to it (God's goodness in Leibniz's case).[43] In the words of Dieter Henrich: "*Nur wenn es ein absolut Zufälliges gibt, ist Notwendigkeit denkbar.*"[44]

The conclusion of this first section (level of formality) is that the actual, insofar as it is possible, is both contingent and necessary. The actual is what it is because it was possible. It not only reveals itself to be what it is but also to have become what it is. This identity with itself is necessity: "Thus actuality in that which is distinguished from it, namely possibility, is identical with itself. As this identity it is necessity."[45] Possibility is what opens the door for "what is," not to *be* what it is, but to have become what it is. This can only occur when "what is" is taken as actual, as having caused itself or having become. Whatever becomes does so due to itself, not to any external power or to any "other." And when actuality and possibility are taken together as a unity, this unity reveals itself to be both contingent and necessary. "What is" cannot be identical with itself in an immediate manner. An immediate A = A is pure abstraction and emptiness. In order for "what is" to be identical to itself it must have become itself, it must be mediated. For Hegel what is actual *becomes* identical to itself by being mediated, by being possible. Neither qualitative/quantitative being nor essence can become what it is. Only what is actual can do so.

3.5.2 Relative necessity, or real actuality, possibility, and necessity

With the unity of formal actuality and formal possibility, characterized as being both contingent and necessary, we have reached real actuality: a real, self-caused actual that became what it is. Now the actual has a particular content, it is a "real" in interaction with others; it effects (*wirken*) them. With formal actuality we saw what an actual would require to become what it was. It would require not being self-contradictory, being possible. Here we shall see what a real actual, an actual entangled in the world, requires to become what it is. Real actuality is in the midst of the world. However, its entanglement with the world does not dissolve it or transform it into some other. Real actuality merely manifests itself in this entanglement. For a real actual to be such, to have become what it is, there must have been a multiplicity of circumstances, the gathering of which determined the becoming of the actual. This multiplicity of circumstances constitutes the actual in its actuality: "The real possibility of something is therefore the existing multiplicity of circumstances which are connected with it…Thus real possibility constitutes the *totality of conditions…*"[46] Looking back from a real actual, one encounters a multiplicity of circumstances that constitute such an actual in its becoming; whereas looking back from a formal actual, one only encounters the principle of non-contradiction. A formal actual is such insofar as it is formally possible; and it is possible insofar as it is not internally self-contradictory. A real actual is such insofar as it is really possible; and its real possibility consists in the totality of conditions constituting it.

Hegel emphasizes another difference between formal and real possibility. This difference has to do with the type of contradictions they bring with them and the manner in which they are sublated.[47] Formal possibility as such brings its opposite with it: if A is possible then ~A is possible too. "Under formal possibility, because something was possible, then—not *itself*—but its *other* was also possible."[48] On the other hand, real possibility, when it gathers itself as such, disappears into actuality. The fulfillment of circumstances determines that a possible become actual. Real possibility does not require some other to sublate it: it sublates itself. Formal possibility was retrospectively posited by formal actuality; it was posited as distinct from it since in its being posited, formal possibility introduced an "other" to it: an "other" possible. This is what determined formal actuality as contingent. Here, real actuality also retrospectively posits real possibility as distinct from it. However, they collapse into one: real possibility *is* real actuality. Whenever a set of conditions is fulfilled they are immediately actualized. This might seem illogical if one forgets that this set of conditions is posited retrospectively and asks: what determines a set of conditions to be fulfilled? Only in retrospect or recollection (*Erinnerung*)[49] are conditions posited as fulfilled in order to determine the becoming of the real actual; only because an actual is already real are its conditions posited as fulfilled. This allows Hegel to assert: "The *negation* of real possibility is thus its *identity*—with self."[50]

The collapse of real actuality and real possibility, the mapping of one onto the other, constitutes real necessity, which is equivalent to relative necessity. What is really possible cannot be otherwise, as opposed to what is formally possible. It is necessary. However, the necessity arrived at is relative. It is dependent on the conditions and circumstances constituting the actual. It has a contingent element, or as Hegel says, "it has its *starting point* in the *contingent*."[51] The real actual will only follow necessarily if the conditions or circumstances of its actualization are given. What determines the necessity of the real actual as relative is precisely this character of "givenness" of the conditions. This does not mean that what makes this necessity relative is the element of contingency it includes within it. Rather, what makes it relative is the apparently external character of this contingency, the fact that the conditions or circumstances are given and not yet reflected-into-self.

Let us turn to Kant for a moment, who by establishing a difference between empirical and intelligible contingency in the fourth antinomy shows that there is necessity in the former. In this manner he disallows any move to a transcendent and necessary being that would account for empirically contingent events. Empirical contingency is subject to time as pure form of intuition insofar as it only appears as alteration, as change within time; whereas intelligible contingency is defined purely formally: that whose "contradictory opposite is possible" (A461 B489). The solution to this antinomy is to show the illegitimacy of dogmatically asserting the existence of a necessary being from the empirical contingency of appearances (it would constitute a *metabasis eis allo genos*). The fact that what is empirically contingent is not an object but a product of an alteration or process shows that one cannot infer the possibility of its contradictory opposite since one is dealing with a state, not a being: "To obtain such a contradictory opposite we require to conceive that in the same time in which the preceding state was, its opposite could have existed in its place, and this can never be inferred from [the fact of] the alteration" (A460 B488). When dealing with an object, it is easy to imagine its contradictory opposite as possible and thus to posit its contingent character. If this were the case, one would then need to ascribe some type of necessity transcendent to it in order to account for its actuality. However, when dealing with a state, one cannot infer that its opposite could have existed in its place. This disallows deducing the existence of a necessary being outside of time, of an absolute beginning. Necessity "must be such as can be thus met with in time, and must belong to the series of appearances" (A 460 B 488). Hegel will proceed in a similar fashion. However, he is not dealing here with objects of experience in the Kantian sense (a sensible manifold subject to the pure forms of intuition and the categories of the understanding) but rather with actualities, with what has developed to become what it is. Both are able to connect necessity to contingency without requiring an external or transcendent standpoint to ground this necessity; and both achieve this by not dealing with objects but rather with states (Kant) or actualities (Hegel). For Kant what is contingent is necessary only insofar as it is given in time. For Hegel actuality is necessary insofar as it is determined as having become what it is, as the endpoint of a process.

The contingent element of real or relative necessity is immediate, merely taken up. The "if → then" structure of the conditional exactly reflects what real necessity is: (1) the conditions are contingent, merely given or presupposed; (2) its necessity is dependent on something external to it (although this relation to externality will be the manifestation of itself); (3) the moment its conditions are given it necessarily follows. Real necessity is contingent since it is dependent on the given conditions that make up real actuality. It is an impure contingency tinged with otherness. The real possible and the real actual are still separate: real necessity "begins from that unity of the possible and the actual which is not yet reflected into itself—this *presupposing* and the *self-returning movement* are still separate."[52] It must become absolute necessity spontaneously determining itself into contingency.[53]

3.5.3 Absolute necessity

The title notwithstanding, contingency and possibility are not excluded or left behind. They become one: absolute necessity, absolute possibility, and absolute actuality all converge. We start off once again with actuality. Real actuality was shown to follow the structure of the conditional: if certain conditions were given, then *x* would be actualized. The actualization of *x* depended on the possibility of its conditions. Thus, the in-itself of real actuality was real possibility. Now the emphasis has fallen back on actuality: it posited (in retrospect) its own conditions of possibility. As so posited they are no longer possible but necessary. The in-itself of actuality is now necessity, not possibility.[54] This constitutes absolute, as opposed to real, actuality: "This actuality, *which is itself as such necessary*, for it contains necessity as its *in-itself*, is *absolute actuality*—actuality which can no longer be otherwise, for its *in-itself* is not possibility but necessity itself."[55] This leads directly to absolute possibility insofar as actuality (absolute actuality) is no longer dependent on a particular set of conditions for its actualization. It has always already actualized them since it posits them in retrospect. Possibility and actuality are completely united now; they have become one. Actuality is no longer dependent on the actualization of some apparently external possible conditions. We have left behind the emphasis on the content, occurring at the previous level, and have reached a level of pure indifference. Absolute actuality is indifferent to any real actual since all actuals necessarily posit their conditions in retrospect; in a sense, all actuals create their conditions. An absolute actual is not dependent on a particular content given by its conditions; it *is* its conditions by positing them. In the same manner absolute possibility is indifferent to any real possibility in the form of particular conditions and circumstances since their particularity is not given but posited, not a starting point but an end posited as starting point.

> But because this *actuality* is posited as being *absolute*, that is, as being *itself the unity of itself and possibility*, it is only an *empty* determination, or, it is *contingency*. This *emptiness* of its determination makes it a *mere possibility*, something which can equally be *otherwise* and can be determined as a possible. But this possibility is itself *absolute*; for it is precisely the possibility of being determined equally as possibility or as actuality. Since it is this indifference toward itself it is posited as an *empty, contingent* determination.[56]

Absolute actuality is empty since it is not dependent on the content of its particular conditions and circumstances for its being actual. This does not lead back to a formal possibility but to an absolute one. An actual that posits its own conditions of possibility does not become actual by having followed the principle of non-contradiction. It has "always already" been actual and has created its own conditions of possibility in retrospect, indifferent to external factors. Everything depends on the retrospective character of an actual that posits its own conditions of possibility insofar as they have already been actualized. This positing act reveals how not only the contingent but also the necessary aspect of actuality becomes. In the act of positing its presuppositions actuality becomes absolutely contingent since, had it been a different actuality, it would have posited different conditions of its own possibility. The contingent element here lies in the fact that there is no external standpoint, no God's-eye view from which to reveal *this* and not *that* as necessarily actualized. Any actual must have become what it is in order to be what it is. There is no neutral standpoint to reveal that it had to be a particular actual *x* instead of any other. Similarly in Leibniz the actualizing of this precise world would have been an absolutely contingent process were it not for the external standpoint of God's goodness, which reveals it to be the best of all possible worlds. Were one to take God out of the picture our world would be absolutely contingent since it would be in equal standing with any other possible world. By positing an external absolute standpoint Leibniz is forced into a tight situation in two fronts simultaneously. He needs to fit contingency and human freedom into the picture of an omniscient, omnipotent God, and he needs to temper God's omnipotence and omniscience by making God rational and infinitely good. The former problem involves the issue of contingency/necessity, while the latter involves that of possibility/actuality. With an absolute standpoint the contingency of some truths will have to be set upon the shoulders of human finitude, since from God's perspective (it is not a perspective, but rather *the* view of "what is") all truths are necessary, all judgments identity statements.[57] The contingency/necessity distinction rests on an issue of temporality: humans are free insofar as they are finite. Concerning the distinction between possibility and actuality, we encounter the problem of why this particular world exists and not any other. Since this absolute standpoint exists prior to actuality, Leibniz must start with possibility and then arrive at actuality. However, if one wants to believe in the inherent rationality of the existing world, in the universality of the laws nature follows, then possibility (understood formally as that whose opposite is not contradictory) will not be a sufficient ground for actualizing itself. This would lead back to the problems encountered by medieval theological absolutism: an irrational

God, whose creation cannot be rationally justified.[58] In order to overcome this, one would need God to be absolutely good and follow not only the principle of contradiction but also that of perfection. "God always acts with the mark of perfection or wisdom."[59] A direct consequence of this is "*that whatever is more perfect or has more reason is true.*"[60] This will allow the step from actuality to necessity: whatever is actual is such insofar as it is most perfect or rational, and this is necessarily so since God cannot but create what is most perfect. Regarding Leibniz, one may conclude with Longuenesse that modality is defined "from the point of view of God."[61]

The necessary aspect of absolute actuality also becomes, precisely for the same reasons as the contingent aspect. Without an external standpoint any process must necessarily become what it is. It cannot become what it is not since what it is is determined in its becoming. For something to become what it is not there must exist a God's-eye viewpoint or a point of view from nowhere to reveal what each actual should have become and be able to contrast it with what it actually becomes. Without this Archimedean point every process necessarily becomes what it is, given that it cannot become otherwise since there is no possibility of ascribing otherness to it.

As Hegel says, absolute actuality "only is as this simple coincidence of the form with itself."[62] It is indifferent to content since its actuality does not depend on a particular content. This indifference to content is precisely the content's unity with form. Indifference to content does not relegate it to the background; it destroys its oppositional character to form. Form is no longer dependent on content being external to it. It brings content, any type of content, with it. With the vanishing of all otherness, of the conditional character of real actuality, actuality has come back to itself in its positing its own conditions of possibility. Real actuality depended on real possibility, on the particular conditions and circumstances surrounding its becoming actualized. However, since it itself posits these circumstances in retrospect, it depends only on itself, necessarily becoming what it is. However, this "what it is" is no longer content-based: a particular x or y. It is a "whatever it may be" since it is self-caused. In other words, a process becomes what it is, whatever it may be.[63] That I became who I am does not exclude that I could have become someone completely different, in which case I would also have become who I was to be. The lack of a God's-eye viewpoint disallows any discrepancy between becoming and being: nothing becomes what it is not. This explains the idea of necessity determining itself into or as contingency.[64] Absolute necessity does not leave contingency behind. It rather radicalizes it by destroying the possibility of an absolute standpoint from which necessity can be ascribed. Another way of expressing the same point is to say that Hegel makes all standpoints absolute insofar as they are all self-caused and therefore do not relate to one another; they do not have an external point of comparison between them. The problem Leibniz encountered with his monadology, and the basis for Hegel's criticism, is the need to balance two contradictory facts: on the one hand, the independence and self-sufficiency of each monad, on the other, the perspectival nature of their Being. Each monad is part of the whole, a reflection of the universe. Leibniz attempts to solve this *aporia* by means of the theory of pre-established harmony.[65] Hegel, by doing away with an absolute standpoint, makes each monad a whole in itself, self-caused and independent from all others. In doing this, the question of whether one or many monads exist ceases to be an issue since there is no way to answer it without such a standpoint. In other words, to posit each monad as a whole is to renounce the possibility of defending either a monistic or a pluralistic view since the only possible standpoint is internal. This would exclude neither the possibility of there being one whole, nor the possibility of there being a multitude of independent, self-caused wholes.[66]

Hegel uses a particular phrase not only to describe what absolute necessity is but also to bring together the Doctrines of Being and of Essence at the threshold of the Doctrine of the Concept: *what is actual is because it is*. This sentence can be divided into three parts, representing each of the three divisions of the *Science of Logic*, and also the in-itself, for-itself, and in-and-for-itself distinction. They are: (1) the actual is; (2) because; (3) it is. The Doctrine of Being focuses on the immediacy of the given: something is and is taken up as such. Pure immediacy cannot claim to be what is true precisely because it has to reveal itself as such, it has to manifest itself to be what is true. The immediacy of pure being allows for any claim. No distinction has yet entered Being. It is purely abstract and empty. Upon reflection on Being, it becomes mediated by some other that causes or grounds it and gives it its being by conditioning it. This is essence, symbolized by the causal character of the connector "because." Everything has a reason, a ground. Nothing is accepted in its immediacy, at face value. Being has acquired a second dimension: the cause of its being. In his search for what is true Hegel reveals the limitations that this conceptual strategy based on two-tiered concepts appearing in the Doctrine of Essence experiences when it manifests "what is." In other words, there are processes that cannot be explained by the reifying act of thinking of objects in terms of ground, cause, essence, condition, and so on. In reaching the concept of actuality, Hegel reveals "what is" as self-caused, explained only in terms of itself, having its own existence as its essence. Here we are no longer dealing with objects, be they immediate or reflected. We are dealing with processes, with the manifesting itself of "what is": "Just as the *light* of nature is neither *something* nor a *thing*, but its being is only its showing or shining [*Scheinen*], so manifestation is self-identical absolute actuality."[67] The process has itself as its cause or ground; its essence is to bring itself into existence, or rather to show itself as having brought itself into existence (the starting point is always the actual).

This unity of Being and essence, of immediacy and mediation, leads to the simple immediacy of what is because it is. However, this is not a return to qualitative or positive Being. Hegel says, "Absolute necessity is thus the *reflection or form of the absolute*: the unity of being and essence, simple immediacy that is absolute negativity."[68] The concept of absolute negativity is directly connected to that of freedom. Let us come back to the example of becoming who one is. Hegel is describing processes that as self-caused can have any outcome, though necessarily so. A human being always becomes who he or she is. It is thus both a necessary process (one cannot become who one is not) and a contingent one (whoever one becomes is never fixed from the outset). Absolute negativity means that the process follows no pre-determined path; it is always free to determine itself otherwise, though strictly speaking, there is no possible *otherwise* due to the lack of an absolute standpoint to deem it so. Absolute negativity is the outcome of the merging of absolute necessity and absolute contingency: an absolute actual can become anything it might become, but must do so necessarily. Absolute negativity is related to simplicity and to simple immediacy. Humans do not have a positive content the way being or essence did since they are a process that can take any direction. And the act of recollection forms the necessary totality of circumstances that a specific human being is.

The three elements constituting an absolute actual are: absolute negativity, absolute necessity, and absolute contingency. I become myself. The fact that I become myself and not that I am myself reveals the absolute negativity in the process. I am never a given but rather a self-actualizing process. I cannot be reduced to *x*, *y*, or *z* properties but am always more.[69] The fact that I cannot but become myself reveals its absolute necessity: I cannot become someone different. The fact that, despite my becoming myself I can end up becoming *x*, *y*, or *z*, reveals its absolute contingency. All three characteristics merge into absolute actuality.

In these passages Hegel uses the metaphor of blindness to characterize absolute necessity: "Absolute necessity is therefore *blind*";[70] "The *blind* transition of necessity is rather the absolute's *own exposition.*"[71] This blindness brings to mind fate and its combination of inevitability and inscrutability, a combination of absolute necessity and absolute contingency in the sense that whatever happens has to happen and it could happen at the least expected moment.[72] The last sentence of this second chapter says: "The *blind* transition of necessity is rather the absolute's *own exposition* [*Auslegung*], the movement of the absolute within itself which, in its alienation [*Entäußerung*], rather reveals itself."[73] This talk of alienation will further clarify what Hegel means by absolute negativity. The word alienation in German is formed by the prefix "*ent*" and the noun "*Äußerung.*" The latter means expression, manifestation; whereas the former conveys the sense of "withdrawal from" or "abandonment of." To be in a state of alienation means not to express oneself, to manifest oneself as other than who one actually is. In alienation one's real nature is concealed. If this is so, Hegel's assertion seems contradictory: the absolute shows itself precisely in its showing itself as what it is not, as being other than itself. It is the nature of the absolute to reveal itself as other than what it is. There seems to be a short circuit here: if it is the nature of the absolute to reveal itself as other then it does not reveal itself as other since this is its nature; it reveals itself as itself, alienation and otherness are its nature. The contradiction vanishes as soon as one ceases to think in terms of positive being: the absolute has a positive being A, whose nature consists in being ~A. Thus, A = ~A. One should bring to mind the concept of absolute negativity here. There is no particular or positive content constituting the absolute. It is rather a process the nature of which is to always reveal itself as a particular content, as A, B, or C at different moments. Its revealing itself is an objectifying of itself. It cannot but objectify itself. What appears is not an object; it is a process. That a human being is more than what is manifest or revealed in her acts does not mean that she has hidden properties that never appear. If this were so, one would never have the experience of being a "complete person," although there would be such a thing. A human being is rather a process in constant development that cannot be reduced to a specific number of attributes since she is always more than their sum. Her nature, however, consists in always revealing herself as those attributes. Human beings are always redefining themselves, exposed to experiences that alter their being, reconfiguring who they are. Nonetheless, they are always themselves.

Hegel has offered an exposition of the presuppositions underlying the concept of "absolute necessity." He has shed light on its posited and historical nature. By means of this it is revealed that "absolute necessity" is constituted by "absolute negativity" and "absolute contingency." To assert of actuality that it is absolutely necessary means to construct its identity as actual through the acceptance of its absolutely negative and contingent nature. To assert that a process is absolutely necessary is to assert that it is cause of itself. To assert that something is cause of itself is to accept that its only justification lies within itself. Therefore, the only standpoint from which absolute necessity can be claimed is an internal one. There is no external God's-eye viewpoint to ground necessity. There is no pre-established goal or telos, either, which would determine in advance the process leading to the present actuality.

As a concluding point one should keep in mind that this concept of absolute necessity does not disappear in the doctrine of the concept. It also applies to the subjective logic and mainly to the endpoint of the system: the absolute idea. This latter is not merely one more concept, the last in a list of concepts dealt with in the *Science of Logic*. It is the process itself of thinking. The absolute idea is the totality of the movement of thinking, the realization that what in truth is, the Platonic *ontos on*, is the totality of its search. As such, the process exhibited in the *Science of Logic* itself is absolutely necessary; that is, it had to take the path it took, *whatever* path it would have taken.

* * * *

Given that the *Science of Logic* deals with conceptual strategies and the concepts that constitute them, the lesson of the section on modality would amount to saying that the concepts used to think "what is" do not *refer* to the immediacy or givenness of qualities, quantities, or measures, on the one hand (doctrine of being), or to mediated appearances, essences, causes, grounds, and so on, on the other (doctrine of essence). They have their meaning constituted through the activity itself of thinking the world. There is no direct contact between a pre-linguistic, objective reality or external world and the concepts that refer to it and through which it is thought. Concepts are movements of thinking whose meaning is constituted by the totality of their history. If this is the case then there is no meaning invariance. All concepts are shot through with contingency; their meaning is always co-determined by the movement of thought in its experience with the world. Concepts become what they are in their continuous readjustment to that experience. This happens not only to concepts of the external, empirical world, but also to pure concepts whose meaning supposedly does not touch the empirical world: the realm of analytic statements, which are true based on their meaning alone. For Hegel, the concept of necessity can only be applied to what is conceptualized as having become what it is, that is, to activities or processes. In the previous sections of the Doctrine of Essence he has shown the contradictory nature of the concept of essence when it is presupposed to be a permanent beyond all appearances, a substratum underlying its manifestations. It is actually posited as presupposed. And insofar as posited it has an alterable constitution since it is determined through manifestation and appearance. There is nothing but appearance. Essence is pure appearance, that is, appearance of itself, not of some essence behind the appearance.[74] The essence of something, its meaning, that without which it would not be what it is, is its having become what it is, which is a constant never-ending process. Therefore, the necessity of any concept lies in the process of its formation. It is necessary since it could not have developed otherwise. And the reason it could not have developed otherwise is not because of any teleological drive pre-existing within it but because its meaning is constituted in recollection, in looking back. It is determined to be the necessary outcome (always already reached) of its development. Hegel makes a deflationary move on the concept of necessity since there is no permanence, either in the world or in our conceptual schemes. This makes the distinction between analytic and synthetic statements, or between necessary and contingent truths, lose its ground. Meaning is never given. It is constructed through and through in the constant to and fro that constitutes human experience. And it is reconstructed in the recollection of that experience. In this recollective movement necessity is ascribed to it. Due to the processual character of meanings they are never settled but subject to continuous re-constitution. The boundary between the analytic and the synthetic is not given but posited. Necessity is not the truth of contingency, a pre-existent *logos* that gives unity to the apparent multiplicity. It consists, rather, in the recollected determination of the becoming of contingency.

4 Everything Rational Is a Syllogism: Inferentialism

4.1 Introduction

The syllogism is of fundamental importance for Hegel insofar as it is intimately connected to our rationality. As the third and last chapter on the section on subjectivity it works as the portal to the constitution of objectivity. It is the moment at which objectivity is born, so to speak. Dealing with the section on the syllogism shall reveal what type of object constitutes "what is." The inferential process at work in the syllogism will reveal it to be the only adequate site for the objectivity of the object to become. The constitution of this object is social; it occurs in Spirit, in the "we" of the community. Thus, it occurs in the syllogism insofar as only by means of it are we capable of holding each other accountable for and entitled or not to the commitments undertaken. We are beings that give and expect reasons for our actions and beliefs. This is what makes us rational.

Hegel's goal in these sections is two-fold. On the one hand, he wants to reveal the inferential nature of objectivity, that is, that a judgment is not capable of possessing objectivity unless it is part of an inferential act in which it appears as a conclusion.[1] Objectivity is not a matter of being. It is rather a matter of becoming. It has to reveal its own process of becoming objective. And this can only happen by giving reasons. Objectivity can only lie in the logical space of reasons. On the other hand, he wants to establish differences in the type of object referred to in judgments and syllogisms. Following the philosophical search for the unconditioned he wants to reveal that infinite objects are more transparent regarding the structure of their objectivity than other more immediate or sensuous types of object. The development encountered from syllogism to syllogism is fueled by the need to find adequate expression for the infinite nature of what Hegel understands by object. For an object to be infinite is for it to always be other than itself while always being itself. It is always more than what it is and can never be exhausted in its determinations. The last syllogism dealt with by Hegel, the disjunctive syllogism, is the most appropriate site for infinite objects to make their appearance insofar as in it objects posit their own becoming. In this syllogism we find that an infinite object is constituted by what it is not. This occurs insofar as we are dealing with processes. The disjunctive syllogism is the site for a process to reveal its having become what it is. It allows infinite objects to reveal their historical character. In other words, it lays bare what conceptuality amounts to.

The fact that these objects are historical means that they are never fully realized. Rather, they are in a constant process of reconstitution. In this manner the object is always itself while always being other than itself. Its identity as object is an ever-changing result that constantly reconfigures its process of having become itself. Infinite objects, therefore, are constituted in their opposition to themselves, through what they are not.

The fact that objectivity is located within the Doctrine of the Notion grants Hegel his idealist badge. The fact that it is reached only by means of the syllogism, an inferential activity, is what the present chapter will attempt to make sense of. The smallest unit of meaning for Hegel is found neither in a concept nor in a judgment. For a concept to have meaning, something needs to be said of it; it needs to be part of a judgment. However, for a judgment to have meaning, it needs to be part of an inferential act. Borrowing hermeneutic terminology, for something to be *thematized* it must be part of a *horizon* of meaning. To thematize something is equivalent to saying something about it. The horizon from which it is thematized is equivalent to the premises from which what is thematized is inferred.

4.2 Detour via Brandom

The first pages of Robert Brandom's *Making It Explicit* are dedicated to shedding light on what distinguishes humans from non-humans, based not on what we are but on what we take ourselves to be. This train of thought leads him to focus on what we are distinctly able to do. His answer is that we are the only beings that subject ourselves to the authority of reasons. This can be offered as a definition of rationality. Brandom says:

> Being rational is...being subject to the authority of reasons. Saying "we" in this sense is placing ourselves and each other in the space of reasons, by giving and asking for reasons for our attitudes and

> performances...for attitudes we adopt in response to environing stimuli count as *beliefs* just insofar as they can serve as and stand in need of reasons, and the acts we perform count as *actions* just insofar as it is proper to offer and inquire after reasons for them. Our attitudes and acts exhibit an intelligible content...by being caught up in a web of reasons, by being inferentially articulated.[2]

This inferential process can assume two forms, following Hegelian vocabulary: mediation or determinate negation. Either we infer that something is to be asserted because it follows from prior reasoned beliefs (consequence), or we infer that something is to be negated because it contradicts prior reasoned beliefs (incompatibility). We embrace the inferential consequences of the commitments we acknowledge, and reject commitments incompatible with them. We are rational beings, not because we relate to the world in a certain way, but because we relate to each other regarding the world in a certain way, because we hold each other accountable for what we express. For this reason a judgment cannot justify itself since it does not include what the reasons for it are. Only in syllogistic inferences is this third dimension, the space of reasons, opened wherein our commitments are shaped and discarded. To be rational is a social process. It does not consist in a two-way interaction between an individual and the world but rather in a triangulated interaction between one individual, another individual or group of individuals, and the world. If it were just a two-way interaction between an individual and the world we would fall into the paradoxes of a dualism that separates the world from our knowledge of it. If it were just a two-way interaction between an individual and a community, then we would fall into some type of social constructivism, and there would be no possible gap between how things really are and how the community takes them to be. What counts as error would be determined by the community, which would just push back the question of objectivity one step: where does the community derive its authority to determine which commitments we are entitled to and which we are not? If the buck stops with the beliefs of the community, the possibility of objectivity itself would be at stake insofar as there would be no getting it wrong on the part of the community (more exactly, getting it wrong would just consist in the community agreeing that it had gotten it wrong). If objectivity is to be saved, it must be possible for the community to get it wrong in a stronger manner. However, without recourse to some variation of the myth of the given, of the belief in coming up against the hardness of the world in an extra-linguistic, purely causal manner, we would seem to lose any possible source of hardness.

Brandom attempts to steer between the pitfalls of a naked empiricism or reductionism, a naïve myth of the given, that imagines the external world as given to us pre-linguistically, on the one hand, and, on the other, a type of coherentism, where the impossibility of standing outside language or a system of beliefs leads to a collapse between how things really are and how they are taken to be. He attempts the former by emphasizing the social space of reasons, where we are committed and entitled, or not, to what follows or what is excluded from what we hold to be true. He attempts the latter by maintaining a source of objectivity in the distinction between commitments and entitlements: it is one thing to be committed to certain reasons. It is quite another to be entitled to them, to have them acknowledged by others. For the possibility of error, and with it objectivity, not to disappear, we need to allow the possibility that everyone (the linguistic community) might be wrong. How can we allow this without steering straight into the other side, crashing against the rocks of a reality external to our linguistic practices and beliefs that causally dictates to us how the world actually is? Sometimes Brandom seems to steers us in this direction: "The status of representings as correct or incorrect, successful or unsuccessful, depends on how things are with what is represented, rather than on the attitudes of representers."[3] He seems to appeal here to the way things really are independent of us to ground the entitlement of our beliefs about the world. At other times, Brandom seems stuck in a normative, linguistic game of asking for, giving, and entitling reasons, without explaining what their entitlement is based on other than an agreement on the part of the community, or the other interlocutor.

Whichever shore Brandom actually comes closer to, he does seem to have a clear understanding of Hegel's own attempt at the helm, whose strategy amounts to saying that in the long run, we will always get it wrong. Brandom calls this "semantic fallibilism."[4] It is structurally built into conceptuality to be in a constant, never-ending process of reconfiguration of meaning. However, this occurs, not insofar as we can never get a good grip on a non-changing, hard, objective world, lying beyond and independent of conceptuality. If this were the case we would founder against the shores of givenness. Rather, it occurs insofar as we are historical beings. Brandom says: "there is, and can *in principle* be no set of determinate concepts such that *correct* application of them—following the norms for their use—will never lead to commitments that are incompatible according to those material conceptual norms."[5] Hegel's maneuver to avoid foundering against the shores of social constructivism lies in his assertion that we will always get it wrong, that, as Brandom puts it, "contradicting ourselves—endorsing materially incompatible commitments—is unavoidable."[6] It projects objectivity insofar as throughout the historical process of conceptualization (semantic constitution) our beliefs are constantly being revealed as false, lying in the interstice between commitments and entitlements.

* * * *

In order to understand Hegel's bold assertions that "*everything rational is a syllogism*"[7] and that "the *rational* is nothing but the *syllogism*,"[8] we must pursue two different paths. The first shall determine how the section on the syllogism is situated within the larger movement of the subjective pole of the Subjective Logic, in which it appears as the third stage, the "in-and-for-itself," of the movement from concept to judgment to syllogism. This path requires that we briefly delve into what Hegel understands by concept and judgment. The second will be located within the section on the syllogism itself, determining its inner development. The driving force of the first path will be the self-unfolding of the concept until it becomes "completely posited."[9] The driving force of the second path will consist in the different types of necessity found in the different types of syllogism. In order to make sense of them we shall make use of the previous chapter on Actuality, in which we encountered formal, real, and absolute necessity. Both of these paths will in turn replicate the movement from Being to Essence to Concept.

4.3 Placement of the section on the syllogism within the *Science of Logic*

We are located within the Subjective Logic, no longer contemplating the movement of the concepts used to think what is, *posited as* other to us (Objective Logic). We are now contemplating the movement of the concepts used to think the conceptual structures by which we think what is, *posited as* other to us. There is a doubling of the object of thought here. We no longer think the concept of something other to it but rather the concept of concept.[10] Let us then give a brief account of what concept and judgment are for Hegel, before dealing with the syllogism.

4.3.1 The concept

The first step in understanding what Hegel means by concept is to distinguish it from what is traditionally called a universal: a sort of abstraction under which many particular instantiations fall. This for Hegel is a mere representation (*Vorstellung*). In the *Encyclopaedia* he says:

> What are also called concepts, and indeed determinate concepts, for instance, man, house, animal, etc., are simple determinations and abstract representations; these are abstractions that take only the moment of universality from the Concept, leaving out particularity and singularity, so that they are not developed in themselves and therefore they abstract precisely from the Concept.[11]

To give a positive answer to the question of what Hegel's concept of concept means we shall follow two different paths. The first path is taken in the Introduction to the Doctrine of the Notion, in the section entitled "The Notion in General." There he makes use of Kant's transcendental apperception by establishing a parallel between the I that must accompany all my representations in the form of the "I think" and the concept. The second path can also be found in the Doctrine of the Notion, as well as in the Introduction to the *Encyclopaedia*, since both contain passages in which Hegel talks about infinite objects.

4.3.1.1 Parallel between the concept and Kant's "I think"

Hegel does not equate the concept to the I of transcendental apperception, though he establishes a parallel between them in order to clarify what he understands by concept.[12] He says:

> I will confine myself here to a remark which may help one to grasp the notions here developed and may make it easier to find one's bearings in them ... Thus we are justified by a cardinal principle in the Kantian philosophy in referring to the nature of the *I* in order to learn what the *notion* is.[13]

There are two elements shared by the transcendental I and Hegel's concept of concept. The first is universality. The "I think" that must accompany all my representations does not consist in a particular content. It constitutes experience but cannot itself be experienced. The I is not a substance that appears differently at different points, always maintaining an unchangeable essence. In the same manner, Hegel's concept of concept is one that will not consist in a particular content. Its content will be given to it by the totality of its determinations. It is determined as absolute negativity. By this, one should understand that it does not negate *any* particular determination (~A or ~B), but rather *each and every* particular determination insofar as it is in a continuous process. In other words, it negates *every* particular determination insofar as it is not tied to *any one* in particular. Hegel says:

> But the *I* is, *first*, this pure self-related unity, and it is so not immediately but only as making abstraction from all determinateness and content and withdrawing into the freedom of unrestricted equality with itself. As such it is *universality*; a unity that is unity with itself only through its *negative* attitude, which appears as a process of abstraction, and that consequently contains all determinedness dissolved in it.[14]

However, the transcendental I cannot exist without what it thinks; it cannot exist without a particular content. The transcendental I cannot merely think without thinking *that*. Thus, it is always determined, individualized. In the same manner Hegel's concept of concept is only constituted in its being determined *as* an individual. It is not tied to any determination in particular, yet it can only appear *as* determined. As he puts it in the *Encyclopaedia*: "It is not merely abstract universality therefore, but the universality that contains everything within itself."[15] It is also mentioned further below: "what is genuine and speculative... being a totality, [it] contains the determinations that dogmatism holds to be fixed and true in a state of separation from one another united within itself."[16] To clarify these two elements characterizing Hegel's concept of concept, let us use as an example the concept of a human being. To take freedom as the concept of a human being means to ascribe to her a universal element insofar as she is not tied to any particular essence: farmer, doctor, or politician. She is only equal to herself insofar as she does not have an essence to characterize her without which she would not be a human being. She negates each and every possible determination as being her essence. However, a human being cannot exist without being determined. There would be nothing left if one stripped away all of her possible determinations. What she is is constituted by her determinations, but not in an essential manner. A human being must exist as an individual, with a particular determination.

For Hegel a concept is constituted by universality, individuality, and particularity. He distinguishes the concept from the universality of a representation by showing that it must always be individualized and cannot exist by itself in abstraction. The Kantian "I think" is always individualized into a "thinking that something is the case." It cannot exist independently of what it thinks. The fact that at any moment it "thinks that..." makes it concrete insofar as it contains a determinate content. In the same manner Hegel's concept of concept must always be a universality rooted in concreteness.

With regard to particularity, the concept does not exist identical to itself, independent of all difference. It *is* in its relation to others. However, as opposed to what occurs in being, these others are determinations of itself (internal determinations). Hegel's concept of concept is the negation of negation. It is not identical to itself immediately but rather as the result of going through and determining itself through its differences.

> The Notion is, in the first instance, the absolute self-identity that is such only as the negation of negation or as the infinite unity of the negativity with itself...The simplicity which constitutes the very nature of the universal is such that, through absolute negativity, it contains within itself difference and determinateness in the highest degree.[17]

In other words, the concept has particularity since it contains difference within it in the form of determinateness. As Hegel says, even the concept of the supreme Being is particular insofar as it is determined as indeterminate. Thus, Hegel's concept of concept is not an abstract universal or simple representation. It is always concrete, embedded in individuality and characterized by particularity. It cannot exist without being instantiated, so to speak. It includes difference within it, particularizing it.

4.3.1.2 Infinite objects

The second path toward determining what Hegel understands by concept is to pay attention to the examples he uses to illustrate what a concept is. We have already seen that he rejects abstract representations or what are commonly called universals. Based on the examples of concepts he gives, it would seem there are only concepts of infinite objects. In the *Science of Logic* and the *Encyclopaedia* he mentions God, freedom, right, duty, the infinite, a true friend, a true work of art, a beautiful work of art, a bad state, a good act, and so on. They all show themselves as infinite. It would seem that there are only concepts of a subset of possible objects of consciousness.

> another circle of *ob-jects* shows up that are not part of this field: *freedom, spirit, God.* The reason that these are not to be found upon that soil is not because they ought not to belong to experience. It is

> true that they are not experienced by the senses, but everything that is in consciousness at all is experienced. (This is even a tautological proposition.) The reason is that these ob-jects present themselves directly as infinite with regard to their *content*.[18]

Read under this light the *Science of Logic* would amount to a progressive search for what is "really real", a search that leads through different subsets of objects of thought since each is revealed to be inadequate insofar as it is self-contradictory when thought through. The endpoint of the enterprise would be arrived at when an object of thought is reached that is able to sustain contradictory determinations within itself. This object of thought would be the Idea: the *adequate concept*, the unity of the concept and objectivity.[19]

Another element that would seem to confirm this reading of the *Logic* as an attempt at delimiting a field of objects of thought as what is "really real" is the following characteristic Hegel ascribes to the concept: its active nature, its developmental and processual character. A concept is a process of becoming other to itself without losing its identity with itself. This identity is not substance-based; it is not determined by a permanent essence that remains while qualities and quantities not essential to it alter. The concept is the totality of its determinations. However, this totality is never completed at any particular moment since it is in a constant process of reconstitution. Therefore we never reach a final set of determinations. Hegel says:

> the movement of the Concept is development, through which only that is posited which is already implicitly present.[20]
>
> But the Concept as such does not abide within itself, without development (as the understanding would have it); on the contrary, being the infinite form, the concept is totally active. It is the *punctum saliens* of all vitality, so to speak, and for that reason it distinguishes itself from itself.[21]

To continue with the example offered above, a human being consists of the totality of her determinations, being always more than what constitutes her at any particular moment. She is constituted by the totality of determinations of her past insofar as they were *necessary* for her to become who she is. She is also in a constant process of self-determination. Following this reading, there can only be concepts of infinite objects. They are in a constant process of becoming other to themselves while simultaneously maintaining their identity as themselves.

However, this identity is not built in opposition to these other determinations the infinite objects have assumed at different moments but precisely through them.

The reason Hegel has apparently circumscribed "what is" to the concepts of infinite objects is the character of absolute necessity they possess. In the previous chapter it was shown that absolute necessity could only exist where there is a development, a process taking place. Something that merely is cannot be ascribed necessity; nor can a substance that manifests itself in its appearing be revealed as necessary. Necessity can only be attributed to that which becomes what it is, to what actualizes its potentiality. These terms point toward Hegel's appropriation of Aristotle. However, he goes beyond Aristotle, revealing the limited character of the natural world insofar as its denizens can only beget further individuals of the same species, perpetuating a particular essence throughout time. Living beings are finite insofar as they are limited by their species, beyond which they cannot go. They carry their death within them and can only dissolve in the universality of their species. This perpetual coming-to-be is for Aristotle "the closest approximation to eternal being."[22] Hegel would view this process as a mere quantitative infinity, an exemplification of the bad infinite insofar as each individual is a mere repetition of a species that remains unchanged. With his talk of infinite objects Hegel goes beyond natural processes into a realm of processes one could describe as spiritual, the basic characteristic of which is their freedom since they are not tied to the development of a particular essence that has existed within them all along, but are rather continuously reconstituting themselves. This freedom does not contradict their absolutely necessary character since due to it they create the conditions for their own possibility, and as cause of themselves they cannot but be what they have become. A spiritual process must be understood to be absolutely necessary insofar as all of its moments determine it to be what it is, making it impossible to have become otherwise since there is no external point of view from which to ground this *otherwise*. In a passage from the *Encyclopaedia* Hegel says: "As the substantial might which is for-itself the Concept is what is free."[23] An example of an infinite object whose concept follows the principle of freedom is the concept of the beautiful, which lacks a particular essence that determines it insofar as it is in a constant process of development and uses only itself, its own development, as criterion for what is beautiful.

Taken together, the processual or developmental character of the concept and its relation to freedom point toward an historical element in these spiritual processes. Beauty, friendship, justice, the state, goodness, duty, right, are concepts whose content cannot be completely displayed without taking them in as a whole, revealing the process in which they have *necessarily* become what they are. Not only are they *accomplished* concepts insofar as at each moment of the process of their development they are an absolutely necessary outcome of the development leading to them, but they are also *ever accomplishing* themselves insofar as there is no essence to be reached, at which point all process and development would come to an end. Only in such a process can absolute necessity be ascribed. This process reveals the developing nature of the concept.

Therefore, the word "object" in the term "infinite object" should be understood as the result of a process due to which it appears as a totality of opposing determinations constituting it through time. To consider a work of art as an infinite object is to go beyond its spatio-temporal nature, beyond the physical attributes constituting it, and to see in it a totality as the result of a process of necessary development throughout history. Without this development it would have no meaning. An infinite object possesses a third dimension, so to speak, a depth that determines it as the *result* of a historical process.

4.3.1.3 Correctness and truth

With this brief characterization of what a concept is for Hegel we now come to the distinction he establishes between mere correctness and truth. Correctness consists in the correspondence of a subjective concept (what a particular individual believes [*meinen*] to be true) to reality taken as mere empirical externality. Verification is an empirical matter. Truth consists in the correspondence of a particular object to its objective concept. An objective concept is constituted by a spiritual process. It has developed throughout history, always revealing itself as different from itself, maintaining its identity nonetheless. In the sentence "This painting is green" we have a correspondence or non-correspondence between my subjective representation of an object, my knowledge of it, and the external object (*Ding*) taken as reality. It is a matter of correctness. In the sentence "This painting is beautiful" we have a correspondence or non-correspondence between an object (*Objekt*) and the concept of the beautiful. In both cases we are predicating something of an individual. However, in the latter case the individual is not taken as a mere individual but as *object*, the result of a process. In the present chapter this process is to be analyzed in its subjective aspect, that is, as a syllogistic process. The object under consideration is thus the result of a syllogism. The painting has a universal element insofar as beauty is ascribed to it. To be able to ascribe the predicate *beautiful* to an object we need more than a perceptual state. We need to know what type of constitution of objects is determined as beautiful. Then we need to assert of the painting under consideration that it is of that type, and therefore, that it is beautiful. In the assertion "This act is good" the subject is an individual act understood from a universal perspective: that of the good. Both the good and the beautiful require more than mere perception to be grasped. They are concepts constituted by the totality of their determinations. They include within them opposing determinations insofar as they are processual, in constant development. What does it mean to say that the concept of beauty includes within it opposing determinations? In its development this concept has at one point been determined as *x*, at a later point as ~*x*. This does not mean that at the later point *x* has been excluded as a determination of it, since only by having at one point been determined as *x* can the concept have developed later on to the point of being determined as ~*x*. ~*x* can only reveal itself as necessary on the shoulders, so to speak, of *x*. The ideal of the beautiful in the late nineteenth century was replaced by a different ideal in the early twentieth century. This new ideal, however, could not be made sense of without acknowledging the previous ideals in reaction to which it sprang.

One can also make sense of this distinction between correctness and truth by means of the characterization of the *Science of Logic* as the pursuit of a field of objects of thought that reveal themselves as what is really real. Following this line of thinking, any talk of truth for Hegel will take place at the level of infinite objects. Beliefs and assertions about external objects are subject to being correct or incorrect. Truth, however, occurs at the level of processes developing in a necessary manner into what they are. There is a normative element at work in talk of truth. Truth only exists where an object corresponds to what it strives to correspond to, where there is a constant summons, a taking up the task.[24] To ascribe greenness to a leaf is a matter of it being the case or not. Its verification is empirical. To ascribe usefulness to a house is a matter of it fulfilling certain external requirements established beforehand. To assert of a painting that it is beautiful, on the other hand, is to compare it to what it ought to be. And what it ought to be is not external to the painting. It is not a set of conditions or requirements existing beforehand, independent of it. The painting itself co-determines the measure of the beautiful compared to which it fulfills it or not. Hegel says: "whereas, to say of a work of art that it is beautiful, or of an action that it is good, the ob-jects in question must be compared with what they ought to be, i.e., with their concept."[25] There is no external point of comparison by which one could say that insofar as this painting resembles it it is beautiful. There is no fixed essence of the beautiful, of which this painting is an appearance. A painting considered beautiful co-determines the concept of the beautiful; it itself becomes a measure for what is to be considered beautiful. This co-determination reminds us of the productive circularity Heidegger and hermeneutic philosophy make use of in attempting to account for a non-linear production of meaning.[26] A beautiful painting is at once an individual insofar as it is determined as a beautiful object, and a universal insofar as it co-determines what is to be considered as beautiful. This concept of concept will help break down the traditional view of the judgment as a bringing together of an individual subject and a universal predicate independent of such a subject.

4.3.2 The judgment

As in all *coming on the scene*, be it that of Science in the *Phenomenology* or of Being at the beginning of the Objective Logic, what comes on the scene must show itself to be what it is, it must become "for-itself" what it is "in-itself," it must be made explicit. Thus, the concept itself must undergo this process in order to exhibit its content and richness. Its content must be unpacked, so to speak. This leads to the judgment as the first moment in which a concept is given some determination. The concept is taken *as* something. Insofar as the judgment takes the structure of a predicative sentence, something is said *of* something. This second something appears in the form of a singular, whereas what is said of it appears in the form of a concept or a universal.[27] The judgment has overcome the immediacy of the concept and posits the concept as separate from itself. Here we shall not deal with each of the different types of judgment Hegel examines, but only with the judgment in general from the perspective of its limitations concerning the manifestation of what is really real.

For Hegel it is the general nature of the judgment to separate the subject from the predicate. This has as a consequence the positing of a self-subsistent, isolated subject (be it an external manifold, as in Empiricism, or a fixed thought or representation, as in traditional Metaphysics) to which an independent and self-subsistent predicate is ascribed. As a result one has a subject with a content limited by the predicate ascribed to it. Insofar as the subject is independent of its determinations no single determination could reveal its truth. Thus, the subject "is richer and wider than the predicate" and "the predicate is only *one* of the *many* determinacies of the subject." The predicate for its part "as what is universal, subsists on its own account, and it is indifferent as to whether this subject is or not; it reaches beyond the subject, *subsumes* it under itself."[28] In this sense, the predicates ascribed to a subject will be a list of determinations indifferent to each other, united by many *ands*. "Moreover, although they are connected with each other because they are predicates of one subject, they are nevertheless diverse through their content, so that they are taken up from outside and in opposition to one another."[29]

In "The First Position of Thought with Respect to Objectivity" in the *Encyclopaedia* (§26–36) Hegel says that although previous metaphysics took as objects of its thinking "totalities that belong in and for themselves to reason, to the thinking of the inwardly concrete universal," it "took them from representation, and when it applied the determinations-of-the-understanding to them, it grounded itself upon them, as ready-made or given subjects, and its only criterion of whether the predicates fitted, and were satisfactory or not, was that representation."[30] This limited nature of the judgment leads to a static view of what is. Insofar as the subject lies beyond its determinations, it is not possible to grasp the developmental and processual character of a concept in a judgment. Its contradictory nature (that it contains within itself opposing determinations) does not come to light in a judgment. Hegel's major concern regarding the judgment is that used in an unreflected manner it leads to the assumption of a substantialist view of "what is." It has ontological implications insofar as what is really real is determined as self-subsistent, independent subjects (substances) to which many self-subsistent, indifferent predicates (accidents) can be ascribed. This view of reality excludes and cannot account for many *facts* (*Sachen*), as he calls the outcome of the syllogism and thus the paradigm of objectivity. Due to this, if one believes that such a substantialist view reflects what is really real, one falls short of being able to give an adequate account of a large portion of what there is.

It is interesting to note the difference Hegel establishes between a mere proposition (*Satz*) and a judgment since this already points toward the overcoming of the limitation of the judgment: meaning can only be ascribed to a judgment when it is taken as forming part of a syllogistic structure, of a horizon from which it is granted. Hegel says:

> We may take this opportunity of remarking, too, that though a *proposition* has a subject and predicate in the grammatical sense, this does not make it a *judgment*. The latter requires that the predicate be related to the subject as one Notion determination to another, and therefore as a universal to a particular or individual. If a statement about a

> particular subject only enunciates something individual, then this is a mere proposition. For example, "Aristotle died at the age of 73, in the fourth year of the 115th Olympiad," is a mere proposition, not a judgment. It would partake of the nature of a judgment only if doubt had been thrown on one of the circumstances, the date of the death, or the age of that philosopher, and the given figures had been asserted on the strength of some reason or other. In that case, these figures would be taken as something universal, as time that still subsists apart from this particular content of the death of Aristotle, whether as time filled with some other content, or even as empty time.[31]

Hegel is emphasizing that there must be reasons underlying a judgment. He is showing that there is no judgment without a context that provides meaning to it. This is why a universal element is needed to form a judgment. It mediates immediacy, creating the space for meaning. The reference to the universality of time points toward the fact that *the fourth year of the 115th Olympiad* would be completely meaningless if one were not able to locate it within the time-continuum of world history. In order to be meaningful (and thus considered a judgment) a proposition must be part of an inference in the form of a syllogism, which gives it the background against which it acquires meaning. The minimum unit of meaning is neither the concept nor the judgment, but rather the syllogism. To judge is not merely to assert that something is the case, but to infer it from something else.[32] And only because there is something else to infer it from does it acquire meaning. Without a horizon of meaning one cannot thematize something in the form "such and such is the case." To make thematic or to judge is to infer. There is no meaning in a simple judgment.

One of the distinctions between Kant and Hegel's concepts of judgment lies in the fact that for Kant the relation between a judgment and the types of judgment there are is a synchronic one, whereas for Hegel it is diachronic.[33] For Kant all judgments are subject to being ascribed a quantity, a quality, a relation, and a modality. Without one of these, it would not be a judgment. The content of the judgment does not alter its having to manifest a particular quantity, quality, relation, and modality. For Hegel, on the other hand, a development takes place from one type of judgment to the next. Keeping in mind the motor of this movement (the different types of necessity manifested in the copula uniting subject and predicate in a proposition), the passage from one type of judgment to another reflects a transformation in the relation between subject and predicate. The force of the copula is transformed as we move from judgment to judgment, from a contingent to an absolutely necessary copula.

How can a judgment, which by its nature determines what there is as constituted by substances and accidents—reflecting the linguistic distinction between subject and predicate—do justice to states of affairs in constant alteration, developing into what they are? How can it capture the tension of the striving of something to realize its ought? Only what becomes what it is can be revealed to be absolutely necessary. Hegel's concept of concept is one whose identity is constituted through its differences, posited by them. It does not congeal into an essence. This attribute pointed toward concepts of what were called *infinite objects* or *spiritual processes* as characterizing what a concept was for Hegel. These concepts therefore reveal themselves as absolutely necessary, containing within them opposing determinations, the totality of which determine them to have become what they are in an absolutely necessary manner. They will make up the predicate of the type of judgment that most closely reveals what is really real. The subject of such a judgment will be characterized by its striving toward this concept, by an element of ought constituting it. This element of ought is achieved in non-achievement. The ought is achieved not by being overcome and turning into an *is*, but by realizing that as ought it *already* is. It is its nature to strive, to posit its fulfillment *as* beyond it.[34] The type of judgment characterized in this manner is called by Hegel the judgment of the concept:

> it is only in the judgment now to be considered [of the Notion] that its relation to the Notion is found. In this judgment the Notion is laid down as the basis, and since it is in relation to the object, it is an *ought-to-be* to which the reality may or may not be adequate. Therefore it is only a judgment of this kind that contains a true appreciation; the predicates *good, bad, true, beautiful, correct,* etc. express that the thing is *measured* against its universal *Notion* as the simply presupposed *ought-to-be* and is, or is not, in *agreement* with it.[35]

Only in judgments in which *infinite objects* or *spiritual processes* are at play does Hegel believe the *is* of the copula completely fulfills its function. This copula reveals an identity between subject and predicate, which was found in neither judgments of existence, nor of reflection nor of necessity. In a judgment of existence there is no necessity at all. It is purely contingent that the wall is green, for example. They are also two different objects of thought: a wall and greenness. A judgment of reflection suffers the same fate insofar as for Hegel it is still reached empirically. The use of *a, some*, or *all* is reached empirically, from below, so to speak. It is a matter of empirical observation, there being no room for necessity yet. The judgment of necessity includes within it an inner and a real necessity. By the former Hegel means a necessity that depends on the givenness of a particular subject. His example is: "The rose is a plant." It is necessary for the rose to be a plant, but it is not necessary for there to be a rose. The emphasis concerning what this judgment is lacking is placed on the posited character of the necessity of the relation between subject and predicate. The predicate does not posit the existence of the subject. The existence itself of the rose is presupposed. It is not granted, so to speak, by the predicate. It is not *causa sui* insofar as it needs a prior rose for it to exist as a plant. Thus, its cause is external to it. The rose is not completely self-contained by being a plant. It has its death within it, dissolving into the universality of its species.[36] In addition a rose cannot but be a plant. There is no room for an element of ought here. There is no striving to become what it is: it merely is. Only with an element of striving does what is striven for appear in its totality. The rose is a limited exemplar of being a plant. The richness of the species plant is curtailed in the rose. A painting that strives to be beautiful, a human being that strives to be moral, will reveal beauty and morality in their totality. In other words, beauty appears in all its vastness in a beautiful painting. This does not collapse the two, either. The beautiful painting does not become the standard for the beautiful, but rather embodies or captures it.[37] In doing so it also co-determines it. The concept of the beautiful determines which paintings are beautiful, while simultaneously it is through beautiful paintings that a sense for the concept of the beautiful is cultivated.[38] This characteristic makes the copula reveal its full force in a judgment such as "This painting is beautiful," manifesting the identity of identity and difference that the copula should express. Only in an object striving to realize itself, attempting to conform to its concept, does the true nature of the copula manifest itself. Only then is the predicate (concept) revealed in all its richness in the subject (object), both as identical to and different from it, as not totally fulfilled or realized.

There are thus three elements to be found in this judgment of the concept, which, according to Hegel, is the only one containing a true appreciation (*wahrhafte Beurteilung*). These three elements depend on the emphasis being placed on the subject, the copula, or the predicate. The predicate brings with it an element of absolute necessity insofar as it is revealed as a spiritual process that includes within it all opposing and prior determinations. The subject brings with it an element of ought or striving insofar as it reveals in its totality the concept that is predicated of it, though not corresponding to it completely. A state is just not insofar as no injustice is experienced in it, but rather insofar as it strives to overcome such instances of injustice.[39] There is no just state if being just is understood as excluding all injustice. The copula brings with it the identity of identity and difference insofar as the predicate is embodied in its totality in the subject (subject = predicate) but as the concept the subject strives for (subject ≠ predicate). There is a realization in non-realization, an accomplishment in non-accomplishment. In other words, this identity is *just as much accomplished as it is eternally accomplishing itself.* Another way of understanding this characteristic is through the vocabulary of fallibility and revisability of judgments. Rationality has a self-correcting nature, not because it slowly but inexorably approximates the world as it really is independent of us, but rather because our own conception of objectivity is in constant change, reconstituting the criteria determining how things really are.

Morality only reveals itself in the striving of a moral being to act morally. Justice only reveals itself in a state's striving to be just. Truth has an element of *non-correspondence in correspondence* constituting it. This element is brought in by the striving character of the object in its attempt to correspond to its concept. Identity for Hegel means identity of identity and difference. Therefore, infinite objects do not overcome this separation. Although their concept is not different from their being, the element of striving toward fulfillment introduces an irreducible element of difference. This separation is internal. It is posited as an ought-to-be striven for. As such, this ought determines the concept in its totality.

Therefore, there are two ways in which one might understand the difference between correctness and truth: either from the point of view of correspondence, by means of which the correspondence in correctness is called formal and takes place between two different things (representation and content) and the correspondence in truth is that of something with itself (object and its concept); or from the point of view of non-correspondence, by means of which the non-correspondence in correctness is one between two different things (body and soul are separate—definition of finite things) and the non-correspondence in truth is a non-correspondence with itself (body and soul are both separate and one in the body's striving to realize its soul).

Before going on to the syllogism, let us take a look at the last type of judgment of the concept: the apodictic judgment. In it one already finds what will later appear in the syllogism: an inferential nature.[40] This character makes Hegel assert of it that it "is *truly* objective; or it is the *truth of the judgment* in general."[41] What is new is the addition of a mediating element, of the particularity that will work as "the *ground* why a predicate of the Notion judgment applies or does not apply to the *whole subject*, that is, whether the subject corresponds to its Notion or not."[42] In the examples given by Hegel in these passages, this particularity appears in the form of *a constituted so and so*. We now have judgments no longer constituted by two elements (subject and predicate) united by a copula, but by three elements: "the house constituted so and so is *good*, the action constituted so and so is *right*."[43] The syllogistic nature of the judgment comes out clearly here. Such and such a constitution in actions is right; this action has such and such a constitution; therefore, this action is right.

Hegel is not only making the point that all judgments in order to be meaningful must be understood as the outcome of a syllogism. He is also making a point about the constitution of actuality. This is so insofar as he breathes life, so to speak, into the purely formal rules of reasoning, revealing how they are not separate from what is *rationally* thought. The only way to adequately gesture toward what is actual is by means of the syllogism insofar as the judgment does not capture the tension, the movement determining actuality as such. Therein lies the importance the syllogism has for Hegel in dealing with what is really real. Only through concepts understood in the Hegelian sense (constituted by a normative element) does this processual character of actuality come to light. This split in actuality between what it is and what it ought to be provides the space for actuality or "what is" to be understood in terms of more than purely mechanical causes and effects, beyond the causal space of perceptions. This split plays a functional role in allowing one to understand "what is," not in a substantialist or static manner but rather from the point of view of purposiveness (*Zweckmäßigkeit*). It would allow for a more accurate description as to why Socrates sits instead of fleeing upon hearing of his condemnation at the hands of the Athenians, than a purely mechanical explanation based on bones and sinews and their motion or lack thereof.[44]

> The *subject* likewise contains these two moments in *immediate* unity as the *fact* [*Sache*]. But it is the truth of the fact that it is internally *split* into *what it ought-to-be* and *what it is*; this is the *absolute judgment on all actuality*. It is because this original partition, which is the omnipotence of the Notion, is just as much a return into its unity and an

absolute relation of *the ought-to-be* and *being* to each other that makes what is actual into *a fact*; its inner relation, this concrete identity, constitutes the *soul* of the fact.[45]

4.4 The syllogism

The perspective from which the section on the syllogism is to be read will be the transformation of the types of necessity, which, as mentioned above, reflects the development the concept of necessity undergoes in the section on Actuality, leading from formal through real to absolute necessity. This already points toward the fact that in the section on Subjectivity Hegel is not dealing with formal rules for reasoning, to which a material content must then be added in order to think about "what is." The fact that we think conceptually in judgments that form part of syllogisms is intrinsically related to what we think. Form and matter are not isolated from one another. To think conceptually in the form of judgments has implications for determining "what is."[46] A certain picture of the world seeps in through a thinking that expresses itself in judgments. This is one of the criticisms Hegel levels at the position that assumes the form of the judgment to be the adequate form of truth:[47] it leaves outside of the scope of "what is" that which Hegel calls *facts* (*Sachen*). These will be revealed to be the outcome of a syllogism, and to acquire objectivity in the process. There is a movement in thinking that leads from one type of judgment and syllogism to another. This movement is propelled by the unsatisfied propensity of reason to attempt to grasp the unconditioned, that which requires nothing beyond itself to determine it as absolutely necessary. The contingent element found in judgments of existence leads beyond them to the judgments of reflection; the external character of the necessity found in the judgments of reflection leads beyond them to the judgments of necessity, and so on.

However, one should not imagine a continuous development leading from the positive judgment all the way down to the disjunctive syllogism, revealing at each new step an ever-increasing autarchy, so to speak, in the type of necessity.[48] It is also difficult to establish a parallel between the development encountered in the section on the syllogism and that encountered in the section on the judgment: whereas the judgment is subdivided into four sections, the syllogism is subdivided into three.[49] There are other reasons not to assume an exact parallel between these developments. For example, while both the judgment and the syllogism of existence are characterized by their contingent nature, this contingent nature assumes a different character in each. A judgment of existence is contingent insofar as it takes up a being in its immediately qualitative aspect: a rose in its redness, a man in his learnedness.[50] This immediacy disallows any type of necessity. A syllogism of existence, on the other hand, is contingent with regard to the way the property chosen to work as the middle term is taken. So long as the middle term of a syllogism is to be taken as an *immediate determination* and not as an *essential Concept determination*,[51] there is an element of contingency insofar as any of an indefinite number of determinations could have been taken as the middle term, leading to contradictory conclusions. To take a human being as a sensible or a spiritual being is completely arbitrary since both determinations are assumed in their immediacy. Depending on which determination we use, humans will either fall under the dichotomy good/evil or will not be affected by it. These are mutually exclusive, though correctly inferred, conclusions about human beings.[52] The contingent element found here is due to the fact that we are not dealing with qualities, as in the judgment of existence, but with determinations in a qualitative manner, which could also be dealt with in a conceptual manner ruling out contingency. For this reason the same example can be used to illustrate a syllogism of existence and one of reflection,[53] whereas in the section on the judgment the examples used to illustrate each type of judgment varied from type to type.[54] Any assertion of a strict parallel existing between the development of the judgment and that of the syllogism should then be disallowed.

The syllogism is "the unity and truth" of the concept and the judgment; it is "the completely posited notion"[55] insofar as already in the judgment the concept is posited: it posits itself as something other to it, it reflects itself as determinate, duplicating itself into subject and predicate. As mentioned above, the movement concept–judgment–syllogism reflects that of Being–Essence–Concept. The judgment is the negation of the concept since it negates immediacy and posits it *as* something other (predicate). The syllogism negates this negation. This means going back to the concept by fully mediating it, that is, including within it its determinations as moments: "In reason the *determinate* notions are posited in their *totality* and *unity*."[56] Only in the syllogism is the concept realized as concept: "Thus the notion is, in the first instance, the *absolute self-identity* that is such only as the negation of negation or as the infinite unity of the negativity with itself."[57]

Absolute self-identity is not the purely formal tautological law of identity A = A, but rather this identity reached as a result, after A has determined itself as many other things until it finally reaches its totality and *determines* itself *as* itself. It is the negation of all abstract one-sided determinations or negations of it. This means that it does not negate each determination or negation but rather their one-sided aspect, taking each of them up now as a moment in a totality. The concept negates neither Being nor Essence; it rather takes them up and recognizes them as moments of its self-positing as concept. The negation of negation is the uniting of it with itself. A concept only negates its one-sided determinations insofar as it unites them in itself.

Causa sui, which is what characterizes the concept as the truth of Essence, consists in something making itself into what it is. It must show that it is *causa sui* and not just assert that it is.[58] Herein lies the importance of the syllogism. Only in it are the different and opposing determinations of a concept to be found united in the identity of identity and non-identity. The constitution of what is really real, already found in the copula of the judgment but only implicitly, *without consciousness,* is made explicit in the syllogism. The middle term is the place where the richness of the concept converges, where its distinctions are held together in identity. In the syllogism the concept is revealed to be completely posited.

Let us now turn to the inner movement of the section on the syllogism. There are two variables at work simultaneously, determining the different types of syllogism, both of which have to do with the middle term. One is connected to mediation; it constitutes the different figures within each type of syllogism by determining the middle term as individual, particular, or universal (the extremes or premises take up the remaining two), while the other is connected to what Hegel calls "the stages of *impregnation* or concretion of the middle term."[59] This means the type of necessity applicable to the middle term, which will generate the distinction between syllogisms of existence, reflection, and necessity. These two variables are intimately connected in Hegelian philosophy. Immediacy for Hegel is equivalent to contingency, arbitrariness, and, therefore, untruth. It is mediation that brings necessity with it. Within each type of syllogism the need for mediation, for the grounding of something, will lead to the revelation of its necessity. However, the necessity reached at the end of each mediating process in the different types of syllogism will be different. The mediating effort will also lead to different results in each type of syllogism. In conclusion, there are two processes at work simultaneously: on the one hand, a process of continuous mediation within each type of syllogism; on the other, one of an increasing autarchy in the type of necessity from one type of syllogism to the next.

Figures → **Necessity ↓**	I–P–U	P–I–U	I–U–P	U–U–U
Existence (I–P–U)	I–P–U	P–I–U	I–U–P	Mathematical
Reflection (U–I–P/P–I–U)	Allness	Induction	Analogy	—
Necessity (I–U–P/P–U–I)	Categorical	Hypothetical	Disjunctive	—

We will be more concerned with the movement downwards than with that from left to right, since this downward movement gives life to the ossified structure of formal logic by bringing in content, revealing different degrees of richness in the determinations that constitute a syllogism. These determinations can, for example, be treated as abstract, isolated determinations taken up in their immediacy, coming together externally in a syllogism. They can also be treated as *posited totalities*, as *posited unities of extremes, embracing a manifold within themselves*, as they are in a syllogism of reflection.[60] Finally, they can be treated as the *reflection-into-self of the determinateness of the extremes*, that is, *reflected simple identity*:[61] not a totality composed of the sum of its parts, but a whole that is more than its parts without being other than them.

The movement from left to right, which reveals an increasing degree of mediation, sometimes seems like a forced attempt at including within the whole process of the movement of thinking all previous types of syllogisms dealt with in both formal and transcendental schools of logic, an attempt at making room for what has been handed down by tradition.[62] To clarify the movement from left to right, we shall deal with the development of mediation occurring in the syllogism of existence since it is a clear example of how for Hegel contingency is overcome by mediation, leading thus to necessity.

4.4.1 The syllogism of existence

The basic shortcoming of a syllogism of existence lies in the fact that, given the way the determinations of thought that constitute it are taken up, it is completely contingent which determination is ascribed to the individual. Since each individual has myriad qualities determining it, a change of the quality ascribed to it as the middle term can result in a conclusion contradicting one previously reached. Hegel's example is of a human being. One can ascribe it spirituality as well as sensuality. Depending on which is used as the middle term one ends up having a human being either falling under the dichotomy good/evil or being neither good nor evil. Insofar as these determinations are taken up in their immediacy as being merely properties, it is totally arbitrary which one to use as the middle term.

In order for a syllogism of existence to reveal a necessity that goes beyond being merely formally necessary, and therefore beyond being merely correct but possibly false, its determinations have to be shown to be derived, not just taken up immediately. This is what the process of mediation consists in, which leads to the movement from figure to figure. Hegel starts off with the figure I–P–U (individual–particular–universal), which, following Aristotle, he calls "the essential form of the syllogism in general."[63] For Aristotle, all types of syllogism can be reduced to syllogisms of this first figure, namely, to Barbara/Celarent. Hegel accepts that they can all be reduced to this figure, but he also asserts that this is an abstract form that needs to be further concretized or mediated in order for it not to remain merely correct, but also to become true. This figure, which works as the "general schema of the syllogism,"[64] is composed of three judgments: I–P, P–U, and I–U. Only the third is mediated since it reveals where it comes from: it shows as its ground or reason the other two. What is needed is to mediate I–P and P–U in order to have a totally mediated and thence necessary syllogism. I–U, having been mediated, can serve as a middle term in order to mediate P–U. We will then have P–I, I–U, and P–U. The latter two judgments are mediated whereas the first still remains immediate. However, it is now P–I, not I–P, as we had in the original syllogism. The only way to maintain an identity between these two is to introduce limitation into P–I: the only way to reverse "All I's are P's" without altering its value is by saying "Some P's are I's." We have then reached the second figure of the syllogism: P–I–U (particular–individual–universal), through which the second judgment (P–U) constituting the first figure (I–P–U) has been mediated. Now we have U as mediated or inferred. This will allow us to mediate the only unmediated judgment remaining from the first figure: I–P. We thus have I–U, U–P, and I–P. I–U was achieved as inference from the first figure. However, the inference from the second figure was P–U, not U–P. Hegel will achieve this change from P–U to U–P through negation. Negation allows the value of P–U to remain unchanged when the judgment turns into U–P: "No P's are U's" is equivalent to "No U's are P's." This is the third figure: I–U, U–P, and I–P.

The movement from the first through the second to the third figure has allowed the mediation of the judgments constituting the first figure: the first figure mediates the conclusion (I–U), the second mediates the major premise (I–P), and the third mediates the minor premise (P–U). However, this mediation of a syllogism of existence could only take place by recourse to limitation and negation. This is Hegel's main point: reality (third judgment: I–U) can only be mediated by limitation (first judgment: I–P = P–I) and negation (second judgment: P–U = U–P).[65] Reality, when taken up in its immediate nature, is purely contingent. Without recourse to limitation and negation it will be led back in an infinite regress of causes determining it. This triad of reality, limitation, and negation found in the syllogism of existence in its attempt to ground itself is equivalent to Kant's sub-division of the categories of quality.[66] However, Hegel's point is not that any object of intuition must a priori be judged to be either real, limited, or negated,[67] but rather that in thinking's quest to grasp by means of syllogisms what is really real (the unconditioned) as qualitative determinations of thought, it is led to an infinite regress from syllogism to syllogism unless an element of limitation and negation is brought in by means of which the syllogism mediates itself.

Hegel has been able to quell the *geometrical progression to infinity*[68] leading from syllogism to syllogism in the attempt to mediate what has been immediately given, by revealing that the middle term of the syllogism is not an immediate determination, as it would first appear to be, but a determination that, by taking up the roles of individual, particular, and universal, is a totality that posits its terms, though still as other to it. In the syllogism of existence the determination as individual presupposed its ground in an other to it. In the syllogism of reflection this determination as universal will presuppose itself as other, that is, it will posit its other (as individual). Limitation and negation determine something through what it is not; they allow this something to reflect on itself as *other to...*

4.4.2 The syllogism of reflection

By having gone through all of the figures of the syllogism of existence, the middle term becomes more concrete; it loses its abstract nature insofar as it has now been mediated by its others. It "is posited as the *totality* of the terms."[69] We are now dealing with posited universals or *genera*.[70] It is no longer a matter of dealing with determinations such as *green*, but rather with *all green things*. The middle term is no longer an abstract quality with no necessary connection to what it is predicated of, and that could therefore lead to contradicting inferences about the same object. The first type of syllogism of reflection is that of allness. Hegel's example for the difference between syllogisms of existence and of reflection is the following: Green is pleasurable, X is green, therefore X is pleasurable. Insofar as green is an abstract quality among many others there can be objects that are green, but that do not share the quality green itself has. There is no essential connection between being green and being pleasurable. On the other hand, when we have: All green things are pleasurable, X is green, therefore X is pleasurable, we are already excluding anything green from not being pleasurable. It is insofar as things are green that they are pleasurable. The weakness of this syllogism lies in its basis on empirical observation. *All green things* means all individuals; it is a universal reached through empirical observation, not through conceptual work. "Allness" is just a totalization reached through quality. The ground of the universal is still posited as external to it, as the sum of all individuals. As Hegel says: "allness is still not the universality of the Notion but the external universality of reflection."[71] Thus the major premise presupposes the conclusion since, were the conclusion false, it would falsify the premise. This creates a logical short-circuit: one starts off with a premise that can only be grounded by the conclusion that it must itself ground.

The only possible solution to this shortcoming of the syllogism of allness is to spell out the *all* dealt with in the major premise in the form of a complete list of individuals as minor premises. In other words, the universality of allness should be taken as *completeness*.[72] This obviously runs up against the wall of a bad infinite. Both the syllogism of allness and that of induction are subject to the type of criticism Hume aimed at causality. Both attempt to constitute universality from below, so to speak, from the empirical side.

The last type of syllogism of reflection Hegel mentions is that of analogy. It is a variation on the previous two. Once again, from agreement in one property we have the inference of agreement in another property. The variations lie in the fact that, on the one hand, we are now dealing with two individuals that share a property and not with an individual subsumed under a universal. On the other hand, the property shared is essential to both (unlike the greenness of all green things). As long as the second property is not essentially related to the first, it cannot be ascribed to those who share that first property, regardless of the fact that this first property might be essential to both individuals. Hegel's example is the following: The earth is inhabited; the moon is an earth; therefore the moon is inhabited. That the earth and the moon are essentially earths (celestial bodies) is not enough to make them share all other properties if these properties are not essentially tied to being an earth. The middle term unites, as it does in both the syllogism of allness and that of induction, an individual (the moon) and a universal (being inhabited) in an immediate manner, that is, externally, since this universal determination of being inhabited has an empirical origin. It still does not reveal its conceptual nature; it is not conceptually tied to being an earth, but rather empirically tied to *the* earth. Therefore, its application to other individuals is in question.

In the two previous types of syllogism of reflection the universal was posited from the individual; it was the negation of the individual (as opposed to the syllogisms of existence, in which there was immediacy and presupposition). Now, the universal posits itself and, doing so, negates its negation of the individual. It is a double negation that has as a result the identity between universal and individual. It is no longer a matter of inherence of a universal in an individual (syllogism of existence), nor of subsumption of an individual under a universal (syllogism of reflection). In the former case, the inherence was completely arbitrary since the starting point was an individual that as individual had as its characteristic to be composed of various qualitative universals. This led from syllogism to syllogism in an attempt to find necessity in the universal ascribed to the individual. In the latter case, the subsumption of individuals under universals brought in necessity, though a relative one insofar as it was still dependent on the individuals composing the universal. This led to the mutual presupposing of premises and conclusions. Now it is a matter of identity between universal and individual, not of subsumption or inherence. There is then neither an infinite regress from syllogism to syllogism nor a mutual presupposing of premises and conclusions, both of which are unsatisfactory for reason's demand for the unconditioned: what is because it has made itself into what it is; what is absolutely necessary and thus *causa sui*.

4.4.3 The syllogism of necessity

In the syllogisms of necessity we will be dealing with the identity of identity and difference between individual and universal. In the categorical syllogism the middle term reveals itself now as genus: not *all green things*, but rather a substance, an essence without which all individuals constituted by this essence would have no identity. It is a substance that runs through all three terms of the syllogism. Hegel says: "we have here *one* essential nature pervading the three terms, a nature in which the determinations of individuality, particularity and universality are merely *formal* moments."[73] The example that has been cropping up throughout the section on the syllogism comes to mind. Gaius is a man and therefore he is mortal. Mankind is Gaius' essence or substance. It is no longer taken as a particular quality (syllogism of existence: a man) nor as a universal quality (syllogism of reflection: all men), but as substance: mankind. Gaius and mankind form an identity when the latter is taken as a substance and not as a particular quality (the way green is a particular quality) or a universal quality (the way *all green things* reveals a universal quality). The problem encountered by this type of syllogism can best be understood by going back to the section on Actuality, in which it was shown that there was no absolute necessity in a substantial relation.[74] Absolute necessity can only be revealed by something becoming what it is, making itself into what it is, not by being what it is. That Gaius is a man is necessary insofar as he would lose his identity if his mankind were to be removed. A green leaf, on the contrary, could be changed into a yellow one without losing its identity. However, Gaius *is* a man; he has not become one. He has not made himself into that which he was to be. Absolute necessity only exists in a process by which something makes itself into what it is. The categorical syllogism is not able to reveal the processual character of that which becomes what it is. It gives a static view of "what is," unable to grasp it in its truth. It still works at a substantialist level. The concept has not yet come to life. The middle term of a categorical syllogism merely *is*; it has not *become*. Something that *is*—albeit essentially—cannot *be* in an absolutely necessary manner; it *merely* is. And just as it is, others that share its essence could also be. There is still a contingent element here. The individual is the universal, though there are other individuals, and the selection of the individual in the syllogism remains contingent.

Only in the last two types of syllogism of necessity (hypothetical and disjunctive) will justice be done, so to speak, to the processual character of what is really real according to Hegel, to what reveals itself as absolutely necessary, as cause of itself. Here it is no longer a matter of substances, as it was in the categorical syllogism, where one essence ran through all three terms and created an identity between them instead of a relation of subsumption or inherence.

4.4.3.1 The hypothetical syllogism

The hypothetical syllogism runs: "If A is, then B is, But A *is*, Therefore B is."[75] It has been reduced to two terms: A and B. Their relation will most adequately exemplify what Hegel understands by identity of identity and difference. In the categorical syllogism there was still a contingent element insofar as the individual (identical to the universal—albeit in an immediate manner) could not show its being as absolutely necessary: why this individual and not any other? This led Hegel to say of this syllogism that it "still continues to be subjective in that the said identity is still the substantial identity or *content*, but is still not at the same time *identity of form*."[76] How can this be resolved by focusing on becoming rather than on being, on a process rather than on a substance? Where does the absolute necessity lie in something for it to become what it is? Once again, the section on Actuality offers us the clue to understand these last two types of syllogisms of necessity. One should keep in mind that Hegel subordinates possibility to actuality. His starting point is actuality: what is, not what is possible. Only because of this can absolute necessity be assigned to it in its looking back in remembrance to its conditions of possibility: what was absolutely necessary for it to become what it is. This is encountered in the hypothetical syllogism. Hegel's emphasis on the fact that A *is*, shows that A is "what is." B is the totality of its conditions of possibility. Thus Hegel starts off with "what is," proceeding then in an absolutely necessary manner to its conditions of possibility, not the other way around. One could say that here Hegel starts off in objectivity. It is not to be reached, but rather posits its own conditions in retrospect.[77] We now have a copula that is not abstract but a "pregnant *mediating* unity."[78] It is a unity of *actuality* and *totality of conditions*. The emphasis is placed on its *mediating* character. However, in this hypothetical syllogism what is revealed is the becoming of "what is" in the form of the totality of its conditions of possibility. "What is" was not; it *became* what it is. Negativity appears then in the type of unity occurring. It is a *negative unity*[79] insofar as the individuality of "what is" negates its conditions of possibility in its positing them in retrospect.[80]

In this syllogism we find the triad with which the *Science of Logic* begins: Being, Nothing, and Becoming. In other words, we have reached Becoming at the level of the concept. The movement itself of thinking has been revealed. The categorical syllogism expressed necessity in its being, in a positive unity. Since it lacked the negativity, the activity of becoming, it still had a contingent element in it. From *something is* one cannot conclude *something necessarily is*. The hypothetical syllogism expresses absolute necessity in its becoming, in a negative unity. From *something is* one can conclude *something necessarily became*. The conditions for something to have become actual are necessary. The actualizing of that something necessitates precisely those conditions and none other. The actual is not *due* to its conditions; it *is* its conditions. They are one and the same. For this reason absolute necessity is encountered here.

> The absolute content of A and B is the same; they are only two different names for the same underlying fact for ordinary thinking [*Vorstellung*] which clings to the appearance of the diversified shape of determinate being and distinguishes between the necessary and its necessity; but in so far as this necessity were to be separated from B, B would not be the necessary.[81]

We have reached the syllogism describing processes that are cause of themselves. Insofar as they are cause of themselves there is no external standpoint from which to assert their dependence on something other than themselves. All historical events, for example, all development of humans as spiritual beings, fall under this type of syllogism. It is in recollection or looking back that they are revealed as having become what they are in an absolutely necessary manner. They are absolutely necessary processes insofar as one only takes up their conditions of possibility. By only focusing on the totality of conditions of possibility of something, it will be revealed to be absolutely necessary. If I look back on my life, on the totality of events comprising it, I cannot but have become who I am. An historical event understood as the totality of its conditions of possibility cannot but have taken place as it did. The hypothetical syllogism focuses on this absolutely necessary aspect of processes when reconstructed in recollection.

4.4.3.2 The disjunctive syllogism

The disjunctive syllogism runs: A is either B, or C, or D; but A is B; therefore A is neither C nor D. The hypothetical syllogism underscored the totality of conditions (B) of A; now, the disjunctive syllogism underscores what A is not (C or D). This brings even further determination to A insofar as it is not only the totality of its conditions but posits itself as one among many possible totalities that could have been.[82] A is now not only together with itself (A = B) but also further determined by excluding from itself what it is not (A ≠ C and D). This includes possibility within actuality. In the hypothetical syllogism the being of A lies in an other to it that is itself, in a negative unity that gives it its being. In the disjunctive syllogism this negative unity is given more concreteness insofar as it includes what could have been within what is. Not only is A its own becoming; A more explicitly *posits* this becoming by excluding C and D from it and only remaining with B. In the hypothetical syllogism we moved from a substantialist to a processual view: becoming overtook being, so to speak. As becoming of itself it was determined by self-identification. Now, this becoming is made more concrete through self-differentiation.

In the chapter on Actuality it was seen that what is absolutely necessary is that which becomes what it is, while simultaneously showing that nothing can become what it is not since there is no external standpoint from which to find a differentiation between what it was to become and what it actually became. Thus, it could have become anything, though in an absolutely necessary manner. These two characteristics formed the unity of absolute necessity and absolute contingency. Only looking back can absolute necessity be ascribed; and it always comes intertwined with absolute contingency. They are two sides of the same coin. The hypothetical syllogism emphasizes one side of the coin: that of absolute necessity. A looks back and posits B as the totality of its conditions for becoming A, and since A is, since the starting point is actuality, it is absolutely necessary. The disjunctive syllogism, on the other hand, emphasizes the other side of the coin: absolute contingency, insofar as it shows that just as A is B it could have been C or D. This disjunctive syllogism makes explicit the act of self-differentiation of the concept. The concept posits not only its own conditions of actualization but also those against which it distinguishes itself.[83]

The disjunctive syllogism reveals how absolute necessity is not reached unless it is complemented by absolute contingency. Only this syllogism is capable of revealing the element of absolute contingency in what is absolutely necessary insofar as it includes within it not only the totality of conditions of possibility that became A, but also that against which A determines itself as what it became. To include within a process certain conditions of possibility it did not follow in its becoming what it is reveals that infinite objects are not only absolutely necessary (they are processes of seeking out in recollection their own conditions of possibility) but also absolutely contingent (since there is no absolute standpoint, no point outside of history, they could have become something other, though necessarily so). To be conscious of what could have become enriches our self-understanding insofar as we embrace the tenuousness and contingency of life. To include what could have become in the determination of what became completes the movement of self-determination of the concept. It includes its other within it. This should not be understood as the disappearance of the other in its being consumed by the concept, but rather as a constant taking the concept to task, a constant keeping it on its feet, so to speak. An element of "could have," of "otherwise," is constitutive of being. Necessity goes hand in hand with contingency; and the hypothetical and disjunctive syllogisms, respectively, bring this out.

The movement encountered in this section on the syllogism is one of increasing mediation where the distinction between mediated and mediating disappears.[84] The mediation encountered in the hypothetical syllogism seemed to be one-way: B mediated A, even though it was posited by A (in recollection). B was posited *as* presupposed by A. Now we have B posited *as* posited insofar as it lies in distinction to C and D. The structure at work is that of a mutual mediation. The relation between actuality and totality of conditions is not unidirectional. Each element mediates and is mediated by the other. A particular event is determined by the totality of its conditions of possibility while simultaneously determining them. This movement of determination or positing becomes more explicit when it lies side by side with other possible conditions, with what could have been. The element of "could have" emphasizes the ascription of meaning, the creation of a narrative. The occurrence of an historical event is determined by the totality of conditions constituting it. However, it simultaneously determines the conditions of its own possibility in its recollection of them. Human beings are always already determined by their past while simultaneously being in a constant process of reconstitution of this past in recollection. A human being is constituted by the totality of life experiences she has had in her past. They have determined her to necessarily be who she has become. However, she gives meaning to these experiences from her present standpoint, reconfiguring them as *her* experiences. This movement of reconfiguration is emphasized when it is contrasted to excluded possibilities or totalities of being (who she did not become). Therefore, not only is who she is determined by who she was; who she is also co-determines who she was, as the narrative she creates of having become herself. This narrative element is brought into further relief in the contrast with who she did not become, though could have.

As a conclusion to this section on the syllogism Hegel says:

> The syllogism is *mediation*, the complete Notion in its *positedness*. Its movement is the sublating of this mediation, in which nothing is in- and for-itself, but each term is only by means of an other. The result is therefore an *immediacy* which has issued from the *sublating of the mediation*, a *being* which is no less identical with the mediation, and which is the Notion that has restored itself out of, and in, its otherness. This *being* is therefore a *fact* [*eine Sache*] that is *in and for itself-objectivity*.[85]

What is the relation between objectivity, on the one hand, and absolute mediation and contingency, on the other? To assert that only in absolute mediation we reach objectivity implies not only that the constitution of the object occurs on this side, so to speak (Chapter 1). It also implies that this constitution only occurs inferentially: a concept only has meaning when it accounts for its own formation, when it *posits* itself as the culmination of a process that necessarily leads to it; in other words, when it reveals where it comes from. However, absolute mediation means that it is not totally constituted by this process, but rather co-determines it in its looking back on it. This is Hegel's hermeneutic understanding of concept constitution, in which a concept is constituted by and co-constitutes its past. Contingency comes in due to this co-constitution since it is posited to have necessarily been constituted the way it was, whatever that constitution might turn out to be; and given our historical nature, there is no final "turning out to be."

Objectivity is constituted with others and within history. It is constituted in recollection, in our making sense of reality, our creating narratives. It deals with spiritual processes (processes of concept-formation) insofar as only they appear as absolutely necessary, fulfilling the requirements that the striving for the absolute demands. Only these conceptual processes can reveal themselves as absolutely necessary, completely self-dependent and thus cause of themselves. They contain their own conditions of possibility. This is the power of recollection. It gives itself its own criterion, and as such, it is a criterion that will always be changing. There will always be a blind spot, so to speak, that allows for the movement of the constitution of objectivity. The concept is never totally transparent to itself since it appears in time, constantly reconstituting itself, yet always identical to itself. The disjunctive syllogism makes evident the becoming, or more precisely, the always already having become, of objectivity.

The syllogism has the function of revealing the temporal character of objectivity. A judgment is a-temporal. It is two-dimensional. What gives it meaning is the third dimension added by making it the conclusion of an inference. This third dimension is time. For Hegel objectivity is reached with concepts that reveal their own constitution. They not only become throughout history, but do so necessarily. What is "really real" are concepts that have been formed in a historical process, continuously reconstituted as such in social recollection.

* * * *

According to his critics, Brandom either seems to lose grip of the hardness of the world by determining as the basis of our beliefs the social game of asking for and giving reasons, where the ultimate ground for those beliefs held and what follows from them lies in the difference between undertaken and entitled commitments (a distinction always determined by others); or, he seems to rely on a not sufficiently problematized notion of *the* way things actually stand, *the* way the world is, to work as the ground of our true beliefs. This latter position is equivalent to a metaphysical realism that would make a distinction meaningful between what is experienced and what really is, or between "how things are" and "how they are taken to be."[86]

By means of the elements of absolute mediation and contingency encountered in the final sections on the syllogism, where the constitution of objectivity takes place, Hegel confronts this Scylla–Charybdis situation, avoiding foundering on the rocks of givenness, on the one hand, and social constructivism, on the other. Absolute mediation undercuts the attempt to find a solid indubitable starting point for knowledge, a given upon which all further knowledge may rest. It stanches the endless, bad infinite bleeding of the search for a first, without falling into another horn of the Agrippan trilemma, circularity, since it is a productive, hermeneutic circle in which its elements co-constitute one another in a continuous re-formulation of meaning.[87] Meaning is not supplied by the causal space of perceptions. There is no one-to-one relation of immediacy between world and mind. This avoids the problem of how to justify what is merely given since as given it would be pure immediacy. On the other hand, Hegel avoids the free-floating element of coherentism or social constructivism by emphasizing the contingent aspect of meaning-constitution continuously exercised by humans in their experience, which due to its negative component tempers said meaning-constitution and narrative-creation. We are constantly reconstituting the totality of conditions determining our beliefs and judgments based on our permanent experience of getting it wrong, both theoretically and practically. The disjunctive syllogism emphasizes this negative aspect of human experience since it shows how our current beliefs are formed by including within this process of concept-formation what could have been and was not. As historical beings, we are constantly reconstituting our own process of having become who we are, wherein the "could have been" and the "otherwise" play a fundamental and constitutive role.

5

The Most Stubborn Opposition: Mind and World

5.1 Introduction

If the history of Western philosophy were to be reduced to one overarching narrative, a potentially fruitful path would be the connection between thought or language and the world. Hegel, as a critic of all type of dualisms—Platonic, Cartesian, Kantian—would be seen as offering a monistic system in which such dualisms are overcome, and the problem of how to connect two very dissimilar entities dissolved. His concept of the absolute would be the unitary ground from which any opposition might spring. In this sense, the identity of the absolute is prior to and makes possible all dualities. If the absolute by definition includes everything, then there is no remainder, no absolutely other that can resist its gravitational pull and not be absorbed by it. In the absolute the opposition between seeming and being, appearance and reality, would be overcome since both belong within it and do not transcend it. The same would apply to the opposition between the is and the ought. The ought is fulfilled insofar as it is immanent to reality. Given this reading of the absolute, Hegelian philosophy is criticized from an epistemological point of view for spinning in a void and losing all friction with an external world; and from a moral point of view for not allowing the otherness of the other to confront us, for not encountering the face of the other in its otherness. However, in the section on the absolute idea, the last section of the *Science of Logic*, Hegel characterizes the idea as the most stubborn opposition. This opposition does not dissolve in the idea. It is just reflected on, made a subject of thought. The stubbornness of human experience will provide Hegel with the hardness and friction of the world and with the absolute otherness of the other. With the absolute idea Hegel will be able to complete the totality while including within it a blind spot that works as a never-ending source of otherness and difference.

5.2 Detour via McDowell

McDowell's *Mind and World* attempts to shed light on the point of contact between humans and their knowledge, on the one hand, and the world, on the other. The guiding question is: How can one grant objectivity to one's beliefs about the world if, given the critique of the myth of the given, there is no immediate connection between them, if any immediate contact would belong merely to the causal space of perceptions and sense impressions, without therefore being able to justify or ground these beliefs, entering into the logical space of reasons?

McDowell offers a model in which conceptuality already lies within content as a part of it, without postulating a purely external source for that conceptual content. He places the logical space of reasons within the natural space. However, he proposes a second nature, following Aristotle's ethics as paradigm. The world given to us at the point of contact with the mind is always already conceptual: a world of facts and not of nervous stimuli causally affecting us. Human experience does not consist in extra-conceptual impacts on our sensibility. There is no ontological gap to overcome since we are already on both sides: on one side we encounter our spontaneity or conceptual capacity. On the other lies our second nature: the world that has always already been conceptually given to us. We can only confront a world as long as it is constituted and sustained by the tradition in which we have been formed as human beings. McDowell appeals to Gadamer's hermeneutics and his concept of *Bildung*. We always have an (already conceptual) world confronting us to which we then apply our conceptual schemes. That world is determined by tradition; it is the store of historically accumulated wisdom.[1]

However, our knowledge cannot have a merely social or linguistic foundation, it cannot be justified by a form of life or a social agreement. A belief would end up being true simply because we all believe it to be true. The beliefs constituting a form of life or a particular society must somehow extend their roots beyond that form of life or society itself. McDowell's problem is that when he attempts to describe this second nature, he ends up making use of social or linguistic formulae very similar to those he was meticulously trying to avoid. We all have a second nature since we are always already part of a world determined by tradition and a particular history. Our immediate relation to the world is given insofar as we are formed as members of a community and as such receive a *Bildung*. Without this there would be no world to which we could relate through our conceptual schemes.

However, what is the relation between first and second natures? Either the first completely determines the second and therefore makes it superfluous since second nature would contribute nothing, or, as Pippin says: "Given the unbelievable variety in human culture, it seems safe to say that first nature radically underdetermines, even while it conditions, any second nature."[2] The distinction between both natures, instead of avoiding the postulation of an aporetic point of contact between mind and world, ends up preserving it, now between a first nature (the world) and a second nature (tradition or history). Instead of being dissolved the question has just taken a step back: how was the tradition in which we are formed as human beings built? The answer to this question cannot lie beyond the world we are a part of. Here Hegel and McDowell would agree. Only by using criteria offered by the tradition itself can we interrogate and alter it in a constant give and take. This capacity for alteration is an example of the role of spontaneity. The criteria used are themselves subject to alteration.[3] The fact that we do not build this second nature but are formed in it does not mean it has not been built. The fact that there is always a world that conditions us but does not completely determine us does not mean that it is not social. In fact, we cannot speak of *the* world but of worlds, in the plural; we cannot speak of tradition but of traditions. The word *nature* in "second nature" reveals McDowell's effort to avoid having meaning be a purely social construct, to avoid having "what is" depend on socially established criteria. Nonetheless, when he unpacks his conception of second nature he speaks of "a store of historically accumulated wisdom." This wisdom is accumulated in the encounter among various social practices and different worlds. Human beings are not formed in *the* world, but rather in *a* world. How does one appeal to the logical space of reasons in order to solve confrontations among worlds if this logical space is given within these worlds themselves?

The specter of relativism shows up again, revealing the incapacity of McDowell's proposal to recover the world always already there by means of the concept of second nature without falling into a social construction of meaning, which would undermine its autonomy.

McDowell ends up replacing a meaning determined by mere community ratification with one that is community-transcendent but not world vision- or tradition-transcendent. This tradition or world vision is what makes the external world already have conceptual content. Second nature, insofar as it is nature, supposedly provides the already conceptual friction that would allow us to cut the Gordian knot of the interminable oscillation between coherentism and the myth of the given. What McDowell does not explore is the element of friction this second nature offers. Where does its hardness come from? It seems the concept of second nature dilutes the hardness of the world McDowell wanted to rescue to avoid falling into coherentism or mere social normativity. If second nature is so underdetermined by first nature that many different worldviews and traditions as dissimilar as exist on this planet can be created, then the element of friction or hardness of first nature cannot play any justificatory role but merely a causal one. We have once again fallen into the scheme/content dualism and the ensuing relativism, now transferred to the relation between first and second nature.

* * * *

Let us take a look at what Hegel has to say about "the most stubborn opposition" in the section on the Idea in the last section of the *Science of Logic*. Curiously enough, this section does not have a content of its own. It is rather the self-reflective moment of thinking about the process itself that leads to it. For this reason Hegel says that the content of the absolute idea is the method. With it the point is reached where totality appears and, as such, includes all preceding moments within it. The absolute idea amounts to the constitution of totality.

Insofar as the search for what is has brought thinking closer to a reflection on its own activity, the ideas Hegel deals with in this section characterize what constitutes a human, thinking being. They are: life, the true, and the good. These ideas determine a human being as possessing the capacity to ask herself "What is?" In other words, these determinations make a human being philosophical. Before dealing with the absolute idea we shall come to terms with the ideas of the true and the good. We shall leave aside the idea of life due to the limitations it suffers, mainly, that it lacks the element of freedom.

5.3 The Idea

I shall begin by making some general comments on Hegel's concept of the Idea, based on certain passages of the Introduction to Section Three of the Doctrine of the Concept. This shall be followed by some comments concerning two of the Ideas Hegel describes: the true and the good. Finally, I shall attempt to characterize Hegel's concept of absolute idea by focusing on certain relevant aspects of this concept. The following are two descriptions of the Idea given by Hegel:

> by virtue of the freedom which the notion attains in the Idea, the Idea possesses within itself also the *most stubborn opposition*; its repose consists in the security and certainty with which it eternally creates and eternally overcomes that opposition, in it meeting with *itself*.[4]

> The Idea is essentially *process*, because its identity is only the absolute and free identity of the Concept, because this identity is the absolute negativity and hence dialectical.[5]

The Idea is the *most stubborn opposition*. It is a process and its identity is absolute negativity. It is no coincidence that when we finally reach the Idea the emphasis is not placed on identity, reconciliation and fulfillment but rather on difference, negativity, and eternal process. The task at hand is to give a reading of what concepts such as identity, fulfillment, realization, absolute, and so on might mean in the context of the Idea when the main emphasis is placed on difference and negation. The former set of concepts is the one most frequently associated with Hegelian philosophy, generally from a critical point of view. This point of view deems Hegel to be the most metaphysical of thinkers, for whom everything is permeated by reason, without any remainder or difference. His system would be a totality completely transparent to reason, and therefore one with it. Let us begin with the following passage:

> But having reached the result that the Idea is the unity of the Notion and objectivity, is the true, it must not be regarded merely [*nicht nur*] as a *goal* to which we have to approximate but which itself always remains a kind of *beyond*; on the contrary, we must recognize that everything actual *is* only in so far as it possesses the Idea and expresses it. It is not merely that the object, the objective and subjective world in general, *ought to be congruous* with the Idea, but they are themselves the congruence of Notion and reality; the reality that does not correspond to the Notion is mere *Appearance*, the subjective, contingent, capricious element that is not the truth. When it is said that no object is to be found in experience that is perfectly congruous with the *Idea*, one is opposing the Idea as a subjective standard to the actual; but what anything actual is supposed in truth *to be*, if its Notion is not in it and if its objectivity does not correspond to its Notion at all, it is impossible to say; for it would be nothing.[6]

In reading this passage the use of the "not merely" (*nicht nur*) should not be overlooked since herein lies the key to avoiding a certain interpretation of the Hegelian Idea as the point at which all difference and disparity are overcome and all goals reached. We have already gathered enough tools in the preceding sections to understand that what is here at stake is once again the idea of a correspondence in non-correspondence. In the English translation there is a slightly negative tone concerning the *goal to which we have to approximate*: the Idea must not be regarded *merely* as a goal. The German original has a more neutral connotation: the Idea must not be regarded *only* as a goal to which we have to approximate. What characterizes infinite objects is precisely this striving toward a goal. It determines them as free insofar as the duality is/ought in which they are located reveals their self-determining nature. They are permanently determining themselves in their attempt to fulfill the ought. For this reason the striving is itself a constitutive element of the Idea. In the following sentence Hegel asserts that what is actual is only because it possesses the Idea, the main characteristic of which has just been described as being a *goal to which we have to approximate*. In other words, it is precisely as a goal to be reached that actuality possesses the Idea. The Idea is posited as external to actuality, but already in the act of positing it it reveals that the Idea is part of actuality. The Idea is possessed in its being posited as *beyond*. A just state is not one in which there is no injustice. It is one in which justice is a goal permanently striven for. A human being is moral, not insofar as she obeys the categorical imperative in each of her acts. She is moral insofar as she is permanently struggling to obey it. In the following sentence Hegel asserts that it is limiting to say that the objective and subjective world *ought to be congruous* with the Idea. But then he goes on to assert that they are themselves the congruence of Concept and reality, not that they *are* congruous with the Idea. They themselves are the Idea insofar as they *ought to be congruous* with it. In other words, when he confronts the belief that there is no perfect congruence between experience and Idea, he does not assert the contrary: that there is perfect congruence. Rather, he asserts that the other extreme, total non-congruence, makes no sense at all; it would be nothing. There must be some congruence for there to be something at all. And there is congruence as long as one does not oppose the Idea to the actual. To possess the Idea is not equivalent to being totally congruous with it. Hegel's Idea does not consist in total congruence. It consists in "congruence in striving." Only one page later Hegel once again attacks the idea of total non-congruence without mentioning its opposite, total congruence. He says:

> But if an object, for example the state, *did not correspond at all* [*gar nicht angemessen*] to its idea, that is, if in fact it was not the Idea of the state at all, if its reality, which is the self-conscious individuals, did not correspond at all to the Notion, its soul and its body would have parted... The worst state, one whose reality least corresponds to the Notion, in so far as it still exists, is still Idea; the individuals still obey a dominant notion.[7]

That he uses as example the state, which is an infinite object, is revealing. There is no state that is totally congruous with its idea. This fact does not prevent it from being an infinite object. Therefore, its infinite element does not lie in total congruence.

The crucial distinction lies between non-congruence and congruence in non-congruence, and not between total congruence and total non-congruence. The latter characterizes finite things or, what is the same, objects without an internal end; the former characterizes infinite objects, those with an internal end, self-determining in their striving to realize such end. The fact that they are constantly striving explains why Hegel asserts that the Idea is eternally creating and eternally overcoming opposition. The Idea is eternally *positing* an ought *as* opposed to it; and in its act of positing it, already eternally overcoming it.

> Finite things are finite because they do not possess the complete reality of their Notion within themselves but require other things to complete it—or, conversely, because they are presupposed as objects, hence possess the Notion as an external determination. The highest to which they attain on the side of this finitude is external purposiveness. That actual things are not congruous with the Idea is the side of their *finitude* and *untruth*, and in accordance with this side they are *objects*, determined in accordance with their various spheres and in the relationships of objectivity, either mechanically, chemically, or by an external end.[8]

Even the worst state, insofar as it is an infinite object, insofar as it has its goal within it and is constantly striving to realize it, is Idea. This is so because its existence consists in striving to overcome its own self, its own positing in the form of an ought. This determines it as a free object. A being either has an ought by means of which it constantly determines itself (more succesfully or less so) or it does not. The Idea is a permanent process in which it distinguishes itself from itself, forming its identity around this constant act of distinguishing itself. This distinguishing itself takes the form of an ought and it requires freedom, something mere living beings lack:

> But the animal does not succeed in being for-itself in its species; instead, it succumbs to the power of the latter. The immediate being mediates itself with itself in the process of the genus; and in this way it elevates itself above its immediacy, but always just to sink back into it again. So, to start with, life simply runs its course into the spurious infinity of the infinite progress.[9]

Freedom is revealed to be the main distinguishing element between finite and infinite objects; it is intimately connected to the capacity for self-differentiation by means of the is/ought opposition. How should one read sentences that deal with the realization of ends if the distinction is/ought cannot be totally collapsed and if the Idea is an eternal process of opposing itself to itself? Let us analyze the following passage:

> The Notion, having truly attained its reality, is this absolute judgment whose *subject*, as self-related negative unity, distinguishes itself from its objectivity and is the latter's being-in-and-for-self, but essentially relates itself to it through itself; it is therefore its *own end* [*Selbstzweck*] and the *urge* to realize it; but for this very reason the subject does not possess objectivity in an immediate manner, for if it did it would be merely the totality of the object as such lost in objectivity; on the contrary, objectivity is the realization of the end, an objectivity *posited* by the activity of the end, an objectivity which, as *positedness*, possesses its subsistence and its form only as permeated by its subject.[10]

The Idea takes the form of the subject of an absolute judgment. The subject of a sentence is what appears as something, the "in-itself" that appears "for-consciousness." However, it is posited as "in-itself" from the standpoint of its "being-for-consciousness." Thus, the "in-itself" changes every time the object "for-consciousness" does so since the object "for-consciousness" is the only point of contact with it. Due to this Hegel here calls it a self-related negative unity. It is negative because it has no particular content. Its content is always in the process of being determined by the object "for-consciousness." It nonetheless gives unity insofar as it holds together the movement of the object for consciousness, its alterations in experience. And it is self-related because the object "in-itself" is a shadow of the object "for-consciousness." Insofar as the former is posited by the latter, they are the same object, merely in a permanent process of differentiating itself. For this reason the end is its own, even though it posits it as distinct from itself. The Idea consists of the urge to realize the end. It cannot be one with its end in an immediate manner; nor can it be one with its end in the sense of total realization or total congruence. Hegel goes on to assert that *objectivity is the realization of the end*. However, this should not be taken to mean total realization. The next sentence shows us why. Objectivity is posited by the activity of the end. It is the end *as* activity (*Tätigkeit*) that produces objectivity. This activity means the process of striving toward the goal, not the result of reaching it in the sense of complete fulfillment. Otherwise, there would be no eternal creation and eternal overcoming. The *most stubborn opposition*, and with it the Idea, would dissolve. Objectivity is *permeated by its subject*. This gives it its subsistence and form. Objectivity is not the endpoint of a process. Rather, we are *always already* in its midst. The subject has been determined as being constituted by an element of striving, by a permanent process of self-determination (since it posits its own ends) in self-differentiation (since it always posits its ends as to be striven for). This makes it free.

Following the element of *stubborn opposition* with which the Idea has been characterized, the three Ideas Hegel lays out in this section-life, the true and the good-should be taken as paradigmatic cases of such an opposition. We shall not deal with the Idea of life due to the limitations it is subject to: it is not self-determining and therefore not free. We have emphasized above the difference Hegel establishes between organic or natural processes, on the one hand, and spiritual processes, on the other. An outcome of this is that organic beings are not properly teleological for Hegel.

Both the Idea of the true and that of the good are characterized by being urges or drives (*Triebe*). The permanent character of these drives, the fact that they are never totally realized—in the sense of complete realization or total congruence—is what constitutes them as Ideas: they are *the most stubborn opposition*. In the *Encyclopaedia* Hegel describes them in the following manner:

> [To start with, there is the movement] to sublate the one-sidedness of the *subjectivity* of the Idea by means of the assumption of the world that [simply] is into oneself, into subjective representing and thinking; and to fill the abstract certainty of oneself with this objectivity (which thus counts as genuine) as its *content*. And, conversely, [there is the movement] to sublate the *one-sidedness* of the objective

> world, which therefore counts, on the contrary, only as a *semblance*, a collection of contingencies and of shapes which are in—themselves null and void—[the movement] to determine this world through the *inwardness* of the subjective, which here counts as what is truly objective, and to in-form it with this subjectivity. The first movement is the drive of knowing toward truth, or *cognition as such*—the *theoretical* activity of the Idea—the second is the drive of the *good* toward its own accomplishment—*willing*, the *practical* activity of the Idea.[11]

The "in-itself," presupposed as independent of our knowledge of it, of its "being-for-consciousness," was revealed to be posited by our knowledge. An independent "in-itself" is the result of knowledge, not its presupposition. Only because we know something as something does the "in-itself" exist in its being posited in the form of the first *something*: the *something* we know as something. This gap between the "in-itself" and the "for-itself" is not overcome through the experience of natural consciousness described in the *Phenomenology*. It is merely internalized within Thinking itself. Therefore, there is also development and movement in the *Science of Logic*, which takes the standpoint of pure Thinking. Within Thinking itself there is a *stubborn opposition* between what is being thought and that as which it is being thought. The fact that what is being thought are now concepts does not mean that what they *appear as* to thinking disappears and we grasp them in their immediacy. In the *Science of Logic* there is also the permanent experience of believing (*meinen*) something that, then, turns out not to be the case. There is never a total collapse between the concept that is thought and that as which it is thought. This distinction is precisely the gap that Hegel now underlines as the *most stubborn opposition*, which characterizes the *drive of knowing toward truth*.

In the case of the good, the opposition consists in what ought to be done in contrast to what is done. What ought to be done disappears as *ought* the moment it is done. To totally realize the ought is to do away with it. And humans cannot live without an ought. If they always did what they ought to do there would be no ought. Put more strongly, there would be no humanity since a distinctive characteristic of humans is the capacity to do otherwise. Without the opposition of the ought to the is there would be no striving and thus no self-determination. The freedom of human beings lies in their being finite, in the stubborn opposition they live in between what they do and what they ought to do. Hegel is trying to do away with any type of moral a priori. This does not mean that he advocates a moral relativism, but rather that the moment one does not accept the *possibility* of having acted wrongly, one will lose one's humanity. This is similar to what was encountered above concerning the fear of error in the quest for knowledge. Hegel asks if the fear to err is not itself the error. With this he does not mean that if we do not fear we will not err, but rather that only by erring will we reach the true. Theunissen points in the same direction by asserting that the true only appears in the unmasking as untrue of what was held to be true. The point, when applied to practical philosophy, is that to have the certainty of doing what ought to be done is to step beyond the boundaries of what it is to be human. Human experience in terms of both the quest for the true and the quest for the good consists in the constant realization that things are other than they are believed to be. Dogmatism in both of these spheres stands in total opposition to human experience, and as such is to be avoided. It undermines the drives that make us human. One should add that the complementary aspect of the fact that human experience consists in this constant hitting up against *stubborn oppositions* is that humans cannot cease positing beliefs about the true and the ought. They cannot be belief-less since to believe is equivalent to striving toward something, and human beings determine themselves in their striving. Without this striving they would not be self-determining and free.[12] This is why skepticism is a "paralysis" for Hegel, an "incapacity for truth." It is incapable of taking up the task, so to speak, of living in permanent opposition, and rather takes refuge in a, for Hegel, non-human state of *ataraxia* or mental tranquility.

5.3.1 The Idea of the true

In Chapters 1 and 2 above, the topics of the true and of the good were separately dealt with. In the section on the Idea, however, Hegel brings them together and establishes a development leading from the Idea of the true to that of the good in the attempt to overcome the limitations encountered in the former. He describes the shortcoming of the Idea of the true as follows:

> But this subject matter of the Notion is not adequate to it; for the Notion does not come to be the *unity of itself with itself in its subject matter or its reality*; in necessity its identity is for it; but in this identity the necessity is not itself the *determinateness,* but appears as a matter external to the identity, that is, as a matter not determined by the Notion, a matter, therefore, in which the Notion does not cognize itself. Thus in general the Notion is not for itself, is not at the same time determined in and for itself according to its unity. Hence in this

> cognition the Idea still falls short of truth on account of the inadequacy of the subject matter to the subjective Notion.[13]

It is surprising to find such a description of the limited character of knowledge due to the externality of its object in the final pages of the *Science of Logic*. One would have thought that such oppositions had long been overcome (perhaps already in the *Phenomenology of Spirit*). However, Hegel comes back to this opposition between cognizing subject and cognized world at the level of the Idea of the true. This reveals how *stubborn* the opposition really is. The opposition between knower and known, subject and object, and so on, is never totally overcome. The fact that the latter is revealed to be posited by the former merely internalizes the opposition without dissolving it; it reveals the posited character of the externality that had previously been presupposed. Nonetheless, there is still externality. This is the constitutive—and thus impossible to overcome—nature of knowledge: the opposition between what is known and what it is known as. Knowledge must be knowledge *of* something; what is known must be known *as* something, regardless of it being proclaimed by natural consciousness or by pure thinking itself (philosophy). The quest for the true is one of the two drives that constitute human nature. The moment they were to be satisfied we would cease being human. Thus, the processes described in the *Phenomenology* and the *Science of Logic* have not brought us one step closer to overcoming the opposition between subject and object; they have just shed light on how it is constituted. This may serve as another example of the seriousness with which one should take Hegel's claim about the circularity of the process being exhibited. This being said, there is still for Hegel some sense of progress at work here, which will lead to the Idea of the good in order to overcome the opposition encountered in the Idea of the true.

5.3.2 The Idea of the good

The oppositional character of the quest for the true will be overcome by the will insofar as the will penetrates what stands in opposition to knowledge and determines it according to its end. In the Idea of the good we encounter the overcoming of the oppositional nature of knowledge. The Idea of the good, here characterized as the subjective concept, is: "the urge to realize itself, the end that wills by means of itself to give itself objectivity and to realize itself in the objective world."[14] It seems to overcome the opposition the subject suffers from the objective world insofar as it acts in and on it, determining it in its acting. However, even in the Idea of the good the independence of this objective world is not totally overcome. Hegel offers a couple of reasons for this:

> The realized good is good by virtue of what it already is in the subjective end, in its Idea; realization gives it an external existence; but since this existence is determined merely as an intrinsically worthless externality, in it the good has only attained a contingent, destructible existence, not a realization corresponding to its Idea. Further, since in respect of its content the good is restricted, there are several kinds of good; good in its concrete existence is not only subject to destruction by external contingency and by evil, but by the collision and conflict of the good itself. From the side of the objective world presupposed for it, in the presupposition of which the subjectivity and finitude of the good consists, and which as a different world goes its own way, the very realization of the good is exposed to obstacles, obstacles which may indeed even be insurmountable. In this way, the good remains an *ought-to-be*; it is *in and for itself*, but *being*, as the ultimate abstract immediacy, remains *also* confronting it in the form of a *not-being*. The Idea of the realized good is, it is true, an *absolute postulate*, but it is no more than a postulate, that is, the absolute afflicted with the determinateness of subjectivity. There are still two worlds in opposition, one a realm of subjectivity in the pure regions of transparent thought, the other a realm of objectivity in the element of an externally manifold actuality that is an undisclosed realm of darkness.[15]

The Idea of the good is not capable of overcoming the *stubborn opposition* originating in the drive of knowing toward truth. On the one hand, any supposed realization of the Idea of the good, that is, its coming into existence, is bound to be *contingent* and *destructible*. This follows logically from the concept itself of *existence*, which necessarily implies externality and contingency. This reasoning goes beyond that found in the critique of the duality is/ought. There it was shown that the moment the ought is (comes into existence) it ceases being the ought. Hegel's point here is that the ought can never come into existence since the moment it did it would be subject to the contingency that constitutes existence. A good act is bound to come up against existence and be absorbed into its arbitrary and unexpected chain of events. This would undo it as a good act.[16] To avoid the possibility of this moral undoing would lead to total inactivity. One would cease to have any point of contact with existence since one would immediately be stained by reality and its complications. This is the ground for Hegel's critique of the beautiful soul in the *Phenomenology*. Thus, any meaningful concept of the good, must have a particular content, must be embedded in a particular set of conditions. If this is accepted then it follows that there are other possible goods that could address this set of conditions. One ends up with a *collision and conflict* between *several kinds of good.* In other words, the moment the good acquires content it assumes a standpoint that, as such, immediately presupposes other standpoints in conflict with it. In the context of a situation demanding action, the good that ought to be done is contingent upon the particular standpoint from which the situation is assessed.

The Idea of the good is subject, then, to a double *stubborn opposition*: internal and external. Concerning the former, both the universalization and the particularization of the Idea of the good would undermine it. Its universalization or formalization would make it disappear, whereas its particularization would destroy it by splintering the strength of the ought into various conflicting precepts to act in different ways. Concerning the latter, as much as it has the capacity to alter and determine the world (existence), the Idea of the good will never be able to completely and transparently determine it and realize itself in it. The contingency of the world is always more than the good can ever completely determine according to its ends. This leads Hegel to call the realm of objectivity an "undisclosed realm of darkness." How can this reality be overcome and what would it mean to overcome it? Hegel says:

> But what is still lacking in the practical Idea is the moment of consciousness proper itself; namely, that the moment of actuality in the Notion should have attained on its own account the determination of *external being*. Another way of regarding this defect is that the *practical* Idea still lacks the moment of the *theoretical* Idea. That is to say, in the latter there stands on the side of the subjective Notion—the Notion that is in process of being intuited within itself by the Notion—only the determination of *universality*; cognition knows itself only as apprehension, as the identity—on its own account *indeterminate*—of the Notion with itself... For the practical Idea, on the contrary, this actuality, which at the same time confronts it as an insuperable limitation, ranks as something intrinsically worthless that must first receive its true determination and sole worth through the ends of the good. Hence it is only the will itself that stands in the way of the attainment of its goal, for it separates itself from cognition, and external reality for the will does not receive the form of a

true being; the Idea of the good can therefore find integration only in the Idea of the true.[17]

5.3.3 Overcoming the Idea of the good

Hegel's solution for overcoming the *stubborn opposition* encountered in the Idea of the good is to fall back on the Idea of the true. One can understand what this means more easily by going back to Chapter 2 above. In it the overcoming of the spurious infinite by means of the true infinite was shown to take place through a process of reflection on this spurious infinite. The text itself confirms the connection between the overcoming of the stubborn opposition encountered in the Idea of the good and the discussion on the bad and true infinite that occurs in the Doctrine of Being. In the next to last paragraph of the section on the Idea of the good Hegel comes back to vocabulary he had already used in the sections on Finitude and Infinity in the chapter on Determinate Being. He talks about "progress to the spurious infinity," "a merely *individual* act," and "reflection."[18] To posit the infinite as separate from the finite is to place it in an unreachable beyond where the attempt to reach it leads to an endless *one after another.* Each *fresh act* attempts to reach the infinite, only to come to the conclusion that it cannot be reached. It then starts the process anew with the next *fresh act.* This was the nature of the "spurious infinity." What was needed to overcome this constant frustration and disappointment was to realize that it was the concept itself of the infinite that made it unreachable. The infinite cannot be reached without being destroyed. Thus, to realize that this is the case, to reflect on the structure itself of the infinite, means to leave behind the individuality of each fresh act and to take in the totality of the structure of the infinite. The infinite is reached precisely by means of the fact that it is posited as unreachable. The move, therefore, that overcomes this impasse and leads to the true infinite is a theoretical one. It is a matter of reflecting on the structure of the infinite, of "[being] aware of what one is saying in order to find the determination of the infinite in the finite."[19]

This procedure also applies to the concept of the ought or the Idea of the good. When a particular ought is taken in an isolated manner, its non-realization—due to the structure itself of the ought and to the *dark* nature of objectivity—leads nowhere. One merely encounters another *fresh* unrealizable ought also taken in an isolated manner, and so on *ad infinitum*. Each ought is a fresh act and each non-realization of an ought leads to an isolated experience of the finitude of humans and their impotence with respect to realizing their ends in the objective world. However, to reflect on the concept of the ought or on the Idea of the good leads to the realization that it is the nature itself of the ought not to be realized. Therefore, it fulfills its nature in its not being realized, in its being striven for. One can play on the double meaning of the English word *realization* in order to understand what Hegel means. To say that the ought cannot be *realized* is to say that it cannot be fulfilled, executed in existence or externality. However, to *realize that* this is the nature itself of the ought leads to a different sense of realization: the fulfillment of its own nature of being non-realizable in the first sense. The ought is realized due to the impossibility of realizing it. We have a movement from non-realization to realization in non-realization. The bridge between them is a second sense of realization: the realization *that this is the case*. Reflection plays this role for Hegel. This is why the Idea of the true leads beyond the stubborn opposition encountered in the Idea of the good. In the next to last paragraph of the section on the Idea of the good, before the section on the Absolute Idea, Hegel says:

> Now if it is supposed that the end of the good is after all not realized through this mediation, this signifies a relapse of the Notion to the standpoint occupied by it before its activity-the standpoint of an actuality determined as worthless and yet presupposed as real. This relapse, which becomes the progress to the spurious infinity, has its sole ground in the fact that in the sublating of that abstract reality this sublating is no less immediately forgotten, or it is forgotten that this reality is in fact already presupposed as an actuality that is intrinsically worthless and not objective. This repetition of the presupposition of the unrealized end after the actual realization of the end consequently assumes this character, that the *subjective bearing* of the objective Notion is reproduced and made perpetual, with the result that the *finitude* of the good in respect of its content as well as its form appears as the abiding truth, and its actualization appears always as a merely *individual* act, and not as a universal one. As a matter of fact this determinateness has sublated itself in the actualization of the good; what still *limits* the objective Notion is its own *view* of itself, which vanishes by reflection on what its actualization is *in itself*. Through this view it is only standing in its own way, and thus what it has to do is turn, not against an outer actuality, but against itself.[20]

In this passage Hegel makes use of the two senses of realization (*Ausführung*): the *unrealized end* uses the first sense, that is, the sense of non-fulfillment, non-execution in existence. The *actual realization of the end* uses the second sense, that is, the sense of fulfilling its own nature of being unrealizable. This second sense focuses on the struggle to realize an end or ought. The first negation Hegel mentions is that of the unrealizable nature of the ought: externality or otherness confronts it, negating it. The second negation negates this externality or otherness by showing that the concept itself *posits* this externality or otherness of the ought. By positing it the concept shows itself to be identical to itself, to include its other within it. It becomes a free concept. It no longer turns *against an outer actuality but against itself.* This means that the realization of the ought in the second sense does not lie in the subjugation and domination of the objective world by the subject or concept. It lies in the subject herself, in her struggle and striving to overcome the externality of the objective world. The ought is not accomplished by perfectly molding the objective world according to the subject's ends. It is accomplished in her striving to accomplish it, in her struggle to realize her ends.[21] The capacity to strive toward something is dependent on the subject herself, not on the malleable character of externality. In the *Encyclopaedia* Hegel says: "The accomplishing of the infinite purpose consists therefore only in sublating the illusion that it has not yet been accomplished."[22] Once again we find the two senses of realization or accomplishment (*Vollführung*). Humans think it has not been accomplished yet since their ends are not realized. However, it is the nature of human ends—of the ought—not to be realized. Thus, the *infinite purpose* is in fact accomplished. It is accomplished in the struggle to accomplish all ends and oughts posited by humans. One could object that the mere striving to realize the ought remains subjective and one-sided insofar as it does not realize it. Hegel himself acknowledges this objection: "In other words, the activity in the second premiss produces only a one-sided *being-for-self,* and its product therefore appears as something *subjective* and *individual,* and consequently the first presupposition is repeated in it."[23] The second premise consists in the negation of the non-realization of the ought, that is, in the realization of its non-realizable nature. However, the struggle to realize the ought does determine and alter externality. History, in Hegel's eyes, consists in the permanent clash and collision of the striving and struggle of humans to realize their self-posited ends. This reveals that the non-realized (first sense) nature of the ought does not leave the gap between concept and *external actuality* untouched. It removes this gap insofar as the struggle to realize the ought already alters and determines actuality, though not in the way it aims to.[24] The concept is actualized. This grants objectivity *a true being*. The concept lies, so to speak, on both sides of the divide:

both on the subjective side in the form of the ought that is to be realized and on the objective side in the form of an actuality altered by the struggle to realize such ought. This allows Hegel to assert:

> The individuality of the subject with which the subject was burdened by its presupposition, has vanished along with the presupposition; hence the subject now exists as *free, universal self-identity,* for which the objectivity of the Notion is a *given* objectivity *immediately to hand,* no less truly than the Subject knows itself as the Notion that is determined in and for itself.[25]

However, one should be careful not to understand this self-identity as a tautological A = A. Such tautological understanding would mean that the subject achieves what she posits as her ought in the objective world by altering and determining it according to her ends. We would then have a subject identical to the object that confronts her insofar as she confronts herself in the form of external actuality. Clear evidence of the fact that this is not what Hegel has in mind is the dominant place he assigns to the "cunning of reason." The self-identity Hegel ascribes to the subject should be understood following two steps. First, external actuality *is* altered and determined by the struggle of humans to realize their goals. This allows the world to be considered as a mirror of the subject. The world is not, however, altered by the realization or achievement of these goals but by the *struggle* to realize them. Thus, the mirror is rather distorted since it never accurately and transparently reflects the realized ends of humans. This is the nature of human experience: things turn out to be other than what one hopes for.

The second step is more controversial since a particular interpretation of it has given rise to a picture of Hegel as a conservative thinker, as upholder of the status quo. According to this picture, Hegel identifies actuality with reason. This is the literal wording of the famous sentence found in the Preface to the *Philosophy of Right*: "What is rational is actual and what is actual is rational."[26] The self-identity of the subject would consist in its embrace of whatever is actual. In this manner the dualities subject/object and is/ought would disappear within the unifying power of reason. It cannot be denied that at times Hegel's rhetoric serves as an accomplice to such a reading. For example, the last sentence in this section on the Idea of the good says:

> the actuality found as given is at the same time determined as the realized absolute end; but whereas in questing cognition this actuality

appeared merely as an objective world without the subjectivity of the Notion, here it appears as an objective world whose inner ground and actual subsistence is the Notion. This is the Absolute Idea.[27]

The original German does not have the expression *as given.* It merely says: "*Die vorgefundene Wirklichkeit ist zugleich...*" Nonetheless, it still seems to offer a passive acceptance by the subject of the actuality she encounters in the world. She not only takes it in but also determines it as her *realized absolute end.*

There are two points to be made against this reading. The first one has to do with the permanent nature of human striving, whereas the second one has to do with the concept of recollection (*Erinnerung*). *Fulfillment* or *realization* for Hegel does not have a connotation of finality, of reaching a certain point after a long struggle. It is rather a constant process in which the fulfillment is being permanently renewed. The stability achieved by fulfillment is that of its permanent renewal.[28] Given this understanding of the concept of fulfillment or realization, it is impossible to uphold a particular status quo as if it were the final, absolute end. The concept itself of *status quo* seems to dissolve into the permanent flux of different ends being striven for among different subjects. In the *Encyclopaedia* Hegel says:

> The good, the absolute good, fulfills itself eternally in the world, and the result is that it is already fulfilled in and for itself, and does not need to wait upon us for this to happen. This is the illusion in which we live, and at the same time it is this illusion alone that is the activating element upon which our interest in the world rests. It is within its own process that the Idea produces that illusion for itself; it posits an other confronting itself, and its action consists in sublating that illusion. Only from this error does the truth come forth, and herein lies our reconciliation with error and with finitude. Otherness or error, as sublated, is itself a necessary moment of the truth, which can only be in that it makes itself into its own result.[29]

If fulfillment had the sense of finality we would lose all interest in the world and cease being human. Humanity is determined for Hegel by its condition of constant struggling and striving. Only humans live split in permanent duality. Only for them does such a thing as an *ought* exist. This ought cannot be fulfilled in the sense of finality (first sense mentioned above). Humans live permanently in error and illusion, which determine them as humans since they are kept split within themselves between the dualities is/ought and being/seeming. To live in error and illusion does not mean to live blindly. It means to constantly have the experience that what was taken to be true is not true after all. This experience is the truth of humankind. Truth does not appear when all falsehood and illusion are unmasked. It appears in the constant unmasking of falsehood and illusion. We have to reconcile ourselves with error and finitude since truth comes forth only from error. This, however, does not mean that we should content ourselves with living in error. What makes us human is that we continue striving, we posit a new belief that such and such is true after having been shown that what we previously held as true was false.[30] Truth is not found. It makes itself. That out of which it makes itself can only be *otherness or error*. There is nothing else. Truth becomes. If this is so, then if it were to cease becoming, truth would cease to be. Therefore, for truth to exist it must require not only error and falsehood but also a constant supply of it. In this manner the becoming of truth never ceases. The permanence of truth is the permanence of its becoming; and this permanence has as its condition the permanence of falsehood and error; that is, the permanence of the human experience of being wrong. Under these conditions it would seem a rather complicated task to uphold the status quo.

If it is true that the actual is rational and the rational is actual, then there must be an element that unifies what is *as* rational. A present state of affairs is not just taken up as found and conferred the status of rational insofar as it is. If actuality is in a constant process of realization, then a present state of affairs cannot be taken up in isolation from the process out of which it resulted. Hegel has asserted: "The Idea is process," and "The True is the whole." To say that the actual is rational is to say that "what is" is to be understood as a necessary outcome or development. The unifying element that confers rationality on actuality is recollection (*Erinnerung*). This shows that the found character of actuality is, after all, not so much found (presupposed) as reconstructed (posited). There is an active process in ascribing meaning (and therefore necessity, according to Hegel) to actuality. It is not the case that it is rational because it is actual. Rather, it is rational because as actual it must be taken as the end of a process or development that necessarily led to it. And this process is reconstructed in recollection. This point in itself is not sufficient to stem the critique. Regardless of the reconstructed nature of the necessity and rationality of actuality, it is still taken as necessary and rational. However, the fact that the process that leads to actuality is reconstructed and not presupposed shows that the rationality of actuality lies in its being ascribed meaning.[31] The necessity of the process leading to actuality and of actuality as absolute end consists in the necessity of making sense of the whole. Actuality is then merely the point from which to look back over the whole. The necessity of actuality is not a moral necessity. It is a hermeneutic necessity, so to speak.[32] In order to make sense of who we are we have to see ourselves as the necessary outcome of our past experiences. What Hegel is saying is not that things had to happen the way they did. Rather, things had to happen the way they did *in order for us to* make sense of things the way we do. Hegel is not Leibniz. He is not establishing a theodicy in which all evil is assigned a necessary place for the furthering of the universal Good. This would assign a moral necessity to it. Let us recall the identity of absolute necessity and absolute contingency. Everything could have been absolutely otherwise. Nonetheless, it had to occur the way it did in order for the outcome to be what it was. A particular actuality could not have been reached by means of any process other than that by which it was reached since, then, this process would have determined a different outcome. A whole cannot remain the same whole if one of its parts changes.

To attempt to make sense of actuality by seeing it as a necessary outcome of a process posited in recollection is not equivalent to sanctifying actuality and upholding the status quo. On the contrary, it could actually work as the first step in a process of self-reflection that leads to a striving to change the conditions of actuality. There is no absolute standpoint, no God's-eye view from which to assert that actuality must be as it is. It is impossible to assert that this is the best of all possible worlds since the only standpoint there is is one internal to this world. And this world is in a permanent struggle to determine itself; each of its stages is a necessary consequence of the previous one. If this were not the case, we would not be able to make sense of it.

5.4 The absolute Idea

Let us now deal with the absolute Idea itself. We shall attempt to comprehend it by shedding light on the following three issues: (1) its lack of content; (2) the meaning of consummation (*Vollendung*) with regard to the absolute Idea; (3) the relation between totality and the absolute Idea.

5.4.1 Lack of content

The culmination of the *Science of Logic* is not a particular concept. The absolute Idea has no content since it consists in the process itself of thinking. It is the mirroring of itself that thinking encounters when it realizes that its object of thought is itself in the form of its own process of thinking. In other words, the absolute Idea consists in the realization that the true is the whole, or more exactly, that the true is the determination of the whole *as* a whole. The conclusion that the true is the whole amounts to the realization that the true is the process itself of positing particular objects of thought—concepts—as being true. Hegel says:

> the absolute Idea itself has issued into *an existence of its own*; but the nature of this its existence has shown itself to be this, that determinateness does not have the shape of a *content*, but exists wholly as *form*, and that accordingly the Idea is the absolutely *universal Idea*. Therefore what remains to be considered here is not a content as such, but the universal aspect of its form-that is, the *method*.[33]

Form can be understood as the manner in which the objects of thought are posited as what is true. It is the way in which *x* turns out to be *y* when thought through. The universal aspect of this form is the method. Method is the unfolding of the process of thinking that leads from one concept to the next guided only by the principle of non-contradiction.[34]

> The method is therefore to be recognized as the unrestrictedly universal, internal and external mode; and as the absolutely infinite force, to which no object, presenting itself as something external, remote from and independent of reason, could offer resistance or be of a particular nature in opposition to it, or could not be penetrated by it. It is therefore *soul and substance*, and anything whatever is comprehended and known in its truth only when it is *completely subjugated to the method*; it is the method proper to every subject matter because its activity is the Notion.[35]

One could argue that the method is directly connected to the principle of non-contradiction. It is described here in terms similar to those used in the Preface to the *Phenomenology* to describe the negative: "the tremendous power of the negative; it is the energy of thought, of the pure 'I.'"[36] What is the negative if not the principle of non-contradiction itself? It is that by means of which *x* is given identity through its differentiation from all others. Only because we think by means of the principle of non-contradiction can difference and opposition take place. This occurs in a double process, one external and one internal. The former process lies in the fact that something can only be itself by distinguishing itself from what it is not. A cannot be itself and ~A without losing its identity as A. However, it requires of this ~A in order to identify itself in opposition to it as A. If A is not to be an empty tautology that can only ascribe itself to itself, in which case it would not have identity since it would not be able to distinguish itself from any other thing that is identical to itself, then it must construct its identity in opposition to what it is not. This is only possible by means of the principle of non-contradiction. Only because A cannot be ~A simultaneously and in the same respect, is it possible to give it a particular content (establish differences) as A. If we did not follow the principle of non-contradiction then A would have the capacity of being all and everything else, disappearing thus in a sea of *in*-difference. There is also a process internal to A itself, which, spurred by human experience—either through thinking or acting—reveals that A is not what we thought it was. We are forced by experience to reveal as untrue what we had taken to be true. This also occurs by following the principle of non-contradiction. Without it, when A were revealed to actually be B, there would be no difference between A and B, and therefore everything would fall under A. Only by maintaining the principle of non-contradiction can something reveal itself to be other than what it was thought to be. Without this principle there would be no human experience, no development or movement in the process of thinking or acting. The principle of non-contradiction could be called then the soul, what moves a thinking and acting being, forcing her to take up different objects of thought and different actions in her process of thinking and acting.[37] The method is said to be *soul and substance*. The principle of non-contradiction is universal.

These two processes fall under the activity of understanding (*Verstand*). Hegel, nonetheless, goes a step further and reveals the connection between A and B, the processual character of human experience. Reason (*Vernunft*), as opposed to understanding, consists in the realization that, although A led to B both form part of the same process or development. Therefore, there is an identity running through A and B; there is something to which both A and B belong. This identity is the concept. To realize that what is true has a processual character is to realize that what is true is the concept. In the passage quoted above Hegel asserts that the activity of the method is the Concept. Therefore, with respect to the question of what is true, when confronted with human experience we are not led to a world of substances that always appear in different manifestations. Rather, we are led to think of concepts, of processes that are in constant development while simultaneously maintaining an identity throughout their development. This identity holds all differences together since it is constituted by them. This fact does not do away with the principle of non-contradiction. On the contrary, it is only possible by means of this principle since otherwise there would be no process. The differences that constitute the identity of a concept occur spread throughout time. Infinite objects are historical. The concept of the beautiful, for example, is constituted both by a classical sense of harmony and by a romantic sense of the infinite. This does not make it a contradictory concept, constituted by both simultaneously and in the same respect. What we understand by the beautiful now is a direct consequence of it having at one point been understood mainly as harmony, at another as the infinite. It can be explained as what it currently is only by taking these two elements as part of its process of development. Only as being constituted as a reaction to classicism and to romanticism at different moments can we make sense of the present concept of the beautiful.

This reveals that the principle of non-contradiction is never given up by Hegel, and more importantly, that it is a condition without which the process of thinking or human experience itself would not exist. It is its condition of possibility. This is the sense of Hegel's assertion that for something to be comprehended in its truth it needs to be *completely subjugated to the method*: completely, because it cannot be satisfied with the activity of the understanding. In its attempt to do so, it will be forced by experience itself or by its own thinking to go beyond objects or substances and think of what is true in terms of concepts or processes. The emphasis has shifted from being to becoming. To think in terms of objects or things is to hold form and matter apart, to believe that the principle of non-contradiction is a formal principle that should be externally filled with content. Hegel calls this the *universality of reflection* and opposes to it the *universality of the Idea*. The former can be connected to understanding, the latter to reason. In the latter the principle of non-contradiction is not merely subjective. It is objective insofar as "what is" is determined as concepts or processes. The emphasis is no longer on a fixed and stable content or matter; it is on the process. In other words, the content of "what is" is its process of becoming. The *substantiality of things* is their becoming—or their constantly having become—what they are. The method reveals this process of becoming of "what is" and the absolute idea is the movement of self-reflection of the method, the realization that the method reveals this unfolding. In the *Encyclopaedia* Hegel says:

> The last step is the insight that it is the whole unfolding that constitutes its content and its interest. Moreover, this is the philosophical

> perspective: that everything which, taken by itself, appears to be restricted gets its value by belonging to the whole and being a moment of the Idea. This is how we have had the content, and what we now have is the knowledge that the content is the living development of the Idea, and this simple looking back is contained in the form. Each of the stages considered so far is an image of the Absolute, but initially in a restricted way, and hence it drives itself on to the whole, whose unfolding is what we have called method.[38]

The absolute Idea is the self-consciousness of the method; that is, the realization that what is true does not lie in any particular object of thought. It does not even lie in the concepts of certain processes that are total explanatory systems (mechanism, chemism, or teleology). Only in the absolute Idea does thinking realize that what is true is the whole process leading to this particular realization. There is a double movement of reflection here. On the one hand, thinking realizes that what is true is not any particular concept posited as true and then revealed to be false, but the whole process of positing concepts as what is true. On the other hand, to realize that what is true is a process is to reach the self-reflective moment of having its own activity as its object of thought. The moment of consciousness of the process and that of the self-consciousness of the activity of thinking are one and the same. The content of the absolute Idea is itself, its own activity of thinking: "the Idea is the Concept of the Idea."[39]

5.4.2 Consummation (*Vollendung*)

There is a qualitative break between the absolute Idea and everything that preceded it. In the Doctrines of Being and of Essence the objects of thought were objective concepts (concepts of objects). In the Doctrine of the Notion the objects of thought were concepts of processes, not of objects (concepts of concepts, to follow the parallel). Life, the True and the Good were concepts of processes, of systems of explanation, and as such, exemplifications of Hegel's concept of concept. Nonetheless, they were still objects of thought. Now, with the absolute Idea, the object of thought is the process of thinking itself that has led from the concept of Being to the Idea of the Good. The object of thought is *the whole unfolding*, not any of its particular moments. And since it has been the activity of thinking that has been thinking all of its objects of thought, the object of thought in the absolute Idea turns out to be itself in its activity of thinking. Hegel says: "As a result the Science [of Logic] concludes by grasping the Concept of itself as the Concept of the pure

Idea for which the Idea is"[40] and "But in the Idea of absolute cognition the Notion has become the Idea's own content."[41] The fact that there is a qualitative break does not mean that the process has come to an end. This would imply the end of thinking itself. This issue brings us to the second point concerning the absolute Idea: the issue of consummation (*Vollendung*). According to this reading, what could it mean for Hegel to talk about an advance that at a certain point reaches its consummation? He says:

> Hence the advance is not a kind of superfluity; this it would be if that with which the beginning is made were in truth already the absolute; the advance consists rather in the universal determining itself and being for itself the universal, that is, equally an individual and a subject. Only in its consummation is it the absolute.[42]

It would seem that there is a sort of advance that reaches a point of consummation or completion, after which all concept of *advance* would become idle.[43] Following the point made above concerning the lack of content of the absolute Idea completion cannot mean that all possible objects of thought have been exposed. It was shown above that the method was the unfolding of the activity of thinking and that consciousness of it presupposed a self-reflective act on behalf of thinking concerning its own activity. If this is the case then the consummation or completion reached lies in the act of self-reflection of thinking concerning its own activity.[44] This is supported by Hegel's assertion, quoted above, according to which: "The last step is the insight that it is the whole unfolding that constitutes its content and its interest." Consummation is a matter of insight, of reflection concerning the whole, and thus of self-reflection concerning itself. To reach a point at which one achieves self-reflection does not mean to stop reflecting on—positing—particular objects of thought. To come to the realization that the true is the whole is not an endpoint in the search for the true. *The whole* is not a particular content comparable to any of the concepts previously dealt with, which now fills in the empty space of the function: "the true is ( )." It is rather the realization about how the search for the true works. The whole does not reach an endpoint when it is posited. It is completed only insofar as it is reflected on. In this sense its completion is its being posited. It is not completed in the sense of having gone through all of its parts. The qualitative break mentioned above concerning the absolute Idea reveals that only now is the whole revealed as whole. However, this does not bring it to a standstill. It does not once and for all fix the parts constituting it. The absolute Idea is the insight of the whole unfold*ing*, not unfold*ed*. The whole that is the true does not have a determinate number of parts constituting it since it is in constant movement and development. This explains the talk of eternal division, distinction, creation and vitality encountered in the *Encyclopaedia*:

> it is the Idea itself which is the dialectic which eternally divides and distinguishes what is self-identical from what is differentiated, the subjective from the objective, the finite from the infinite, the soul from the body. Only in this way is the Idea eternal creation, eternal vitality and eternal Spirit. While the Idea itself is this passing-over or rather self-translation into the *abstract understanding*, it is also eternally *reason*.[45]

That the Idea is *reason* means that it sees itself as a whole and that it therefore attempts to make sense of all of its parts. That it is *eternally* reason means that the moment it sees itself as a whole it will always remain a whole. However, at the same time, it *eternally divides and distinguishes*. It is *passing-over* and *self-translation into the abstract understanding*. This means that the parts constituting the whole are always different since understanding is always in the process of positing *x*, *y*, and so forth as true. Understanding permanently negates and differentiates. Thus, the whole is also always different depending on the parts posited by understanding. That it is *eternally reason* gives the sense of completion of the absolute. That it *eternally divides and distinguishes* gives the sense of its non-completion. This reading of the assertion that *the True is the whole* and that the *absolute is consummation* has its parallel with regard to the good when Hegel asserts that *the final purpose of the world is just as much accomplished as it is eternally accomplishing itself*. Thus, we have a reading of the absolute Idea that is mirrored both in the Idea of the true and in that of the good. In neither of them does completion mean an endpoint. For this reason they are called *the most stubborn oppositions*. They are never overcome.[46]

5.4.3 Totality

Let us deal with the concept of totality and how it should be understood following the interpretive line offered in the course of this work. The function of this concept consists in avoiding the epistemological problems of accounting for truth on the basis of a separation between subject and object, mind and world. If they are posited as separate, how can truth take place when it is understood as correspondence? The concept of totality attempts to avoid any type of strict duality, which would make problematic any relation between the two parts. An objection to this concept of totality concerns its objectivity: if there is no external object, what then works as the ground for the objectivity of knowledge? Kant's transcendental philosophy still held on to an ambiguous concept of a thing-in-itself that supplies the understanding with some type of content: it must be external to us, yet simultaneously related to us. Jacobi's famous remark already reveals this fundamental ambiguity. How can one account for objectivity within a totality? How does one avoid falling into dogmatism or coherentism, both of which seem to have nothing but themselves to rely on when attempting to demonstrate their objectivity? Hegel wants to avoid, on the one hand, both empiricism with its belief in the objectivity of the world in the form of sense impressions, and dogmatism/coherentism with itself as its only guarantor of objectivity;[47] and on the other, skepticism: a renunciation of the search for truth and, therefore, of philosophy. Hegel steers between these three poles by means of a triple movement. He avoids the first pole by revealing the posited character of the true: what is determined as true is not given but posited as true. Consciousness has an active role in determining what it takes to be true. "What is" has a constructed character insofar as it is determined by the activity of thinking.[48] He avoids the second pole by showing the tremendous power of the negative: how what is posited as true always ends up revealing itself to be other. This is what feeds the process of human experience. It also avoids any type of dogmatism. What is true reveals itself only in the shadow of what is unmasked as untrue; and it reveals itself as what replaces the untrue. What distinguishes this position from skepticism? Skepticism renounces the search for what is true, and in its state of *ataraxia* challenges any type of progress or development. It ends up being an upholder of the status quo. In the confrontation with skepticism we encounter the third step. This will give an answer to the question of how, if all assertions are equally valid, the Science that comes on the scene will be able to show itself to be true. It is the only *bare assertion* that does not posit a particular object of thought—be it an object or a concept—as true, and is therefore not subject to being revealed as false by human experience or the process of thinking. A process that includes all of its prior moments within it (all of which at a certain point have been negated) cannot be false.[49] Rather, it continues developing after each particular experience of untruth, which, as such, now forms a part of it. This is the meaning of the assertion that *the True is the whole*. The *Science of Logic* is the only Science that reaches this conclusion, and therefore it is the Science that comes on the scene in the *Phenomenology*, and in its development proves to be what it claims to be. There is nothing left outside of it since it is constituted by the whole process of human experience in the search for what is true, for the absolute. As such, it is a totality immune to being revealed as untrue. Only particular positings within it are revealed to be untrue. The totality is always true insofar as it can always account for each particular part that has been negated, by revealing its place within the totality, that is, by revealing both what it was a reaction to (what preceded it) and what it was in turn negated by (what followed it). The totality, insofar as it is always a totality, is always *accomplished*; whereas insofar as there is always a process of differentiation and negation occurring within it, it is *eternally accomplishing itself*.

The "tremendous power"[50] of the negative consists in its power to dissolve any particular positing, to break down any dogmatic position. In this manner, it maintains the movement that exists between the poles of being and seeming (search for the true), on the one hand, and of the is and the ought (search for the good), on the other. Hegel has determined the source of this movement as the *most stubborn opposition*.

A totality can be determined as such only from its endpoint. There can be no totality projected from a starting point since it could not enclose the non-existent or unknown. On the contrary, the endpoint encloses everything that has preceded it. Philosophical activity, therefore, is constituted in a "looking back," as Hegel asserts in the Preface to the *Philosophy of Right*. Philosophy has nothing to do with projection toward the future insofar as its activity is to determine "what is" by ascribing meaning to it and determining how it has become. To ascribe meaning in terms of the future is the most arbitrary and dogmatic of acts. "What is" cannot be justified by means of what will be insofar as what will be lies beyond the limits of humankind. This would be equivalent to jumping into an abyss. Thus, the role of recollection in Hegel: it is only in recollection that a whole can be determined as such and meaning ascribed to it. The whole that philosophy deals with in the *Science of Logic* is that of its own activity. Only by looking back toward Parmenides, Heraclitus, and the other thinkers, and by attempting to show the necessity of all of the parts of its own activity in order to account for its own positing—its assertion that the true is the whole—is the whole constituted as such by means of the exposition of its development. Hegel says:

> In the absolute method the Notion *maintains* itself in its otherness, the universal in its particularization, in judgment and reality; at

> each stage of its further determination it raises the entire mass of its preceding content, and by its dialectical advance it not only does not lose anything or leave anything behind, but carries along with it all it has gained, and inwardly enriches and consolidates itself.[51]

A totality cannot leave anything behind. However, the act of *carrying* what it has gained is the same act of positing what it has gained. The retrospective act of recollection is one of positing *as* presupposed. This is why, as was said above, the beginning is in the end: only in the end can the beginning be posited as such, mediated as immediate, determined as indeterminate.

> It is in this manner that each step of the *advance* in the process of further determination, while getting further away from the indeterminate beginning is also *getting back nearer* to it, and that therefore, what at first sight may appear to be different, the retrogressive grounding of the beginning, and the *progressive further determining* of it, coincide and are the same. The method, which thus winds itself into a circle, cannot anticipate in a development in time that the beginning is, as such, already something derived.[52]

In this image of the circle we encounter once again Hegel's triple fight against empiricism, dogmatism, and skepticism. A straight line is constituted as a line from the start. There is no particular point at which it determines itself as a line (point of self-reflection). On the other hand, the circle is determined as such after being completed, after it encloses itself. Therefore, all of the parts constituting the circle are posited from that point of self-reflection. They are not given but rather posited in the self-reflective act of looking back and constituting the circle. This avoids the dangers of empiricism and the myth of the given. However, the circle does not end its movement when it is completed. It maintains itself in perpetual motion. Consummation (*Vollendung*) is not the endpoint of a process but rather a point of self-reflection. Due to this perpetual motion the parts constituting the circle will always be different, constituting a different circle throughout time. The constituting gaze that looks back will always be different since it will always occur from different standpoints spread throughout time. It is a historical gaze. This subjects it to the negative element of human experience by means of which what is held to be true or good turns out not to be so. This perpetual motion of the circle avoids any type of dogmatic assertion insofar as all assertions, subject as they are to time, are also subject to being falsified. To have closed the circle means to have reached historical self-consciousness, to have realized that the true and the good occur on a historical plane. They are constituted in time. If this is the case then we are always in truth since we are historical beings by nature. Truth is constantly being constituted and put into question. This constant character of the process confronts any skeptical position. There is truth because we as historical beings constitute it. The fact that it is constantly being revealed as untruth does not question its existence. It just reveals its historical character. The image of the circle is helpful since, after reaching the point of self-reflection, after the circle encloses itself, there will always be a circle, albeit, different at each moment. And the circle—or the whole—is the true. This can only be understood as a relativization of truth if one continues to work within the dichotomy relative/absolute. However, there is nothing outside this circle. There is nothing outside of time (or history). To be more precise, it makes no sense to talk of something outside the whole, outside time. It makes no sense to assert that we are located within a particular standpoint if it is not possible to jump out of this standpoint, into the absolute standpoint itself. We cannot jump out of the whole, just as we cannot jump over our own shadow.[53] This does not mean that there cannot be opposing or mutually exclusive standpoints. What it means is that the process of confrontation between them is not resolved by appealing to an external, objective point.[54] It can only be resolved internally within the whole.[55]

Another advantage of this image of the circle is that it avoids any criticism of the model of *infinite regress* or *vicious circle*. One is not led back in an infinite regress from ground to ground, or given to given, since all grounds or givens are posited as presupposed. The act itself of positing underlies all activity in the search for the true. To say that the beginning is in the end, that it is posited, might lead to a vicious circle: the beginning determines the end (as presupposed) while the end simultaneously determines the beginning (as posited). This is not a vicious circle since neither of them completely determines the other.[56] That we as human beings are determined by our past experiences is obvious. It is also obvious that we do not have a direct and immediate access to these past experiences, but rather reshape them in recollection according to our present experiences. Thus, our present experiences reshape our past and determine it. There is a simultaneous co-determination of beginning and end, the workings of which will never be completely and transparently unraveled since the process of co-determination never ceases.

> By virtue of the nature of the method just indicated, the science exhibits itself as a *circle* returning upon itself, the end being wound back into the beginning, the simple ground, by the mediation; this circle is moreover a *circle of circles*, for each individual member as ensouled by the method is reflected into itself, so that in returning into the beginning it is at the same time the beginning of a new member.[57]

A more appropriate image for the Hegelian system might be that of a spiral. The moment the first rotation, so to speak, is complete it determines the beginning and trajectory of the spiral in retrospect, in recollection. However, it does not reach an endpoint there but rather continues its movement, at each point of which the constitution of that 360° curve is different since it forms part of a spiral. At any point of the spiral after the completion of that first rotation, there is only one point that constitutes the whole by looking back and encompassing all previous points, which were themselves wholes at particular moments and are now reduced to being parts. The spiral never reaches an endpoint; it continues on indefinitely. It also continuously alters the constitution of all of the parts preceding it, including its beginning. There is nothing left outside it.

Concerning Hegel's own standpoint within the history of philosophy—the search for "what is"—a qualitative break is reached, although it is not equivalent to the endpoint of a process. It is rather the point at which the process reaches a consciousness of itself. The totality reached with Hegel's appearing on the scene and asserting that the true is the whole is the first, not the last, in the perpetual process of the determination of "what is". Hegel is the first to reach the absolute since he is the first to assert that it is the whole, rather than being this or that particular part, as had done all thinkers prior to him. The true is its becoming, and it never ceases to become. Hegel cannot and does not account for the future process of the becoming of the true. He does not know what particular positings will occur. He only knows that they form part of one and the same process, one and the same whole. Hegel occupies the blind spot without which there could be no truth. It is a spot that cannot be occupied by a particular content posited as true. Rather, this blind spot is constituted by time. Therefore, Hegel has reached the absolute insofar as he has revealed the temporality of truth. The truth of being is its becoming; in other words, *that* it becomes, not *what* it becomes, since what it becomes will always be different. With Hegel the system becomes conscious of its openness rather than reaching its point of closure.

The absolute idea is the point at which thinking reflects on its fractured nature. Through the absolute idea thinking realizes that the opposition it was to overcome both in the theoretical and the practical realm is constitutive of it. Human beings live in a fractured state that determines them as free. And they do so due to their temporal nature. This gives priority to becoming over being. It determines the place of truth to consist of concepts understood as processes. To be constituted as temporal means to always be subject to having one's beliefs falsified. It also amounts to always being subject to having one's acts determine unintended consequences. With the absolute idea this blind spot is revealed in the movement of self-reflection of thinking upon its own activity. To reveal it does not amount to overcoming it. It cannot be overcome since it constitutes us. Hegel situates himself within the history of Western thinking as the philosopher who revealed this blind spot, the temporal-historical character of humans. "What is" is constituted *insofar as* it is temporal. For this reason Hegel can include all prior thinkers as forming part of the true since the true *becomes*. This determines that the true is—and cannot but be—the whole.

* * * *

According to McDowell, Hegel resides on the coherentist side of the seesaw permanently oscillating between coherentism and the myth of the given, by collapsing the difference between "outside thinking" and "outside what is thinkable."[58] This is the rhetoric of Absolute Idealism that must be domesticated.[59] There is nothing outside what is thinkable. However, to save the independence and hardness of the world there is an other to thinking: being.

Hegel does not reject the independence of a reality lying outside thinking. He rather reveals the contradictory character of such a concept of reality. To think or refer to what is outside thinking is a performative contradiction: it already makes it thinkable. The only option is to think being *as* outside thinking. This is the structure of the "in-itself-for-consciousness" from the Introduction to the *Phenomenology*. Hegel does not deny reality its independence from thinking; what he does is deprive such a concept of any possible meaning. We cannot stand outside of ourselves and connect with reality in a pre-conceptual, prelinguistic manner. It would be equivalent to jumping over our own shadow. Therefore, the distinction McDowell wants to defend at all costs in order to save the friction necessary for the independence of reality is not a distinction Hegel collapses, allowing the waters of thinking to penetrate every corner of the universe. Rather, he simply shows that it is a distinction made by us and therefore internal to thinking itself. Hegel's position is more a comment on the limitations of being human, on the fact that we cannot inhabit God's viewpoint, the point of view from nowhere, and stand outside of ourselves experiencing being in its absolute independence. This point of view does not exist. How then does Hegel account for the friction needed in order not to lose contact with the world? Hegel's absolute idea is constituted by the ideas of the true and the good, and these in turn are riveted by the most stubborn opposition. We have seen how the opposition within the idea of the true between our knowledge and what it is about is overcome by the idea of the good and its aim of shaping the world according to our will. However, this leads in turn to the opposition within the idea of the good between what we will or intend and what in effect ends up happening. This opposition can only be overcome by returning to the idea of the true and becoming aware of the structure itself of these two ideas. The absolute idea amounts to this awareness. The stubbornness of our human experience always turning out to be different from what we originally thought, both in theory and in practice, provides the friction of the world for Hegel. We relate to the world in its independence insofar as we get it wrong. We would not get it wrong if it were not hard, pressing up against us. Hegel appeals to the everyday human experience of error to account for the friction that does not allow us to spin in a coherentist void without any contact with the world. We can only overcome the gap between mind and world by showing that there never was one to begin with, that we are always already in contact with the world. Knowledge as guarantor of the bridge between mind and world will lead to skepticism, precisely because of the separation it presupposes. This is what, according to Hegel, happens to Kant: he cannot assure that we get the world right because, despite renouncing knowledge of things in themselves, our knowledge of them as they affect us still requires some orderliness in the noumenal world determining the order in the appearances. Without this orderliness, the application of the categories of the understanding could always be different. Kant is stuck between either making things in themselves not so in themselves or making them absolutely irrelevant to our knowledge.[60] Due to the structure itself of the ideas of the true and of the good the gap between mind and world is revealed to be posited and not presupposed. However, Hegel avoids concluding with this that we get the world right. Instead of starting off with a gap and attempting to overcome it through knowledge, Hegel starts off with a unity of mind and world, and overcomes it through negativity, making this unity structurally fractured since mind and world never totally match. Hegel's emphasis on the negativity of human experience, the power of the negative, provides the friction necessary to avoid the pitfalls of dogmatism and coherentism. His philosophy does not describe the process of getting the world right. It describes the process of getting the world in our getting it wrong.

Conclusion

This book has offered an analysis of selected sections of the *Phenomenology* and the *Science of Logic* that would furnish the tools for a non-metaphysical interpretation of Hegelian philosophy. The concepts selected are of paramount importance since they serve as load-bearing walls for the whole edifice of his system: the object-in-itself-for-consciousness, the infinite, absolute necessity, rationality, and the absolute idea. Applying these tools, one encounters a system that is open instead of closed, developing instead of fully developed, teleological only in the sense of positing in retrospect the goal that accounts for actuality having become what it is. The identity between being and thinking for which Hegel admires the Greeks is grounded on difference. The necessity of the whole system stands precariously on itself, which makes it also absolutely contingent.

In contemporary philosophy one encounters a debate that consists in seeking how best to navigate the pitfalls of the myth of the given and of coherentism. On the one hand, we have the belief that there is a way the world is and that we would be capable of getting it right if only we could avoid interfering in its impingement on us and just take it in, so to speak. On the other hand, we have the belief that there are many ways the world could be insofar as there are many conceptual strategies to think or relate to it, and the criteria to choose among these different strategies or schemes lie within our belief systems themselves. In this case there would be no standpoint external to thinking (an extra-linguistic, causal space of perceptions) that could serve as secure foundation or ground for our knowledge. Thinkers such as Quine, Davidson, McDowell, and Brandom have all been entangled in this debate at different times, attempting to find a course between these dire straits.

The trenchant critique of givenness or immediacy offered in Hegelian philosophy already steers him clearly away from the shores of the myth of the given. The urgent task that would allow Hegel to be saved from the metaphysical dustbin of the history of philosophy would be to understand how he avoids running aground the other shore: that of a frictionless void where the difference between how things really stand and how they seem to us to stand cannot escape being determined by what merely seems to us. We would thus be inextricably caught within a web of beliefs that have lost all mooring with the hardness of the world.

Hegel appeals to the human experience of getting it wrong, in both our practical and theoretical relations to the world and others. The source of friction and anchoring to the world lies not in what is the case or what we get right, but rather in what is not the case or what we get wrong. In this consists the stubborn opposition of the ideas of the true and the good. The fact that our beliefs are shown to be wrong provides all the friction needed to avoid spinning in our web of beliefs. If the world were not more than our beliefs about it then we would never suffer the negativity of human experience. In the Preface to the *Phenomenology* Hegel describes Being as constituted by negativity. He says:

> But the life of Spirit is not the life that shrinks from death and keeps itself untouched by devastation, but rather the life that endures it and maintains itself in it. It wins its truth only when, in utter dismemberment, it finds itself. It is this power, not as something positive, which closes its eyes to the negative...Spirit is this power only by looking the negative in the face and tarrying with it. This tarrying with the negative is the magical power that converts it into being.[1]

To tarry with the negative means not to turn our backs on experience that contradicts our held beliefs but rather to stare the contradiction down and find a way to overcome it by asking for and giving reasons, by figuring out what our beliefs commit us to and what we are actually entitled to based on this new experience. The non-being that contradiction brings with it, which undermines our most tightly held beliefs, is transformed into being since it leads us to posit other beliefs that seem consistent with experience. However, this being does not amount to a positive object full of content since every object posited will in time be revealed to be false. Rather, it consists in the process of experience itself, through which the world in its hardness reveals itself to us by revealing what it is not, by our coming up short against it. In this context, "being" would mean rather "having been." "What is" is revealed in "what is no longer." Our knowledge of the world is shaped by what we held to be true but no longer do so. The truth of perception, for example, is that "what is" is *not* the immediacy of sense-certainty; that of force and understanding is that it is *neither* the immediacy of sense certainty *nor* the object of perception, and so forth. Error is the unending source of objectivity that allows Hegel to situate the world within our knowledge, as the shadow of our false beliefs, without reducing it to such knowledge since as false these beliefs point beyond themselves. "What is" lies just beyond what it has revealed itself not to be. This explains the importance of determinate negation in Hegelian philosophy: what something is not is fundamental for what it is, not merely because it makes it more explicit, but because *only* through what it is not can "what is" appear. Hegel says:

> In speculative [*begreifenden*] thinking…the negative belongs to the content itself, and is the *positive*, both as the *immanent* movement and determination of the content, and as the whole of the process. Looked at as a result, what emerges from this process is the *determinate* negative which is consequently a positive content as well.[2]

The negative not only belongs to the content as a part of it, but *is* the content itself since any posited content will in time be revealed not to hold in the face of experience, and as such will become part of the constitutive process of "what is" through what it has been, its *immanent movement and determination.*

Hegel's position does not lead to skepticism since the nothingness or negation is "a determinate nothingness, one that has a content." For skepticism belief cannot coexist with truth; they are mutually exclusive, and from the former we can never be certain about having reached the latter. Hegel shares with the skeptics the fact that we cannot leave the territory of the former. However, he positions truth within it through the concept of determinate negation. What is true does not lie beyond seeming or belief, but is rather constituted *in* these various particular positings, through their determinate negation. Experience will reveal them as what is not, not in contrast to "what is" but to the latest positing formed by this experience, to the new object (what *now* seems to us):

> We have here the same situation as the one discussed in regard to the relation between our exposition and skepticism, viz. that in every case the result of an untrue mode of knowledge must not be allowed to run away into an empty nothing, but must necessarily be grasped

> as the nothing *of that from which it results*—a result which contains what was true in the preceding knowledge.[3]

Falsehood can only be reached from a new belief or positing "held as true."[4] Thus, we are always in a "holding as true" whereas the skeptic seeks refuge in a seeming that has been revealed as seeming. She does not move but rather remains in her "certainty of self." She has given up on truth in order to reach tranquility.

To assert that human beliefs will always come up short against the world or others is not a claim about being but rather about time. Our temporality is the source of objectivity since its constant movement makes any claim subject to falsification, and error has been revealed to supply the hardness and friction needed to avoid losing the world. The material of truth can only be *error*. There is nothing else. Truth becomes. If it ceased becoming it would cease being. Therefore, for truth to exist there must be a constant supply of error: the never-ending human experience of getting it wrong.

This negative element of human experience offers a possible exploratory path through which to meet the second challenge raised by Horstmann to the current renaissance experienced by Hegelian philosophy: avoiding an epistemic relativism that Hegel certainly rejected.[5] The first challenge, that of offering a non-metaphysical interpretation of the *Science of Logic*, I hope to have met in the present study.

Notes

Introduction

1. This explicit turn toward Hegel on the part of analytic philosophy is not new. One could go back to the middle of the twentieth century to find analytic thinkers that, more implicitly in some cases, more explicitly in others, have struck a Hegelian chord. Both Quine and Sellars touched on issues that Hegel had already dealt with. In the seventies, Donald Davidson in his philosophical conversation with Quine also takes up a Hegelian position on the scheme/content dualism, albeit with no explicit reference to him. In using Davidson as a point of reference within which to frame certain Hegelian themes we will be focusing narrowly on some of his articles from that period. The views formed in his later development, regarding triangulation, for example, lie beyond its scope.
2. For a critique of this cherry-picking procedure see Horstmann (1999, 284–285): "Hegel's philosophical legacy consists in a very intricate combination of an impressive multitude of elements which in their entirety form one huge complex. To choose only some of these elements and to claim that just these constitute the philosophically important parts of his legacy means to have a very special notion of what could be done to a philosophical theory without changing its content so much that the theory has in fact been abandoned. I am not going to suggest that such a selective treatment of Hegel's philosophy is not possible in the sense that it might not lead to interesting results, all I am prepared to say is that such a treatment has its problems if it is supposed to be compatible with genuinely Hegelian philosophical aims." Horstmann (2006, 70) sets up two challenges to whomever takes this task upon herself: to make sense of the *Science of Logic* from the perspective of this non-metaphysical interpretation of Hegel, and to explain how this interpretation can avoid falling into an epistemic relativism, which Hegel himself "clearly repudiated." The following work attempts to take up the first task by focusing on the *Science of Logic* (except Chapter 1), and hint at the second by, in the final paragraphs of the Conclusion, offering a possible interpretation of negativity, to be explored in a later project, that would provide a response to skepticism and relativism.
3. For a reading of Hegel as a metaphysician following this definition of metaphysics, see Horstmann (2006, 71 ff.). Possibly one of the earliest readings of Hegel as a non-metaphysician is Hartmann (1972).
4. Two excellent books that tackle these issues are Redding (2007) and Nuzzo (2010).
5. For the contrary view according to which Hegel believes the *Science of Logic* to be a necessary a priori sequence, see Kolb (2010, 47–50).

6. In the Preface to the second edition, written in 1831, 15 years after the *Science of Logic* was finished, Hegel wishes to have been able to revise it 77 times, compared with Plato's seven revisions of the *Republic*, given that the whole described by him in his project includes an extra 2,000 years of "material."
7. Hegel's is not a claim to truth but a claim about claims to truth. The character of absoluteness of his absolute is structural; it does not regard content. Claims to truth cannot but be temporally anchored. However, the claim about the temporality of claims to truth, even though it appears with Hegel, becomes permanent because it reveals the necessary structure of any claim to truth: its being temporal.
8. Pinkard (2010, 102) makes a similar point: "The classical epistemological issues simply dissolve, yielding themselves to considerations of how it is that certain types of claims have come to exercise their hold on us and how those kinds of ways they exercised that hold on us themselves require a historical, developmental account of those norms."

1 The In-Itself-For-Consciousness

1. Hegel (1969, 759).
2. Davidson (1984a).
3. Davidson (1984a, 198).
4. Davidson (1983, 426).
5. Davidson (1984b, 200).
6. McDowell (1994).
7. Hegel (1977, 52).
8. Hegel (1977, 52).
9. Hegel (1977, 46).
10. Hegel (1977, 48).
11. Hegel (1977, 47–48).
12. Hegel (1977, 48).
13. Hegel (1977, 47). There is a problem in Miller's translation. Whereas in the German the subject of the second part is *das Wahre,* he translates it as "the truth." *Das Wahre* is not a noun per se, but rather an adjective turned into a noun. This would point toward an attempt to show that the absolute is not a beyond, absolutely independent of us, but is rather found in our midst. The absolute is not Truth, untouched by our attempts to grasp it; it is the true, what is determined as true. Hegel does not isolate the absolute from our constructions of "what is" by means of schemes. It is "with us, in and for itself, all along, and of its own volition" (Hegel, 1977, 47). Pinkard translates it as "the true" (http://terrypinkard.weebly.com/phenomenology-of-spirit-page.html). See Brockard (1970, 38 ff.).
14. The absolute would only need to be felt or intuited. See Hegel (1977, 4–5).
15. Reflection works by means of propositions. All propositions taken separately are one-sided. The absolute cannot be expressed by a proposition. Reason brings together opposing and contradictory propositions, thus being able to reveal the absolute. See Marx (1967, 22).
16. Hegel (1969, 93).

17. Hegel (1977, 47). Robert Solomon (1983, 298) draws an explicit parallel between cognition understood as instrument and as medium, and Kant's distinction between the two faculties of knowledge: understanding and sensibility. The fact that Kant mixes both metaphors just shows how his goal is to overcome the limitations of both rationalism and empiricism. Hegel's critique of Kant in what follows shows how he thinks Kant still stumbles on the metaphor of the medium due to the concept of the thing-in-itself. For this reason, in the *Encyclopaedia* Hegel sets together empiricism and critical philosophy as constituting the second position of thought with respect to objectivity: Hegel (1991, 76 ff.).
18. Hegel (1977, 47).
19. Hegel (1977, 47).
20. Hegel (1977, 47).
21. Hegel (1977, 49).
22. See Walker (1989 105 ff.).
23. Hegel (1977, 47).
24. Hegel (1969 (841, emphasis added).
25. Heidegger (1970, 64 ff. and 153 ff.) says that Hegel presupposes the absoluteness of the absolute, and criticizes him for doing so. It does not seem to be a fair criticism insofar as the absolute as it appears is meaningless; it has no absolute nature (its absoluteness). This nature will only construct itself. Thus, the basic step is the first one: that of presupposing the absolute. This is something one either does or does not. If one does, as is the case with Hegel, then one reaches the absoluteness of the absolute. One can also choose not to.
26. However, his own position can only be reached through the dogmatic attitude of positing specific truth claims in the form of the different figures of consciousness in the *Phenomenology*.
27. Possibility is understood here merely as the opposite of impossibility. However, by means of the activity of recollection, it will be assigned the character of *dynamis*, of an "in-itself" posited from the "for-itself" it is.
28. Hegel (1977, 123–126). See also Sextus Empiricus (1985, 31).
29. Hegel's self-understanding vis-à-vis skepticism distinguishes ancient from modern skepticism. Modern skepticism does not let go of its certainty regarding the sensuous or common sense. It is directed against thought, leaving reality unquestioned. What it is skeptical about is knowledge of the universals, of the absolute; whereas ancient skepticism held common sense and perception as devious. See Hegel (1985a). A consequence thereof is that for moderns the doubt feeding a skeptical position is merely a methodological step in order to guarantee the solidity of their certainty; whereas for ancients it is almost imposed on them by the things themselves, leading them rather to despair (Hegel, 1977, 49). Skepticism, through suspension of judgment, becomes a way to alleviate this despair in an attempt to reach mental tranquility (*ataraxia*). It concerns the whole of human experience rather than being a mere epistemological move. What Hegel criticizes from ancient skepticism is that in avoiding any assertion and preceding every opinion with an "it seems to me" it remains one-sided insofar as it maintains pure difference. It does not realize that reason, while continuously opposing itself, gives identity to this difference. Hegel's point is that the true does not lie beyond the "it seems to me" (the universal we are never quite sure

of in our subjectivity or particularity), but is constituted in these various particular positings. This shall not mean that any particular positing is equal to any other, falling thus into a purely relativistic situation, but rather that the criteria by which certain positings take precedence over others are in constant movement and will never be totally transparent to those in the act of positing. Truth is not an easy business, remaining in itself, waiting to be revealed unperturbed. The sceptic is aware of this. However, her response is to sacrifice its search in favor of tranquility, rather than to take on the task. "Skepticism is, in fact, such paralysis—an incapacity for truth which can only reach certainty of self, and not of the universal, remaining merely in the negative, and in individual self-consciousness" (Hegel, 1968, 329–330). For Michael Forster (1989), Hegel attempts to overcome the equipollence criticism raised by Sextus by showing how the absolute is not another one-sided position relativized by others but includes all opposition and therefore all claims within it. I am stressing Hegel's concept of an impermanent absolute that reveals itself as what it is in its non-correspondence to our knowledge, through error.

30. Hegel (1977, 49).
31. Hegel (1977, 49).
32. Hegel (1977, 50).
33. Hegel (1977, 47).
34. See Hegel (1977, 17): "We take up the movement of the whole from the point where the sublation of *existence* [*Dasein*] as such is no longer necessary."
35. Hegel (1978, 81).
36. Hegel (1977, 52).
37. Robert Pippin (1988, 102) describes this natural consciousness as "characterized by an internal dualism, a separation of subject and object" and relates it to a reflective consciousness characterized by such a dualism.
38. Hegel (1977, 50).
39. Hegel (1977, 56–57).
40. Reflection should be understood here in a simple manner: as a position of thinking, which not only believes in the total separation of subject and object, but also makes one-sided claims avoiding assigning contradictory attributes to one and the same object. These two characteristics are closely connected.
41. Marx describes the nature of natural consciousness as: "all the circumstances in the total situation which consciousness inhabits and which determine it. The natural consciousness 'exists' essentially in immediate unity with the total situation which at any given time dominates and determines it; it belongs thereto, although the situation may rank for it as a sphere of objecthood standing opposed to it" (Marx, 1975, 3). He emphasizes the presuppositional character of natural consciousness, the fact that taken in its immediacy at any given historical period consciousness is caught in myriad unchecked presuppositions that it must become conscious of in order to reach the true. He is aware of how, from a historical perspective, natural consciousness is not overcome.
42. It is the description of different types of conceptual strategies through which we think of the world as independent of our thinking of it (objective logic) and as determined in our thinking (subjective logic).

43. Heidegger (1970, 62–63) is also aware of the fact that natural consciousness should not be equated with a sensuous consciousness, and that it is not a historical consciousness but rather a philosophical one.
44. In paragraph 80 Hegel talks about the characteristic of consciousness of going beyond itself. What he has to say about this can be applied to its being incapable of accepting contradiction: "Thus consciousness suffers this violence at its own hands: it spoils its own limited satisfaction. When consciousness feels this violence, its anxiety may well make it retreat from the truth, and strive to hold on to what it is in danger of losing. But it can find no peace. If it wishes to remain in a state of unthinking inertia, then thought troubles its thoughtlessness, and its own unrest disturbs its inertia" (1977, 51).
45. The *this* cannot be the most concrete particular and an abstract universal simultaneously; the *thing* cannot be an exclusive one and a multiplicity of attributes simultaneously.
46. Hegel (1977, 51).
47. Hegel (1977, 51).
48. This goes against Flay's reading of the "natural attitude" with which the *Phenomenology* begins. He says: "In the unreflectiveness of this attitude there is no conscious distinction between self and world, nor between physical facts and events and institutional facts and events within that world… the naïve realism of sense-certainty is completely unreflective in its approach to the world" (1984, 14). However, in a footnote he does accept that "there is implicit in the naïve natural attitude the drive to reflection" (1984, 278); and a couple of pages later he states: "The only thing assumed is that an individual in the attitude of sense-certainty is willing to become reflective to the extent that he becomes aware of the nature of his attitude toward reality" (1984, 16). I would argue that natural consciousness, in the figure of sense-certainty, is already in a reflective state, albeit minimally and naïvely; that by pointing to the "this," it is already attempting to give an answer to the question about what is true. Without reflection there would be no question.
49. Hegel (1977, 52).
50. Hegel (1977, 52).
51. Hegel (1977, 47).
52. See Sellars (1997, Chapters I and VIII).
53. Hegel (1977, 52–53).
54. See Tugendhat (1986, 279): "Knowledge is a species of that intentional relation which is called belief [*meinen*], and belief involves a claim to truth in contrast to other intentional relations."
55. Hegel (1977, 52).
56. Hegel (1977, 53).
57. See Cramer (1978, 362–365).
58. As Heidegger puts it: "The true is the object 'for it'. Truth is the object 'for us'" (1970, 99).
59. See Tugendhat (1986, 279–283).
60. This is one of the reasons for the fleeting character of what sense certainty takes to be true. An object without any determination is ungraspable; it vanishes in the constant spatio-temporal flux.
61. Therefore, I do not agree with Cramer, who says: "*Soll 'Wissen' in der Perspektive des Bewußtseins interpretiert werden, scheint 'die bestimmte Seite dieses Beziehens'*

ganz ungeeignet, 'Wissen' zu definieren. Denn die formale Struktur gerade dieser 'Seite' am Bewußtsein erfüllen ebenso gut unsinnige Annahmen, leere oder bloße Meinungen, Glauben, Irrtum und Wahn" (1978, 364).

62. He says: "We say that someone not only believes but knows that something is the case if he not only claims that it is true, but (1) it also is true, and (2) he also can justify that it is true ... Second, if something like knowledge is intended here, the discrepancy between knowledge and mere belief that is characteristic for the reference to truth is overlooked; and this is connected to the fact that the *differentia specifica* of knowledge is overlooked, that is, the relation to justification that is fundamental for the reference to truth" (Tugendhat, 1986, 279–280).
63. Gadamer (1976, 88) takes this *Meinen* that appears in the *Science of Logic* to be limited to the beginning insofar as "we are still at the level of incipient thought." *Meinen* then shall vanish as soon as thinking gets started, so to speak. I do not agree with this view since the element of meaning something different from what is actually expressed accompanies the whole process of thinking exhibited in the *Science of Logic*. It is structural to thinking itself not to be able to achieve a complete self-transparency of what is being expressed in thinking (despite overcoming the external nature of its object in the *Phenomenology*). See Hegel (1969, 139 ff.), where *Denken* means to have reached the truth of the infinite, only to have it be revealed as a finite infinite. The German original reads: "ihn zum Bewußtseindarüberzubringen,daß, in dem er seine Befriedigung in der Versöhnung der Wahrheit erreicht zu haben *meint*, er in dem unversöhnten, unaufgelösten, absoluten Widerspruch sich befindet ..." (emphasis added). This example suggests that, in opposition to Gadamer's claim, the revealing of *meinen* as *meinen* is not merely limited to its first section concerning Being and Nothing. For a similar view, see Theunissen (1980, 83), where, as the subtitle of the book suggests, the *Science of Logic*, at least the objective logic, has a critical element to it, through which it unmasks the untruth, or the *meinen* character of Western thinking up to Hegel. See also Hösle (1988, 174), who also maintains a discrepancy within concepts to be what gives the *Science of Logic* its movement, although for him it is revealed in the discrepancy between what the concept means (*bedeutet*) and what it is.
64. Hegel (1969, 143).
65. Tugendhat (1986, 280).
66. Westphal (1998, fn. 35) is also critical of Tugendhat's interpretation of Hegel.
67. This is a concern shared by Cramer and Tugendhat.
68. Hegel actually takes a step further in the *Science of Logic* and asserts that the space where truth and falsehood occur is not the proposition but the syllogism, since the syllogism includes the justification of its claim. A proposition does not inhabit the logical space of reasons; a syllogism does. See Chapter 4 below.
69. Hegel (1977, 53).
70. Heidegger (1970, 94–96).
71. Pinkard's translation is more neutral: "Consciousness in itself provides its own standard" (http://terrypinkard.weebly.com/phenomenology-of-spirit-page.html).

72. Hegel (1977, 53).
73. For this distinction see especially the paragraphs in the chapter on Judgment (§166–§180) in Hegel (1991). See also Chapter 4 below.
74. Concerning the above talk of content of consciousness and concept of that content, these would correspond respectively to what is being termed "object for-consciousness" and "object in-itself."
75. See Sellars (1997, Chapter I). Theunissen (2002) proposes an understanding of the correspondence of object to concept as the condition of possibility for the correspondence of concept to object.
76. Hegel (1977, 54). "*Der Gegenstand scheint zwar für dasselbe nur so zu sein, wie es* ihn *weiß*" (emphasis added).
77. Hegel (1977, 54). "*Allein gerade darin, dass es überhaupt von einem Gegenstande weiß, ist schon der Unterschied vorhanden, daß ihm etwas daß Ansich, ein anderes Moment aber das Wissen oder das Sein des Gegenstandes für das Bewußtsein ist.*" Pinkard's translation acknowledges the preposition: "Yet precisely because consciousness itself has knowledge of an object, the distinction is already present, namely, that in its eyes something is the in-itself, but another moment is knowledge, that is, the being of the object for consciousness" (http://terrypinkard.weebly.com/phenomenology-of-spirit-page.html).
78. Hegel (1977, 53, emphasis added).
79. See §60–62, 65 and 66 of the Preface to the *Phenomenology*, where Hegel touches on the subject/predicate distinction, and note 63 above. Westphal (1998, 87 ff.), gives a more complex analysis of this distinction by adding to the above established "object to consciousness" and "object for consciousness" an "object itself" and an "object according to consciousness." However, the former plays no possible role given its conceptual impossibility, whereas the latter cannot, in my opinion, be distinguished from the "object to consciousness" since "naïve realism" precisely believes that its conception of the in itself, as opposed to its knowledge of it, is the in itself. Westphal seems to think that this four-fold distinction is what makes possible the internal self-criticism of the different forms of consciousness. In my opinion, this self-critical position can already be achieved by the simple distinction between "object to consciousness" and "object for consciousness" since the gap it structures forces it into a permanent self-critical mode due to the negative character of the experience of consciousness, disallowing any possible coincidence between the world and our conception of it.
80. This image of the shadow is taken from Longuenesse (2007, 20).
81. Hegel (1977, 54).
82. Hegel (1977, 54).
83. "The Subject is assumed as a fixed point to which, as their support, the predicates are affixed by a movement belonging to the knower of this Subject, and which is not regarded as belonging to the fixed point itself; yet it is only through this movement that the content could be represented as Subject. The way in which this movement has been brought about is such that it cannot belong to the fixed point; yet, after this point has been presupposed, the nature of the movement cannot really be other than what it is, it can only be external. Hence, the mere anticipation that the Absolute is Subject is not only not the actuality of this Notion, but it even makes the actuality

impossible; for the anticipation posits the subject as an inert point, whereas the actuality is self-movement" (Hegel, 1977, 13).

84. One could object that there are multiple other relations to the table that appears to me as red, which sustain it all throughout the cognitive process: it is rectangular; it stands on the corner, I broke my forehead against it as a child, and so on. This is true. However, none of these constitute the essence of the table, without which it would cease to exist. Each of these attributes is falsifiable individually, but not all simultaneously, as Sellars says in (1997, 79): "For empirical knowledge, like its sophisticated extension, science, is rational, not because it has a foundation but because it is a self-correcting enterprise which can put any claim in jeopardy, though not all at once." The object is thus a projection from its attributes, constantly changing in the process of falsification of its attributes.
85. For a different reading of the nature of this second object see Brandom (2011, 10 ff.), where he asserts that the second object is not an in-itself, but an in-it-self-for-consciousness, that is, the first in-itself revealed as false, as merely for-consciousness. Following Brandom's own example, the first object would be "the stick is bent," whereas the second object would be "the stick is bent is false (for-us)." In my reading, the first object is "the bent stick is bent," whereas the second object would be "the straight stick is straight."
86. Theunissen (2002, 7).
87. Hegel (1977, 47).
88. Hegel (1977, 55).
89. "We learn by experience that we meant something other than we meant to mean" (Hegel, 1977, 39).
90. Kuhn (1962, 77) reaches a similar conclusion concerning the manner in which scientific investigation takes place: "the act of judgment that leads scientists to reject a previously accepted theory is always based upon more than a comparison of that theory with the world. The decision to reject one paradigm is always simultaneously the decision to accept another." Hegel's claim is somewhat more radical since he would doubt the very possibility of comparing a theory with *the world*.
91. Hegel (1977, 55).
92. Hegel (1977, 36).
93. A possible interpretation of the beginning of the *Science of Logic* is that it actually starts with becoming rather than being. Being and nothing would then be retrospectively posited presuppositions. For this interpretation see Gadamer (1976, 87–91).
94. (Hegel, 1977, 54–55). The latter part of the quote reads in German: "*und die Prüfung ist nicht nur eine Prüfung des Wissens, sondern auch ihres Maßstabes.*" Pinkard offers a more accurate translation: "and the examination is not merely an examination of knowledge but also that of the standard of knowledge" (http://terrypinkard.weebly.com/phenomenology-of-spirit-page.html).
95. Mention must be made of de Boer's work on the negative in Hegel since her understanding of absolute negativity as the development of what she calls the dialectical strand of tragedy, in opposition to the tragic strand (tragic negativity), offers an understanding of the role of negativity in the *Phenomenology* and the *Science of Logic* that stands in exact contrast to the one offered in this work. For de Boer absolute negativity amounts to the resolution of contrary

determinations. Therefore the sway of the negative turns out to be the sway of resolution, at least in Hegel's later works. See de Boer (2010, 2 ff.). In my understanding, absolute negativity is precisely our coming to terms with the impossibility of an absolute resolution that avoids further entanglement. It is one of the main goals of the present work to pave the way for an understanding of the negativity exhibited in the *Phenomenology* and the *Science of Logic* as tragic through and through.

96. For the ancient skeptic the revelation that our most tightly held beliefs about the world are countered by opposite, equally valid beliefs leads to despair. She emphasizes the element of pure difference given the variety of opinions held in all matters, the only response to which can be to bracket the desire to know: she merely reports her impressions of things at the moment. She does not realize that truth appears in the negative experience of revealing particular beliefs as false. In other words, the capacity to explain why our false beliefs are false requires that we be in contact with the truth, tracking it in its movement, always arriving late, so to speak. The skeptic starts from the presupposition that there is an objective and permanent world that seems to lie beyond the reach of our beliefs about it. Hegel's starting point is the impermanence of the world, its becoming. Therefore, the gap between our knowledge and the world, between conceptual scheme and content, is necessary because of this impermanence. As such, it is not a source of disturbance: we encounter the world as it is in itself insofar as it reveals itself as impermanent every time our knowledge attempts to grasp it; whereas for the skeptic the gap creates disturbance since her goal is the permanent, independent world. Her solution is to seek *ataraxia* by disengaging from the world and suspending belief. For Hegel, this retreat into subjectivity goes against one of the drives that constitutes us as human: our desire to know. In skepticism error keeps us from the truth, which is its opposite; for Hegel, we can only reach truth in error.

2 The True Infinite and the Idea of the Good

1. Hegel (1991, 152).
2. Hegel (1991, 152).
3. Derrida (2005).
4. Derrida (2005, 130).
5. For a redescription of this issue in the realm of anthropology see Peter Winch's confrontation with E.E. Evans-Pritchard and Alasdair McIntyre in (1964).
6. Derrida (2005, 148–149).
7. While expounding Hegelian philosophy as the epitome of a metaphysics of presence, Derrida admits that "within the limits of this continuum, breaks do occur, discontinuities regularly fissure and reorganize the theory of the sign... it would be more than foolish to erase the differences of these restructurations in order to produce a smooth, homogeneous, ahistorical, all-of-a-piece cloth, an ensemble of invariant and allegedly 'original' characteristics" (1982, 72).

8. (Derrida (2005, 149).
9. Derrida (2005, 191).
10. Rocio Zambrana, asserts that "the dialectic of the finite and the infinite in the Seinslogik is the first moment in the Logic when this metalogical standpoint is achieved" (2012, 217). The standpoint she refers to is the vantage point from which an account of account-giving is given in the final section of the *Logic*: the section on the Absolute Idea. It is no longer a matter of describing the specific conceptual strategies offered by philosophical thinking in its process of thinking what is, but rather portraying or giving an account of human beings as account-givers of "what is".
11. Hegel (1977, 100–1001).
12. Hegel (1969, 137–138).
13. Stephen Houlgate also acknowledges a difference of perspective between the two works instead of seeing them side by side on a continuum (2006, 162).
14. Probably the first commentator to interpret the *Science of Logic* in this manner was Klaus Hartmann. For him the text is a reconstruction of the major categories by which philosophy and science have attempted to grasp "what is real". For this reason what we have before us is a "categorial theory... philosophy devoid of existence claims" (1972, 110). As he says, in philosophy "there need be no metaphysics" (1972, 117).
15. This might sound rather paradoxical since the *Science of Logic* is supposed to be: "the exposition of God as he is in his eternal essence before the creation of nature and a finite mind" (Hegel, 1969, 50); that is, it should represent an ahistorical perspective. However, it is only when humans become conscious of their historical nature that they reach an ahistorical standpoint insofar as their historical nature will remain throughout time, becoming their *eternal essence*. In other words, the standpoint of the *Science of Logic* does not lie "outside of history," but rather in its dead center, where we finally realize that human beings cannot but be historical.
16. This "becoming conscious of itself" is not the step from consciousness to self-consciousness—insofar as here we would still be dealing with individual consciousnesses—but rather the endpoint of the whole *Phenomenology*: Spirit becoming conscious of itself as Spirit.
17. Pinkard makes a similar claim regarding Hegel's own view of the *Phenomenology* only a couple of years after its publication, He says: "It thus also began to seem to Hegel in Nuremberg that at most one would need only the first part of the *Phenomenology* to introduce the 'we,' after which it could be discarded in favor of a more purely "logical" investigation" (2000, 336). However, it seems that when writing the *Encyclopaedia* some years later, the position it occupied in the system would no longer be that of an introduction to it, but would rather be absorbed within "subjective spirit."
18. Kant (1965, Bxi–xii).
19. Hegel (1969, 74).
20. Hegel (1969, 50).
21. Hegel (1969, 50).
22. For a critique of such talk of being and nothing from the side of analytic philosophy, see Tugendhat (1992, 50–57). For a reply to this critique see Theunissen (1980, 95–115).

23. To objectify is here understood as *vergegenständlichen*: to reify. It does not mean to make objective, i.e. universally valid.
24. Hegel (1969, 119).
25. Hegel (1969, 124).
26. Hegel (1969, 123).
27. Hegel (1969, 133).
28. Such is the title of Fichte's book, *Die Bestimmung des Menschen* (*The Vocation of Man*).
29. The attempt here is to give a more satisfactory account of why Hegel introduces talk of the ought at this point than that offered by McTaggart: "Why then did Hegel use the word ought? I believe he did so because it gave him a chance of introducing an attack on the ethics of Kant and Fichte (G.L. I 142; Enc. 94). This was a temptation which he was never able to resist" (1964, 29).
30. Hegel (1969, 123).
31. Marcuse (1987, 53ff.) correctly emphasizes the importance of the concept of "determination" in order to understand what the finite means. However, since he does not link it to its other meaning as vocation, and through this, to the talk of man's determination/vocation, he merely emphasizes the limited element in the concept of determination without realizing how it already points toward the infinite through the element of vocation that takes part in it. I will touch upon this at length below.
32. Hegel (1969, 129).
33. A similar process occurs in the chapter on Perception in the *Phenomenology*: the contradiction it falls into while attempting to think what is as a thing with properties is due to the fact that it *posits* itself now as perceiving the attributes it then ascribes to the exclusive one, now as cutting off the attributes out there to form an exclusive one. The contradiction lies in its acting in such a way, in its own positing.
34. Hegel (1969, 130).
35. Hegel (1969, 129).
36. Hegel (1969, 129).
37. It is interesting to note that the point at which talk of *life* appears in the *Phenomenology* is when self-consciousness makes its appearance at the end of the chapter on "Force and the Understanding," the same self-consciousness that, a couple of pages later at the beginning of the chapter with the same title, is defined as desire (Hegel, 1977, 195). Desire is the reverse side of lack.
38. Appearing in this context, the concept of the finite will be one whose function is to bridge the passage from objects understood as relational, dependent on others ("something" and "other'), to beings that carry their self within them ("being-for-self" is the outcome of this section). This allows for the conceptualization of living beings. This reading of what the finite means in the *Science of Logic* goes against a reading such as Guyer (1979), who understands the passages on the finite as those in which the individual thing is revealed to be relational, and incapable of standing by itself, its claim to self-sufficiency leading to contradictory results. I do not deny the occurrence of this process in the chapter on Determinate Being, but I believe it occurs already in the passages dealing with determinate being, "something" and "other," while the step to the finite is one to a type of being qualitatively different from

that relational one described as a "something." The finite introduces a self-subsistent being that carries its telos within itself, as opposed to a "something." For readings similar to the one proposed in the following pages, see Theunissen (1980, 267–297, especially 279) and Houlgate (2006, 377–378).

39. The title of the section about to be analyzed is *The Immediacy of Finitude*.
40. The contradiction lies in determining "what is" as a constant coming-to-be and perishing, while simultaneously making its finite character permanent. In other words, to determine objects as finite is to ascribe them a permanent (and thus non-finite) character. The concept of the finite requires its own negation in order to say what it means (*meinen*), so to speak.
41. Hegel (1969, 130).
42. Hegel (1969, 130).
43. Hegel (1969, 130–131).
44. Hegel (1969, 131).
45. Hegel (1969, 135).
46. Hegel (1969, 134).
47. Hegel (1969, 132).
48. Hegel (1969, 132).
49. Hegel (1969, 132–133).
50. Hegel (1969, 135).
51. Hegel (1969, 136).
52. Hegel (1969, 134).
53. Hegel (1969, 133).
54. Hegel (1969, 136).
55. For Theunissen the concept of the finite, defined as concept and reality, soul and body, being separable, must be completed by showing their simultaneous correspondence. He says: "Nevertheless, Hegel approaches Plato's metaphysical dualism only in order to repel it. He also sublates the *ontological* notion of the truth of metaphysics mainly through the fact that he questions the opposition between truth and untruth. On closer inspection, finite reality, to wit, should also correspond to its notion in its non-correspondence. This is precisely what defines finitude: that it simultaneously corresponds and does not correspond to its notion. *All* finitude in Hegel is defined in this way, not only that of 'things,' which, regarding their mode of being, are in every respect separated—from their notion, from consciousness and from one another—but also that of subjective spirit, which still has not raised itself to the absolute" (2002, 15). This expanded, completed concept of the finite is precisely what the true infinite consists in. The true infinite is merely the finite correctly seen.
56. This holistic element of the infinite is emphasized by Brandom when he defines infinity as the "holistic conception of the conceptual" (2002, 184). He is referring here to the section on Consciousness in the *Phenomenology*. However, this definition applies equally well to the *Science of Logic*.
57. Hegel (1969, 135).
58. Hyppolite reveals a parallel structure concerning the whole and the logos: "The whole is there [in the medium of the logos] insofar as it is excluded, sublated; it is there because it is lacking" (1997, 162).
59. Hegel (1977, 46–47).
60. Hegel (1977, 46).

61. Hegel (1969, 136).
62. Hegel (1991, 302, emphasis added).
63. Hegel (1991, 302).
64. Hegel (1969, 139).
65. Hegel (1969, 138).
66. Hegel (1969, 139).
67. For a similar interpretation see Houlgate (2006, 380).
68. Hegel (1969, 146–147).
69. Hegel (1969, 151).
70. There is a slight similarity between this assertion and Leibniz's critique of the *lazy sophism* (1993, 153ff.). For him, although there are no contingent acts it is up to humans to act or not (seen from their perspective). For Hegel, although there is never certainty of realizing the ought, not acting at all would contradict it. The difference between them, however, is that whereas in Leibniz there is an absolute point of view (God's) from which humans' acts are necessary, in Hegel there is no such external viewpoint from which the ought would appear *as* realized. The equivalent of God's viewpoint in Hegel is the act of recollection (*Erinnerung*), of looking back, a viewpoint that is in constant transformation.
71. Hegel (1985a, 340–341).
72. Mure also denies that the true infinite has a final term: "the true infinite is neither a final term in the indefinite regress, nor again the opposite of the finite...an awareness of totality as immanent in but also transcending, and so neither a final term nor the unreachable "sum" of this endless qualitative regress" (1950, 51).
73. Hegel (1969, 142–143, bold emphasis added).
74. Hegel (1969, 146–147).
75. Hegel (1969, 145).
76. Hegel (1969, 129).
77. Hegel (1969, 822, bold emphasis added).
78. Hegel (1991, 302).
79. It is precisely the processual character of the agreement (*Übereinstimmung*) between being and the ought that does not allow a reading of Hegel as always accepting the status quo as a necessary development of Spirit (See Chapter 3 below for an understanding of Hegel's concept of necessity). Within this development there are forces constantly at work, striving toward the good, determining this agreement in non-agreement. Obviously the purpose of the world does not reveal itself in the process itself of this agreement in non-agreement, but rather only in looking back, in recollection (*Erinnerung*). A consequence of this is that the final purpose of the world is not final since the process of its realization is permanent. An alternate reading of this would be that the final purpose of the world is accomplished precisely insofar as there is no final purpose since the process is a continuous one.
80. Hegel (1991, 302).
81. Hegel (1969, 136).
82. Hegel (1969, 144–145).
83. Hegel (1969, 145).
84. This brings Heraclitus to mind, of which Hegel says: "there is no proposition of Heraclitus which I have not adopted in my Logic" (1968, 279). A unity of

the unity of the finite and the infinite and their difference, as opposed to a mere unity of the finite and the infinite, runs parallel to a synchronic unity of opposites found in Heraclitus. See fragments 8, 51, and 125. What gives unity to something is not the bringing together of opposites (spread through time), but rather the simultaneous bringing together of their being opposites and of the unity they produce. The bow is not formed merely by being tensed in opposite directions (unity of opposites), but rather by the unity of its being tensed in opposite directions *and* its condition of being one bow (unity of opposites and unity). It is this condition that reveals its tension.

85. This distinction is similar to that Houlgate makes between "moment" and "process" in Houlgate (2006, 423).
86. Hegel (1969, 148).
87. Hegel (1969, 89).
88. Hegel (1969, 89).
89. Theunissen (2002, 8).
90. There are various parallels here with Houlgate's comments on the relation between Hegel and Levinas. See Houlgate (2006, 432–435). However, I am emphasizing a notion of immanent absolute alterity based on the negativity of the human experience of the other.
91. For a critique of Derrida's position vis-à-vis Hegel as falling back on the dichotomizing aspect of the Doctrine of Essence and its reflective thinking, see Kisner (1995).

3 Necessity is Contingency

1. Spinoza (1985, 409).
2. Quine (1953, 38).
3. Quine (1953, 42).
4. See Bergstrom (2004, 109): "In Quine's view, truth still seems to be relative to theory in the sense that the truth of a sentence presupposes a whole theory or system of the world to which the sentence belongs and from which it gets all the meaning it has... A sentence is true if and only if it is implied by our system of the world."
5. Quine (1953, 43).
6. Quine (1960, 76).
7. Quine (1953, 44). One is reminded here of Protagoras's position as laid out by Socrates in the *Theaetetus*, where it is held that for the healthy man the wine tastes sweet, whereas for the sick man it tastes sour, neither positon of which lies closer to the fact of the matter since there is no fact of the matter. However, we all prefer to be in health, for practical reasons, which allows us to apply the concepts of better and worse, and thus to defer to the doctor in matters of health. Science would thus be considered better since "it has proved more efficacious than other myths as a device for working a manageable structure into the flux of experience" (Quine, 1953, 44).
8. Quine (1953, 46).
9. De Rosa and Lepore make this point succinctly: "Either observation sentences are theory-free and hence have independent empirical content but confirm nothing except themselves, or they are theory-laden and hence (dis)confirm

the theory but lack independent empirical content. How does the stimulation of sensory surfaces to which observation sentences are conditioned get translated into the rational evidence that observation sentences express?" (2004, 80).

10. The following reflections on the relation between necessity and contingency will go beyond those of previous commentators, such as Henrich and Houlgate. Henrich has the merit of revealing the necessary character of contingency itself in Hegel's system. It is necessary that there be contingency in actuality. However, there is still a conceptual distinction maintained between them. Houlgate takes one step further by declaring that necessity is the necessity of contingency. He also asserts that contingency and necessity do not form two distinct sets of events, but rather are one and the same process understood from different respects. In what follows we shall take the next step and show that absolute necessity is completely identical to absolute contingency, without any appeal to "respects" or "regards."
11. For a deflationary, non-normative reading of Hegel's famous remark in the Preface to the *Philosophy of Right* regarding the rationality of the real, see Stern (2009, 81ff.).
12. Kant (1965, A219).
13. By this I mean that all the elements exhibited in the Transcendental Aesthetic and the Transcendental Analytic must work simultaneously in order for there to be knowledge.
14. Hegel (1969, 50).
15. Charles Taylor reads the Doctrine of Essence as having necessity as its underlying character, and actuality as the point where it rears its head, manifesting itself. "The section on *Wirklichkeit* develops this idea of manifest necessity, manifested essence, through two main dialectics which are common to both versions: the first is a study of modal terms, of necessity, actuality, and possibility. This is destined to vindicate for actuality the status of manifested necessity, and also at the same time to explicate the relation of necessity to contingency. We finally, therefore, come to grips here with the concept of necessity which has been underlying Essence all along" (1975, 279–280). Necessity, contingency, and possibility manifest themselves in actuality.
16. Hegel (1969, 536).
17. Hegel (1969, 531).
18. Hegel (1969, 531).
19. Hegel (1969, 541).
20. He takes up this idea of "cause of itself" from Spinoza despite the fact that it has still not appeared as a concept in the thinking process described by the *Science of Logic*. It is a concept implicit at this point, to be made explicit only later.
21. Spinoza (1985, 408).
22. "Hence the necessity of the advance of the absolute to unessentiality is lacking and also the dissolution of the unessentiality in and for itself in the identity; or, there is lacking the becoming both of identity and of its determinations" (Hegel, 1969, 538). A pointed critique of Hegel's reading of Spinoza on this and other issues can be found in Macherey (2011).
23. Hegel (1969, 536).

24. If we apply what has just been said above concerning the modal concepts to this assertion, it would seem that for Hegel "what is," understood as Being (qualitatively or quantitatively) or Essence, cannot be ascribed necessity or contingency. Only when thinking "what is" in its becoming, in its movement or realization, are such concepts applicable. That is, only when "what is" is taken as becoming what it is, as a self-developing process, can it be thought of as contingent, possible, or necessary. The concept Hegel assigns to "what is" in its becoming itself is actuality. Things can be neither possible nor necessary; they merely are or are not. The point here is that the concepts of "possibility" or "necessity" are not applied to thinking "what is" as objects (Objective Logic). Naturally, one can talk about the possibility or necessity of an object. However, what is being referred to is not the object as such but rather the process in which it is referred to as means for a particular end; and this end is external to it. What Hegel describes in the subsection on Relative Necessity, though, should not be thought in terms of this type of externality (of means) but rather of an externality of circumstances and conditions for an object to manifest itself.
25. This is not the first time a sense of process is emphasized in the *Science of Logic*. One could make the case that the concept of the infinite appearing in the Doctrine of Being brings an element of process to the understanding of "what is." However, at that point "what is" is still understood through objective concepts of Being. In other words, it is an objective process still thought of as "other" to thinking. The character of process belonging to actuality is of a different nature. It will pave the way for the understanding of "what is" as a continuous process of the "self-becoming" of thinking. The endpoint of the *Science of Logic* is a consideration of the thinking process itself, a consideration of the pure activity of thinking that thinks "what is." This means that "process" will no longer be understood as a manifesting of something or of an essence but rather of itself as process. In other words, the character of process encountered in the concept of the infinite reveals the constant becoming of a Being (Being-for-self), whereas that encountered toward the end of the *Science of Logic* reveals the constant becoming of the activity itself of thinking that thinks the world; it is a becoming of concepts.
26. Hegel (1991, 237).
27. There is a certain parallel between what I term spiritual processes and what McCumber calls "parameters," which exist within "situating reason" (1993, 26ff.). However, I do not believe Hegel leaves out the "demarcative side" of situating reason, as McCumber asserts. To say that his narrative becomes absolute obviously requires a definition of the absolute, which Chapter 5 below will attempt to provide.
28. Hegel (1991, 236).
29. See the concept of absolute negativity in the section on Absolute Necessity below.
30. This point is fundamental. If one were to begin with an absolute that is simply logically possible, the step from a logical possibility to reality would have to be explained. Put in Leibnizian terms, we would need to account for the step from an infinity of possible worlds to the actualization of this world. By beginning with actuality Hegel has no need for an external point

(Leibniz's infinitely good God). Slavoj Žižek is right in saying: "Hegel always insists on the absolute primacy of actuality: true, the search for the 'conditions of possibility' abstracts from the actual, calls it into question in order to (re)-constitute it on a rational basis; yet in all these ruminations actuality is presupposed as something given. In other words nothing is stranger to Hegel than Leibnizean speculation about the multitude of possible worlds out of which the Creator picks out the best: speculation on possible universes always takes place against the background of the hard fact of actual existence" (1993, 157).

Also Longuenesse stresses the actual as Hegel's starting point: "Another originality of Hegel's exposition is that he makes actuality the pivot of all modal reflection, whatever the figure of thought envisaged may be. This is because the reflection of modal categories takes root in the very presence of the object that is thought. It is wrong, according to Hegel, to start with the definition of the possible, for this is never where thought begins" (2007, 122).

31. Hegel (1969, 542).
32. Longuenesse acknowledges only the first two in (2007, 146).
33. Hegel (1969, 542).
34. Hegel (1969, 543).
35. Hegel (1969, 543).
36. Hegel (1969, 544).
37. The contradictory character of the possible only occurs insofar as we started off with actuality. Were we to start with possibility there would be no contradiction since the concept itself of possibility allows for its opposite (as possible). Having started off with actuality, possibility always remains under its shadow, so to speak. This goes against Charles Taylor's analysis of this passage in the section entitled "Possibility, reality, and necessity," where he says: "Hegel starts off his discussion of these modal concepts with the concept of possibility" (1975, 282). Since Taylor starts with simple logical possibility, it is not clear how one reaches the concept of real possibility: "But this [bare possibility] is a thoroughly uninteresting concept of possibility. We can think of it as covering a wider scope than the actual, but it only does in a rather Pickwickian way. We move therefore to a fuller, more grounded sense of 'possible', what is really possible" (1975, 283).
38. Hegel (1969, 544).
39. Put more precisely, what reveals contingency is the lack of a strict unity. Since what is actual is a subset of what is possible this allows opposites to be simultaneously possible, the actualization of one of which is then determined to be contingent since it could have been otherwise. Henrich also considers possibility to be the gateway for contingency: "*Zufälligkeit ist die Weise, in der Möglichkeit als realisierte gesetzt ist. Etwas, das nur möglicherweise existiert, ist, wenn es wirklich ins Dasein tritt, mit Rücksicht auf diese bloße Möglichkeit zufälligerweise wirklich geworden. Also ist das wirklich gewordene Mögliche insofern zufällig, als der Bereich des Möglichen den des Realisierten umgreift*" (1967, 162).
40. For Houlgate the step from an abstract or formal possibility to an actual one lies in the distinction between "the abstract possibility of A or B or C," on the one hand, and the actual "possibility of A or not A," on the other (1995, 40). I disagree with this view insofar as the ground for formal possibility is precisely the principle of non-contradiction: that A cannot be itself and ~A

simultaneously. What allows the step from formal to real possibility (and therefore to necessity) is the fact that we started off in actuality. Therefore, the reflected actuality we come back to after having gone through formal possibility is the actualization of a particular possibility (of A as opposed to ~A). The emphasis on possibility leads to contingency, whereas the emphasis on the reflected actuality we come back to from possibility leads to necessity. Therefore, necessity arises from contingency. Since we reach reflected actuality only from the contingency of formal possibility (through possibility being the possibility of a particular actuality), this introduces the concept of necessity. In this point I do agree with Houlgate when he says: "it is usually not noted that the very idea of necessity first arises in Hegel's logic in the context of contingency itself" (1995, 41). However, this does not occur because "necessity is initially nothing but the necessity *of* contingency" (1995, 41) but rather because the possibility of an actuality (this is what reflected actuality consists in) is necessary.

41. Hegel (1969, 545).
42. Hegel (1969, 546).
43. Absolute necessity only occurs as *causa sui*. It has thus no ground for its necessity other than itself: it is because it is. Had it been otherwise it would also be because it is. This shall be dealt with in more detail in the section on Absolute Necessity below.
44. Henrich (1967, 164).
45. Hegel (1969, 546).
46. Hegel (1969, 547).
47. "'Possible' is the category in which contradiction appears" (Longuenesse, 2007, 147).
48. Hegel (1969, 548).
49. I introduce this term *Erinnerung*, which is not to be found in these passages from the *Science of Logic*, mainly due to Hegel's emphasis of actuality over possibility: we "always already" find ourselves in the midst of actuality and only then determine—or posit—the possibilities from which this actuality arose. This act is one of *Erinnerung*.
50. Hegel (1969, 549).
51. Hegel (1969, 549).
52. Hegel (1969, 550).
53. Hegel (1969, 550).
54. This movement parallels that between formal and reflected possibility above, which paved the way for real necessity. Here, the way is being paved for absolute necessity.
55. Hegel (1969, 550).
56. Hegel (1969, 550–551).
57. However, even for God there is a difference between the identity between subject and predicate encountered in truths of fact and that encountered in truths of reason. The latter will take an infinite amount of time to be reached, whereas the former will be achieved in a finite number of steps.
58. Blumenberg deals with this issue when he says: "The God Who is subject only to the logical principle of contradiction is at the same time the God Who can contradict himself, Whose creation does not exclude the will to destruction, Who stands over every present as the uncertainty of the future,

in other words, finally, the God Whose activity does not allow us to assume immanent laws and Who puts all rational 'constants' in question" (1983, 161). See also Part II, chapter 3: 145–179.

59. Leibniz (1989b, 30).
60. Leibniz (1989a, 19).
61. Longuenesse (2007, 117).
62. Hegel (1969, 551).
63. This will allow us to understand Hegel's concept of absolute content, found in the section on The Absolute. Absolute content is any content, regardless of its content, so to speak.
64. Hegel (1969, 550–551).
65. For a critique of this solution, see Hegel (1969, 539–540). For a comparison between Leibniz and Hegel on this issue, see Guyer (1979).
66. There can only be one totality for Hegel. To assert more than one would be contradictory. However, within this totality there is space for an other that cannot be totally subsumed and always maintains itself like an internal blind spot. The fundamental Hegelian concepts of negation and experience are related to this blind spot. This is an issue, however, that extends beyond the limits of the present analysis.
67. Hegel (1969, 554).
68. Hegel (1969, 552).
69. For a description of this "being more" see Theunissen (2002, 19).
70. Hegel (1969, 552).
71. Hegel (1969, 553).
72. There is a saying in the Spanish language, which asserts that nobody dies on the eve of their death: *Nadie muere la víspera*. If one dies, one was fated to do so at that precise moment. If one survives a terrible accident, or barely misses one, it was just not one's day to die. Death arrives unexpectedly, and it does so unerringly; it cannot arrive on its own eve.
73. Hegel (1969, 553).
74. Hegel says absolute actuality is "*illusory being posited as illusory being*": "*der als Schein gesetzte Schein*" (1969, 554). Absolute actuality is *Schein*, not of an essence, but of itself; it is a manifesting of manifestation. It is both being and essence; according to the former it is itself (*Schein* is *Schein*); according to the latter it is mediated by itself (*Schein* as *Schein*). The identity is not immediate, tautological. It is an identity in otherness, always being a *manifesting of*, a *scheinen as*.

4 Everything Rational is a Syllogism

1. This is one of the main themes Brandom takes up from Hegel for his inferentialist project. See (1994, 92ff.).
2. Brandom (1994, 5).
3. Brandom (1994, 78).
4. I take "semantic fallibilism" to mean what Quine's first dogma of empiricism amounts to: there are no necessary meanings.
5. Brandom (2014, 18).
6. Brandom (2014, 19).

7. Hegel (1969, 664).
8. Hegel (1969, 665).
9. Hegel (1969, 664). "Completely" here distinguishes the posited character of the concept in the syllogism from the merely posited character it has in the self-differentiating moment of the judgment, in which it posits itself as other to itself.
10. This leads to the question: is there only one true concept, *the concept*? Or is the concept being thought in the Subjective Logic a genus-type concept, under which all prior concepts thought in the *Logic* fall? The former possibility seems to necessarily lead to the assertion that for Hegel there is only one true object. This object would be the absolute idea. What this actually means would depend on how one understands the absolute idea. The latter possibility would indicate that whatever the conclusions arrived at in the Subjective Logic may be, they must apply to all prior concepts. Thus, the insufficiency of these prior concepts in their attempt to give an account of what is would be due to a lack of reflection on what it entails to be a concept. This makes sense if we believe that at the end of the movement we come back to the concept of being, having given it content and determination (this can be taken as the first step toward an externalization of logic into nature).
11. Hegel (1991, 242).
12. For a similar view on the relation between the I and Hegel's concept of concept see Horstmann (1984, 89–90). For a reading of Hegel's concept of concept as equivalent to Kant's transcendental apperception see Pippin (1988, 232ff.). For a critique of Pippin's view see Houlgate (2006, 139ff.).
13. Hegel (1969, 583, 585).
14. Hegel (1969, 583).
15. Hegel (1991, 57).
16. Hegel (1991, 70).
17. Hegel (1969, 601).
18. Hegel (1991, 32).
19. Hegel (1969, 755–756).
20. Hegel (1991, 237).
21. Hegel (1991, 245).
22. Aristotle (1941a, 336b 27–337a 1).
23. Hegel (1991, 236).
24. This normative element in truth for Hegel can be read in different ways, depending on how one understands the "ought." One possibility would be to ascribe to Hegel a conservative and justificatory claim about the rationality of the world as it is insofar as this rationality is intrinsically good: what is, is what ought to be, and what ought to be is. Such a reading is given by Schnädelbach (1993). One need only clarify what Hegel understands by the *ought* to avoid this reading of Hegel. For an alternative reading of Hegel's *ought* see Marquard (1964). See also Brandom (1994, 7ff.), where he explains a concept to be a rule of use instead of a sign standing in for or representing an object independent of it. Concepts specify how something ought to be done. The rules of use of our concepts are determined by us, not by the objects they refer to. For this reason we are responsible for them.
25. Hegel (1991, 249).

26. See Heidegger (1962, 194ff. and 362ff.). See also Gadamer (1993, 266ff. and 291ff.).
27. Hegel (1969, 624).
28. Hegel (1991, 247).
29. Hegel (1991, 68).
30. Hegel (1991, 68).
31. Hegel (1969, 626).
32. Some commentators read this passage as saying that in order for a proposition to be a judgment it requires an assertive force, that "it is the case that..." or "I believe that..." should precede any proposition in order to turn it into a judgment. See Pinkard (1988, 82, footnote 29).
33. There is a similar parallel concerning the overall aim of Kant's first *Critique* as opposed to Hegel's *Science of Logic*.
34. Natural processes have the characteristic of not being free to be otherwise than they are, and therefore of not being constituted by an element of ought. In other words, in natural processes there is no room for striving. An acorn does not strive to be a tree, whereas a human being does strive to be moral, and it is precisely this striving that constitutes her as a moral being.
35. Hegel (1969, 657–658).
36. There is an Aristotelian element at play here insofar as for Aristotle the next best thing to eternal being (like that of the celestial bodies) is an eternal coming-to-be. The species remains throughout time.
37. In the *Encyclopaedia* Hegel uses this image: "the predicate is, as it were, the soul of the subject, by which the latter, as the body of this soul, is determined through and through," (1991, 250).
38. One can name this characteristic *interdependence*, as Brockard (1970, 105–106) does. A rose does not co-determine what a plant is in the way a beautiful painting co-determines what beauty is. It is just subsumed under it.
39. "The nation without deeds is without blame" (Hegel, 1969, 721).
40. See Theunissen (1980, 467–468), and Taylor (1975, 312).
41. Hegel (1969, 662).
42. Hegel (1969, 662).
43. Hegel (1969, 661). The German original has "constituted" in italics: *beschaffen*
44. See Plato (1989b, 97c–99c); also quoted and referred to by Leibniz in (1989d, 283–4), and (1989c, 53).
45. Hegel (1969, 662).
46. Kant had already discovered this in his transcendental project, though limiting "what is" to what appears to us.
47. Hegel (1991, 66–68).
48. There are different degrees of autarchy in the concept of necessity. For example, there is greater autarchy in the concept of absolute necessity than in that of relative necessity insofar as the latter depends on something external to it. It follows the hypothetical structure: "If, then."
49. Both are divided into existence, reflection, and necessity; the concept is the extra type of judgment dealt with. In the Addition to §171 of the *Encyclopaedia* Hegel explains why there are four types of judgment. Since they reflect Being, Essence, and Concept, the one falling under Essence will itself be subdivided into two since Essence is the stage of difference, that of separation from self. The question that crops up is: Why is it not the same

with the syllogism, if the names their sub-division takes are the same as those of the sub-division of the types of judgment?

50. Hegel (1969, 632).
51. Hegel (1969, 670).
52. Hegel (1969, 671).
53. It is interesting to note that the syllogism: "All men are mortal; Gaius is a man; therefore he is mortal", can be found to exemplify a syllogism of existence [first figure (Hegel, 1969, 669)] and one of reflection [allness (Hegel, 1969, 688)], but it is no longer found in the syllogism of necessity. This is due to the fact that mortality for man is not his *concept*; his *concept* is freedom. Mortality can be an essential determination for man, but it is not man's *concept* since it is a plain biological fact without any normative element characterizing it. Mortality is not a spiritual process. For it to be one it must belong to a free being.
54. The following are examples Hegel uses to illustrate the different types of judgments: The rose is red [existence: (Hegel, 1969, 632)]; Things are perishable [reflection: (Hegel, 1969, 643)]; The rose is a plant [necessity: (Hegel, 1969, 651)]; This action is good [notion: (Hegel, 1969, 659)].
55. Hegel (1969, 664).
56. Hegel (1969, 664).
57. Hegel (1969, 601).
58. This is one of the criticisms Hegel raises against Spinoza's substance. See (1969, 535 ff.) and (1968, 257 ff.). For a reply to this critique as an inaccurate reading of Spinoza see Macherey (2011, 49 ff. and 91 ff.).
59. Hegel (1969, 703).
60. Hegel (1969, 686–687).
61. Hegel (1969, 695).
62. This attempt is obviously parallel to the more general one in the *Science of Logic* of bringing together and putting into motion and development all the major thought determinations and conceptual strategies in Western thought.
63. Hegel (1969, 668).
64. Hegel (1969, 668).
65. One is reminded here of the section on reality and negation in the Doctrine of Being: (1969, 111–114).
66. Kant (1965, B106).
67. "In this manner there arise precisely the same number of pure concepts of the understanding which apply a priori to objects of intuition in general, as, in the preceding table, there have been found to be logical functions in all possible judgments. For these functions specify the understanding completely, and yield an exhaustive inventory of its powers," (Kant, 1965, B105).
68. Hegel (1969, 673).
69. Hegel (1969, 686).
70. Hegel (1969, 687).
71. Hegel (1969, 687).
72. Hegel (1969, 691).
73. Hegel (1969, 697).

74. In this section also he asserts that accidentality "is the relationship peculiar to substance" (1969, 696).
75. Hegel (1969, 698).
76. Hegel (1969, 697).
77. Ubaldo R. Perez-Paoli makes this point by saying: "*Da die Sache ist, so muß auch die Totalität ihrer Bedingungen sein. Aber jene wird so unter diese subsumiert, daß sie das Zusammenfassende der Bedingungen ist, und dieses Zusammenfassen ist nicht wie im Schluß der Reflexion-wo es umgekehrt war: das Allgemeine faßte die Einzelnen zusammen-ein Verlangen nach Objektivität, sondern ein schon geschehenes: das Eingetretensein in die Wirklichkeit, weil durch die Negativität der Einzelheit bestimmt. Somit schlagen die Bedingungen in die Seite des Bedingten um: sie setzen die Sache voraus*" (1977, 144–145).
78. Hegel (1969, 699).
79. Hegel (1969, 700).
80. The connection between negativity and becoming is encountered in various passages from the Preface to the *Phenomenology*: "pure negativity or ... *simple becoming*" (1977, 11); "purpose... as such is Subject. Its power to move ... is *being-for-self* or pure negativity" (1977, 12); "this is the tremendous power of the negative; it is the energy of thought" (1977, 19). Its connection to thinking lies in the fact that thinking dissolves all solidifying, substantializing activity. It leads from a world of being to a world of becoming.
81. Hegel (1969, 700).
82. This does not threaten Hegel's claim "that Reason is but one" and that "there cannot be distinct Reasons" (1985b, 275) since, given the reading of certain Hegelian concepts offered in the present work, this claim is deflated and assumes the role of being a predecessor to Davidson's claim against the possibility of incommensurable schemes.
83. Perez-Paoli says of the disjunctive syllogism that "*Das Resultat dieser Entwicklung ist nicht nur das Mit-sich-zusammen-geschlossen sondern ebensosehr das Von-sich-ausgeschlossen-sein des Begriffs*" (1977, 163).
84. Hegel (1969, 703).
85. Hegel (1969, 704).
86. The following is the full quote: "A semantically adequate notion of correct inference must generate an acceptable notion of conceptual content. But such a notion must fund the idea of objective truth conditions and so of objectively correct inferences. Such proprieties of judgment and inference outrun actual attitudes of taking or treating judgments and inferences as correct. They are determined by how things actually are, independently of how they are taken to be. Our cognitive attitudes must ultimately answer to these attitude-transcendent facts" (Brandom, 1994, 137).
87. For a similar hermeneutic reading of the section on the syllogism, albeit, one in which the emphasis is placed on understanding the syllogism as the logical term for the structure of recognition, see Redding (1996, Chapter VII).

5 The Most Stubborn Opposition

1. McDowell (1994, 126).
2. Pippin (2002, 69).

3. "Thus in what consciousness affirms from within itself as *being-in-itself* or the *True* we have the standard which consciousness itself sets up by which to measure what it knows... Hence it comes to pass for consciousness that what it previously took to be the *in-itself* is not an *in-itself*, or that it was only an in-itself *for consciousness*. Since consciousness thus finds that its knowledge does not correspond to its object, the object itself does not stand the test; in other words, the criterion for testing is altered when that for which it was to have been the criterion fails to pass the test; and the testing is not only a testing of what we know, but also a testing of the criterion of what knowing is" (Hegel, 1977, 53–55).
4. Hegel (1969, 759).
5. Hegel (1991, 290).
6. Hegel (1969, 756).
7. Hegel (1969, 757–758).
8. Hegel (1969, 757).
9. Hegel (1991, 294).
10. Hegel (1969, 758).
11. Hegel (1991, 295).
12. This self-determination and freedom should not be understood in the sense of empirical unrevisability. It consists rather in the self-determination of constantly reconstituting the criteria (conceptuality) of what we hold to be true and to be good in the face of the negativity of human experience. To reach the Doctrine of the Notion does not amount to having suppressed the empirical but only to have absorbed it within the conceptual. There is still a hardness that we experience and that makes us revise our conceptual schemes. It is just not pre-conceptual, merely given. There are no one-to-one connections between statements we make or beliefs we hold and elements of the empirical world, as Quine's second dogma attests to. Empirical revisability occurs only through conceptual revisability. This would dissolve the tension Pippin finds between Hegel's more recollective account of the process of "determinate negation" encountered in the *Science of Logic* and the "empirically unrevisable, internally self-determining, 'free' Notional level, constitutive of all possible knowledge of objects" (1988, 255).
13. Hegel (1969, 817).
14. Hegel (1969, 818).
15. Hegel (1969, 820).
16. One could argue that what makes an act good is not its effectiveness but rather the intention with which it is done (for duty's sake). However, Hegel's emphasis here is at the phenomenal level: observing what happens when humans act in the world: they usually hit up against it in the most unexpected ways.
17. Hegel (1969, 821).
18. Hegel (1969, 822).
19. Hegel (1969, 143).
20. Hegel (1969, 822).
21. For a similar view, see Wallace (2005, 260). I would hesitate, however, to speak of the world being objectively good without being careful in explaining how this does not amount to a normative assessment.
22. Hegel (1991, 286).

23. Hegel (1969, 822–823).
24. This is the ground for what Hegel calls the "cunning of reason" (*List der Vernunft*).
25. Hegel (1969, 823).
26. Hegel (2008, 20).
27. Hegel (1969, 823).
28. For an understanding of the concept of correspondence (*Entsprechung*) that follows this description, see Theunissen (2002).
29. Hegel (1991, 286).
30. This reveals the importance for Hegel of confronting not only Cartesian but also ancient skepticism.
31. By "ascribing meaning" I understand subjecting actuality to the principle of sufficient reason.
32. For a non-normative reading of Hegel's remark that parallels our hermeneutic reading, see Stern (2009, 81ff.).
33. Hegel (1969, 825).
34. Terry Pinkard describes the method as "simply the means of relating the concepts with one another" (1979, 431).
35. Hegel (1969, 826).
36. Hegel (1977, 19).
37. Hegel in fact calls the negative "the soul or that which moves [the I and substance]" (1977, 21).
38. Hegel (1991, 304).
39. Hegel (1991, 303).
40. Hegel (1991, 307).
41. Hegel (1969, 843).
42. Hegel (1969, 829).
43. *Completion* is closer to the German term *Vollendung*.
44. For a similar view regarding the meaning of *Vollendung*, see Pippin (1989, 257).
45. Hegel (1991, 289).
46. Christoph Menke underscores a similar structure regarding Hegelian dialectics, though he locates it in the distinction between life and knowledge, immediacy and mediation. I would place the emphasis more on the distinction between understanding and reason, taking up understanding as the permanent positing of different ideas of the true and the good. See Menke (1992, 58ff.).
47. It is interesting to note that Hegel places Kant and critical philosophy together with empiricism as conforming the Second Position of Thought with Respect to Objectivity. The other two positions are metaphysics and immediate knowing. See Hegel (1991, 76–108).
48. Kant's project is a failed attempt at offering this solution given how it still holds on to an external standpoint, which is what allows Hegel to classify it as belonging together with empiricism in its relation to objectivity.
49. This point is made in Forster (1989).
50. He also calls the force and work of the understanding, which is what negates, the "most astonishing and mightiest of powers, or rather the absolute power" (1977, 18).
51. Hegel (1969, 840).

52. Hegel (1969, 841).
53. The metaphor used by Hegel is that of overleaping one's own age, of jumping over Rhodes: "It is just as absurd to fancy that a philosophy can transcend its contemporary world as it is to fancy that an individual can overleap his own age, jump over Rhodes" (2008, 21).
54. If there were an external point, we would have the problem of incommensurability of schemes, which Davidson makes thematic in his criticism of the third dogma of empiricism. See Chapter 1 above.
55. A weak spot of Hegelian philosophy might lie in the fact that there seems to be no space for simultaneous alternative reasons, which in the present reading, would amount to saying that there can only be one meaning-conferring narrative of history at a time. There can be no competing narratives. See Menke (1992, 12).
56. Just as the critique of relativism disappears when the dichotomy relative/absolute is put into question, in the same manner the critique of circularity disappears by questioning the dichotomy ground/grounded or beginning/end.
57. Hegel (1969, 842).
58. McDowell (1994, 28).
59. McDowell (1994, 44).
60. This might be one of the differences between the first and second editions of the *Critique of Pure Reason*. See Walker (1989, 160).

Conclusion

1. Hegel (1977, 19).
2. Hegel (1977, 36).
3. Hegel (1977, 56).
4. Hegel (1977, 22–23).
5. Horstmann (2006, 70).

Bibliography

All references to Hegel's original texts are taken from G.W.F. Hegel, *Werke: [in Zwanzig Bänden]*, (ed.) E. Moldenhauer and K.M. Michel (Frankfurt am Main: Suhrkamp, 1986).

Aristotle (1941a) "On Generation and Corruption," in *The Basic Works of Aristotle*, (trans.) Harold H. Joachim (New York: Random House), 467–531.

Bergstrom, L. (2004) "Underdetermination of Physical Theory," in *The Cambridge Companion to Quine*, (ed.) Roger F. Gibson Jr. (Cambridge: Cambridge University Press), 91–114.

Bernstein, J. (2002) "Re-enchanting Nature," in *Reading McDowell: On Mind and World*, (ed.) Nicholas Smith (New York: Routledge), 217–245.

Blumenberg, H. (1983) *The Legitimacy of the Modern Age*, (trans.) Robert M. Wallace (Cambridge, MA: MIT Press).

Brandom, R. (1994) *Making It Explicit* (Cambridge, MA: Harvard University Press).

—— (2002) *Tales of the Mighty Dead: Historical Essays in the Metaphysics of Intentionality* (Cambridge, MA: Harvard University Press).

—— (2011) *Munich Hegel Lectures*, http://www.pitt.edu/~brandom/currentwork.html.

—— (2014) "Hegel and Analytic Philosophy," http://www.pitt.edu/~rbrandom/present.html.

Brockard, H. (1970) *Subjekt: Versuch zur Ontologie bei Hegel* (München: Pustet).

Cramer, K. (1978) "Bemerkungen zu Hegels Begriff vom Bewuβtsein in der Einleitung zur Phänomenologie des Geistes," in *Seminar: Dialektik in der Philosophie Hegels*, (ed.) Rolf-Peter Horstmann (Frankfurt: Suhrkamp), 360–393.

Davidson, D. (1983) "A Coherence Theory of Truth and Knowledge," in *Kant oder Hegel? Über Formen der Begründung in der Philosophie* (Stuttgart: Klett-Cotta), 423–438.

——— (1984a) "On the Very Idea of a Conceptual Scheme," in *Inquiries into Truth and Interpretation* (Oxford: Clarendon Press), 183–198.

——— (1984b) "The Method of Truth in Metaphysics", in *Inquiries into Truth and Interpretation* (Oxford: Clarendon Press), 199–214.

de Boer, K. (2010) *On Hegel: The Sway of the Negative* (London: Palgrave Macmillan).

de Rosa, R. and Lepore, E. (2004) "Quine's Meaning Holisms," in *The Cambridge Companion to Quine*, (ed.) Roger F. Gibson Jr. (Cambridge: Cambridge University Press), 65–90.

Derrida, J. (1982) "The Pit and the Pyramid: Introduction to Hegel's Semiology," in *Margins of Philosophy*, (trans.) Alan Bass (Chicago: The University of Chicago Press), 69–108.

—— (2005) "Violence and Metaphysics," in *Writing and Difference*, (trans.) Alan Bass (London: Routledge), 97–192.

Flay, J. (1984) *Hegel's Quest for Certainty* (Albany, NY: State University of New York Press).

Forster M. (1989) *Hegel and Skepticism* (Cambridge, MA: Harvard University Press).

Gadamer, H.-G (1976) *Hegel's Dialectic: Five Hermeneutical Studies,* (trans.) Christopher Smith (New Haven, CT: Yale University Press).

—— (1993) *Truth and Method,* (trans.) Joel Weinsheimer and Donald G. Marshall (New York: Continuum).

Guyer, P. (1979) "Hegel, Leibniz and the Contradiction in the Finite," *Philosophy and Phenomenological Research,* 40, 75–98.

Guzmán, L. (2006) "El Carácter Contingente de la Necesidad Absoluta en la *Ciencia de la Lógica* de Hegel," *Ideas y Valores,* 131(August), 3–31, Bogotá, Colombia.

—— (2012) "Totalidad y Negatividad en la *Ciencia de la Lógica* de Hegel," *Signos Filosóficos,* 27(XIV), 71–88, Mexico City, Mexico.

Hartmann, K. (1972) "Hegel: A Non-Metaphysical View," in *Hegel. A Collection of Critical Essays,* (ed.) Alasdair MacIntyre (Notre Dame: University of Notre Dame Press), 101–124.

Hegel, G.W.F. (1968) *Lectures on the History of Philosophy,* Vol. II, (trans.) E.S. Haldane and Frances H. Simpson (New York: The Humanities Press).

—— (1969) *Science of Logic,* (trans.) A.V. Miller (Atlantic Highlands: Humanities Press).

—— (1977) *Faith and Knowledge,* (trans.) Walter Cerf and H.S. Harris (Albany, NY: State University of New York).

—— (1977) *Phenomenology of Spirit,* (trans.) A.V. Miller (Oxford: Oxford University Press).

—— (1978) *Hegel's Philosophy of Subjective Spirit: Vol. I,* (trans.) M.J. Petry (Boston: D. Reidel Publishing Company).

—— (1985a) "Relationship of Skepticism to Philosophy, Exposition of its Different Modifications and Comparison to the Latest Form with the Ancient One," in *Between Kant and Hegel. Texts in the Development of Post-Kantian Idealism,* (trans.) George di Giovanni and H.S. Harris (Albany, NY: State University of New York Press), 311–362.

—— (1985b) "The Critical Journal of Philosophy. Introduction on The Essence of Philosophical Criticism Generally, and its Relationship to the Present State of Philosophy in Particular," in *Between Kant and Hegel. Texts in the Development of Post-Kantian Idealism,* (trans.) George di Giovanni and H.S. Harris (Albany, NY: State University of New York Press), 272–291.

—— (1991) *Encyclopaedia Logic: Part I of the Encyclopaedia of Philosophical Sciences with the Zusätze,* (trans.) T.F. Geraets, W.A. Suchting and H.S. Harris (Indianapolis, IN: Hackett Publishing Company).

—— (2008) *Elements of the Philosophy of Right,* (trans.) H.B. Nisbet (Cambridge: Cambridge University Press).

Heidegger M. (1962) *Being and Time,* (trans.) John Macquarrie and Edward Robinson (New York: Harper & Row).

—— (1970) *Hegel's Concept of Experience,* (New York: Harper & Row Publishers).

Henrich, D. (1967) "Hegels Theorie über den Zufall," in *Hegel im Kontext* (Frankfurt: Suhrkamp), 157–186.

Horstmann, R.-P. (1984) *Ontologie und Relationen* (Königstein: Athenäum-Hain).

—— (1999) "What is Hegel's Legacy and What Should We Do With It?," *European Journal of Philosophy,* 7(2), 275–287.

—— (2006) "Substance, Subject, and Infinity: A Case Study of the Role of Logic in Hegel's System," in *Hegel: New Directions*, (ed.) Katerina Deligiorgi (Montreal: McGill-Queen's University Press), 69–84.

Hösle, V. (1988) *Hegel's System. Band I: Hegels Systementwicklung und Logik* (Hamburg: Felix Meiner Verlag).

Houlgate, S. (1995) "Necessity and Contingency in Hegel's *Science of Logic*," *The Owl of Minerva*, 27(1), 37–50.

—— (2006) *The Opening of Hegel's Logic: From Being to Infinity* (West Lafayette, IN: Purdue University Press).

Hyppolite, J. (1997) *Logic and Existence*, (trans.) Lawrence Lawlor and Amit Sen (Albany, NY: State University of New York Press).

Kant, I. (1953) *Groundwork of the Metaphysic of Morals*, (trans.) H.J. Paton (New York: Harper Torchbooks).

—— (1965) *Critique of Pure Reason*, (trans.) Norman Kemp Smith (New York: St. Martin's Press).

Kirk, G.S., Raven, J.E. and Schofield, M. (1983) *The Presocratic Philosophers* (Cambridge: Cambridge University Press).

Kisner, W. (1995) "*Erinnerung, Retrait*, Absolute Reflection: Hegel and Derrida," *The Owl of Minerva*, 26(2), 171–186.

Kolb, D. (2010) "The Necessities of Hegel's Logics," in *Hegel and the Analytic Tradition*, (ed.) Angelica Nuzzo (London: Continuum), 40–60.

Kuhn, T. (1962) *The Structure of Scientific Revolutions* (Chicago: The University of Chicago Press).

Leibniz, G.W. (1989a) "On Freedom and Possibility," in *Philosophical Essays*, (trans.) Roger Ariew and Daniel Garber (Indianapolis, IN/Cambridge: Hackett Publishing Company), 19–23.

—— (1989b) "On Contingency," in *Philosophical Essays*, (trans.) Roger Ariew and Daniel Garber (Indianapolis, IN/Cambridge: Hackett Publishing Company), 28–30.

—— (1989c) "Discourse on Metaphysics," in *Philosophical Essays*, (trans.) Roger Ariew and Daniel Garber (Indianapolis, IN/Cambridge: Hackett Publishing Company), 35–68.

—— (1989d) "Two Sects of Naturalists," in *Philosophical Essays*, (trans.) Roger Ariew and Daniel Garber (Indianapolis, IN/Cambridge: Hackett Publishing Company), 281–284.

—— (1993) *Theodicy*, (trans.) E.M. Huggard (La Salle: Open Court).

Longuenesse, B. (2007) *Hegel's Critique of Metaphysics* (Cambridge: Cambridge University Press).

Macherey, P. (2011) *Hegel or Spinoza*, (trans.) Susan M. Ruddick (Minneapolis: University of Minnesota Press).

Marcuse, H. (1987) *Hegel's Ontology and the Theory of Historicity*, (trans.) Seyla Benhabib (Cambridge, MA: MIT Press).

Marquard, O. (1964) "Hegel und das Sollen," *Philosophisches Jahrbuch*, 72, 103–119.

Marx, W. (1967) *Absolute Reflexion und Sprache* (Frankfurt: Klostermann).

—— (1975) *Hegel's Phenomenology of Spirit: Its Point and Purpose – A Commentary on the Preface and Introduction*, (trans.) Peter Heath (New York: Harper & Row Publishers).

McCumber, J. (1993) *The Company of Words. Hegel, Language and Systematic Philosophy* (Evanston, IL: Northwestern University Press).
McDowell, J. (1994) *Mind and World* (Cambridge, MA: Harvard University Press).
—— (2002) "Responses," in *Reading McDowell: On Mind and World*, (ed.) Nicholas Smith (New York: Routledge), 269–305.
McTaggart, J. (1964) *A Commentary on Hegel's Logic* (New York: Russell and Russell Inc.).
Menke, C. (1992) "Der 'Wendungspunkt' des Erkennens. Zu Begriff, Recht und Reichweite der Dialektik in Hegels *Logik*," in *Vernunftkritik nach Hegel: Analytisch-Kritische Interpretation zur Dialektik*, (ed.) Christoph Demmerling and Friedrich Kambartel (Frankfurt: Suhrkamp), 9–66.
Mure, G. (1950) *A Study of Hegel's Logic* (Oxford: Clarendon Press).
Nietzsche, F. (1954a) "Twilight of the Idols," in *The Portable Nietzsche* (New York: Penguin Books), 463–563.
Nuzzo, A. (ed.) (2010) *Hegel and the Analytic Tradition* (London: Continuum), 96–112.
Perez-Paoli, U. (1977) *Hegels Lehre vom Schluß* (Braunschwieg: Inaugural Dissertation).
Pinkard, T. (1979) "The Logic of Hegel's Logic," *Journal of the History of Philosophy*, 17(4), 417–435.
—— (1988) *Dialectic: The Explanation of Possibility* (Philadelphia: Temple University Press).
—— (1994) *Hegel's Phenomenology. The Sociality of Reason* (Cambridge: Cambridge University Press).
—— (2000) *Hegel: A Biography* (Cambridge: Cambridge University Press).
——— (2010) "Hegel's Non-Analytic Option," in *Hegel and the Analytic Tradition*, (ed.) Angelica Nuzzo (London: Continuum).
Pippin, R. (1988) *Hegel´s Idealism: The Satisfactions of Self-Consciousness* (Cambridge: Cambridge University Press).
—— (2002) "Leaving Nature Behind: or Two Cheers for Subjectivism," in *Reading McDowell: On Mind and World*, (ed.) Nicholas Smith (New York: Routledge), 58–75.
—— (2005) "Brandom's Hegel," *European Journal of Philosophy*, 13(3), 381–408.
Plato (1989a) "Theaetetus," in *Collected Dialogues*, (trans.) F.M. Cornford (Princeton, NJ: Princeton University Press), 845–919.
—— (1989b) "Phaedo," in *Collected Dialogues*, (trans.) Hugh Tredennick (Princeton, NJ: Princeton University Press), 40–98.
Quine, W.V.O. (1953) "Two Dogmas of Empiricism," in *From a Logical Point of View* (Cambridge, MA: Harvard University Press), 20–46.
—— (1960) *Word and Object* (Cambridge, MA: MIT Press).
Redding, P. (1996) *Hegel's Hermeneutics* (Ithaca, NY: Cornell University Press).
—— (2007) *Analytic Philosophy and the Return of Hegelian Thought* (Cambridge: Cambridge University Press).
Rockmore, T. (2005) *Hegel, Idealism, and Analytic Philosophy* (New Haven, CT: Yale University Press).
Rorty, R. (1998) "Robert Brandom on Social Practices and Representations," in *Truth and Progress* (Cambridge: Cambridge University Press), 122–137
Schnädelbach, H. (1993) "Hegel's Lehre von der Wahrheit," *Deutsche Zeitschrift für Philosophie*, 41, 799–813.

Sellars, W. (1997) *Empiricism and the Philosophy of Mind* (Cambridge, MA: Harvard University Press).

Sextus Empiricus (1985) *Selections from the Major Writings on Scepticism, Man, & God*, (trans.) Sanford Etheridge (Indianapolis, IN: Hackett Publishing Company).

Solomon, R. (1983) *In the Spirit of Hegel* (Oxford: Oxford University Press).

Spinoza, B. (1985) *The Collected Works of Spinoza*, (trans.) Edwin Curley (Princeton, NJ: Princeton University Press).

Stern, R. (2009) *Hegelian Metaphysics* (New York: Oxford University Press).

Taylor, C. (1975) *Hegel* (Cambridge: Cambridge University Press).

Theunissen, M. (1980) *Sein und Schein: Der Kritische Funktion der Hegelsche Logik* (Frankfurt: Suhrkamp).

—— (2002) "Notion and Reality: Hegel's Sublation of the Metaphysical Notion of Truth," (trans.) Luis Guzmán, *Graduate Faculty Philosophy Journal*, 23(2), 3–34.

Tugendhat, E. (1986) *Self-Consciousness and Self-Determination*, (trans.) Paul Stern (Cambridge, MA: The MIT Press).

—— (1992) "Das Sein und das Nichts," in *Philosophische Aufsätze* (Frankfurt: Suhrkamp), 36–66.

Walker, R. (1989) *The Coherence Theory of Truth* (London: Routledge).

Wallace, R. (2005) *Hegel's Philosophy of Reality, Freedom, and God* (Cambridge: Cambridge University Press).

Westphal, K. (1998) "Hegel's Solution to the Dilemma of the Criterion," in *The Phenomenology of Spirit Reader*, (ed.) Jon Stewart (Albany, NY: SUNY Press), 76–101.

Winch, P. (1964) "Understanding a Primitive Society," *American Philosophical Quarterly*, I, 307–324.

Zambrana, R. (2012) "Hegel's Logic of Finitude," *Continental Philosophy Review*, 45, 213–233.

Žižek, S. (1993) *Tarrying with the Negative. Kant, Hegel, and the Critique of Ideology* (Durham, NC: Duke University Press).

Index

Made in the USA
Las Vegas, NV
28 October 2024

10599888R00125